THE MODERN HISTORY OF
SOVIET CENTRAL
ASIA

The Praeger Asia-Africa Series

ASIA—AFRICA SERIES OF MODERN HISTORIES

Editor: Bernard Lewis; *Professor of the History of the Near and Middle East, University of London*

THE MODERN HISTORY OF
SOVIET CENTRAL ASIA

GEOFFREY WHEELER

FREDERICK A. PRAEGER, *Publishers*

NEW YORK · WASHINGTON

BOOKS THAT MATTER

Published in the United States of America in 1964
by Frederick A. Praeger, Inc., Publishers
111 Fourth Avenue, New York, N.Y., 10003, U.S.A.

Library of Congress Catalog Card Number: 64–19966

Printed in Great Britain

CONTENTS

ILLUSTRATIONS

(between pages 148 *and* 149)

Acknowledgments

The author wishes to thank the following for supplying photographs for this book: Josephine Powell; pl. 9: Royal Geographical Society; pls. 1 and 10; Society for Cultural Relations with the U.S.S.R.; pls. 2, 3, 4, 5, 6, 7, 8, 17, 18, 19, 20, 21.

vii

MAPS

ACKNOWLEDGMENTS

I owe a particular debt of gratitude to Richard Pierce and Alexander Park of whose books *Russian Central Asia, 1867–1917* and *Bolshevism in Turkestan, 1917–1927* I have made extensive use in Chapters V, VI and VII, and to Mary Holdsworth whose *Turkestan in the 19th Century* was of great value to me in writing Chapter III.

My thanks are also due to Professor Bernard Lewis, Miss Violet Conolly, Mrs K. West and Mr Donald Cumming for their many valuable suggestions, to the past and present staff of the Central Asian Research Centre, to Mrs Dorothy Thompson for her patient transcription and retyping of the manuscript and finally to the Institute of Race Relations and the Oxford University Press for permission to include a few passages from my book *Racial Problems in Soviet Muslim Asia.*

NOTE ON TRANSLITERATION

The consistent spelling of geographical and personal names in a work dealing with an area subjected to different cultural influences – Arab, Persian, Turkic and Russian – presents an insuperable problem. Before the Russian period names were written in the Arabo-Persian character and were usually transliterated by Western writers according to their individual tastes. After the coming of the Russians the matter was complicated by the introduction of Russian and Russianized names which again were transliterated according to taste. With a view to the requirements of modern readers not necessarily possessing a knowledge of the basic languages from which names originate the following principles have been adopted.

(a) All geographical names in use today have been transliterated according to the PCGN/BGN system, that is, as they appear on all maps of the area published in Britain and the USA during the past 20 years. Thus, Dzhalalabad rather than Jalalabad, Chardzhou rather than Charjui, and Termez rather than Tirmidh.

(b) Geographical names and Arabic, Persian and Turkic words in use before the Russian period but since completely changed or fallen into disuse are transliterated according to conventional English usage. The same applies to Muslim names of persons living before the Russian period. Diacritical marks to indicate pronunciation have been omitted.

(c) Muslim names of persons living during the Tsarist and Soviet period are usually transliterated according to the PCGN/BGN system from the Russian spelling, this in order to facilitate reference to Russian source material.

(d) The use of classical names (e.g. Oxus for Amu-dar'ya) has been avoided.

(e) All Russian personal names and words are transliterated according to the PCGN/BGN system.

PREFACE

This book is concerned with the five Asian republics of the Soviet Union which lie to the south of Western Siberia and east of the Caspian Sea. In accordance with the aims of the Asia-Africa series, I have concentrated mainly on the social, cultural and intellectual developments of the peoples themselves since the beginning of the Western impact rather than on the political, economic and diplomatic history of the republics. The distinction, although clearly important, is by no means easy to achieve, for virtually the whole region came under Russian domination in the middle of the nineteenth century and since then the government, the economy and the system of education and social and cultural activities of all kinds have become progressively less informed by the inspiration and initiative of the Central Asian peoples.

The present work does not claim to be the product of any original research or to develop any new point of view. It merely sets out to follow the fortunes of the peoples of Central Asia during the past two centuries after a very brief backward glance at their earlier history. In dealing with the impact on them of European civilization I have tried to make the best and most objective use of Tsarist, Soviet and other available source material. A list and description of the principal works consulted is given at the end of the book.

The plan of the book is a simple one. An introductory chapter about the land and the people is followed by a very condensed review of early history. Chapter III describes the situation immediately before the appearance of the Russians, and the next two chapters deal with the Russian conquest and administration of the area. Three chapters are devoted to the Revolution and the Civil War, the Consolidation of Soviet Power, and Central Asia under Soviet Rule. The last chapter is concerned with the culture of the peoples of Central Asia as it developed before the coming of the Russian, and during the Tsarist and Soviet regimes.

xi

CHAPTER I

THE LAND AND THE PEOPLE

STRICTLY SPEAKING the term Soviet Central Asia refers only to the area which in Tsarist times was known as Russian Turkestan and which today consists of the Soviet Socialist Republics of Turkmenistan, Uzbekistan, Tadzhikistan and Kirgizia. What in Tsarist times was known as the Steppe Region (Stepnoy Kray) and is now broadly speaking the republic of Kazakhstan has always been treated by both Tsarist and Soviet geographers as a separate area. Justification for treating all five republics together for modern, if not for ancient, historical purposes can be found in their ethnographical and cultural affinities, a fact generally recognized by Soviet writers. The geographical distinctiveness of Kazakhstan, however, has had a considerable effect on its history. For example, the Arab conquests of the eighth century virtually stopped short where the sown lands bordered on the Steppe. The extension of the Russian conquests from the Steppe Region into the oasis and mountainous regions lying to the south of it had the double effect of drawing the whole region together as part of the Russian Empire, and of still further separating Turkestan from Muslim South and South West Asia of which it is still culturally, and to some extent, historically and ethnically, a part.

Soviet geographers divide Central Asia and Kazakhstan into four regions: the *steppe*, constituted by northern Kazakhstan, or what is now known as the Tselinnyy Kray or Virgin Lands Region; the *semi-desert* consisting roughly of the rest of Kazakhstan; the *desert* region lying to the south of the semi-desert and reaching the Persian frontier in the west and the Chinese frontier in the east; and the *mountain* region of which the main features are the Pamirs and the Tien-shan.

The mountains in or abutting on the region 'in at least three ways provide opportunities for settlement and exploitation. Their varied topographic zones allow "alpine" high-level pasture in summer, fruit growing and the cultivation of cereals in their valleys up to very high levels (10–14,000 feet), and mineral exploitation, notably in the desert plateau of Pamir, which has been called a miniature Tibet. Secondly, they make possible irrigated agriculture (and thus the concentration of population) along piedmont zones, in enclosed basins (notably those of Fergana and Vakhsh), on lakesides and in river valleys in the otherwise desert plain. Thirdly, they provide an effective insulation between the USSR, Persia, Pakistan and Sinkiang (Chinese Turkestan), though at the same time they afford a few practicable lines of movement, e.g. from Andizhan in Fergana to Kashgar in Sinkiang."[1]

Settlement based on agriculture has been largely regulated by physical geography. The dry semi-steppe of northern and eastern Kazakhstan with its chestnut or brown soils has given rise to villages, and later to collective farms, with fields of spring-sown wheat. Southwards aridity increases and there are numerous salt pans. Farther south again is the true desert extending from the eastern shore of the Caspian beyond the Aral Sea to Lake Balkhash. Here permanent settlement has been so far confined to the oases such as those of Bukhara and Mary (Merv) and the valleys of the larger rivers such as the Amu-Dar'ya and Syr-Dar'ya where there is essential water for crops. In proportion to the vast areas of clay, stone and sandy desert the cultivated and populated land is very small. The area of artificially irrigated land is, however, being rapidly extended and this must result in an increase in the settled areas.

The subject of irrigation is inseparable from the history of ancient as well as of modern Central Asia. During the early years of the Soviet regime, and indeed until quite recently, the official policy was to minimize all positive achievements which took place both before and during the Tsarist regime. Tsarist achievements in irrigation were, it is true, quite unremarkable, the only two major projects which were completed – those of the Golodnaya Step' and on the Murgab River – falling far short of expectation. Russian administrators and economists were well aware of their shortcomings in this matter and in 1912 a vast irrigation programme was planned which would have made possible the cultivation of an additional 12,500 square miles of land.

Long before the appearance of the Russians, however, artificial irrigation had been practised on traditional lines for many centuries. The Greek historian Strabo, in his geography written at the beginning of the first century AD, remarked on the exceptional fertility of Hyrcania resulting from an irrigation system that was developed from the waters of the River Atrek. (Relics of the system can still be seen today. The dam on the Atrek seems to have been destroyed during the Mongol invasion.) In many other areas such as the valley of the Zeravshan and even the Golodnaya Step' traces of irrigation works can still be found which date back to remote antiquity. The traditional system existing at the time of the Russian conquest consisted of a main *aryk* (irrigation canal) leading from a river, from which a number of smaller channels branched off to feed the individual fields of each village. The smaller *aryks*, having separated at an angle from the main branch, generally took a course parallel to it. Sometimes as many as ten villages would be distributed along the main *aryks*, and the water, after feeding the canals of one system, would flow on to another village. The systems were therefore interdependent, for by retaining the water in one, the water in another would be diminished. The canals and dams, particularly the older ones, were very skilfully constructed; they were not deep, which made them easier to regulate and maintain, and they were built in such a way that the current of the water could be kept under control. The main *aryks* were connected to the rivers by simple weirs made of mud, sand, gravel, willow branches and occasionally stones. Materials used for some of the dams and other constructions in these irrigation systems were usually of the best quality and were capable of lasting many hundreds of years.

In each village it was the local cultivators themselves who dug and maintained the canals and as a rule no comprehensive plan would be adopted for irrigating the largest area possible; the network would be laid down as necessity demanded. The administrators of the irrigation system were known as *aryk-aksakals* (literally 'canal greybeards') and were elected by the local farmers. Their duty was to look after the distribution of water and see to repairs. According to Moser[2] the Tsarist Government attempted to change this traditional system and make the *aryk-aksakals* employees of the Government; but the plan proved unsatisfactory and they were obliged to revert to the old methods. To a large extent the old methods still persist in Persia and Afghanistan, but they have been completely abolished by the Soviet regime in Central Asia.

In his *History of Irrigation in Turkestan*, Barthold gives details of many of the irrigation works carried out under native administration before and during the Tsarist regime. During the eighteenth and nineteenth centuries projects were carried out in the Fergana Valley, and the waters of the Naryn and Kara-Dar'ya were used for the first time. In the valley of the Zeravshan a dam was built on the largest canal and a number of canal systems were cleaned or in part re-dug. In the 1860s a canal was built from the Amu-Dar'ya to the village of Kenges in Karakalpakia, and in the 1870s dams were constructed on the rivers flowing into Lake Daykara. New canals were also dug in the delta of the Amu-Dar'ya, which increased the area of cultivable land in the region. In 1831 a canal was built from Lake Laudan to irrigate Staryy (Kunya) Urgench; and in 1846 when water from this lake penetrated the old bed of the Amu-Dar'ya, a dam was built to conserve it and irrigate more land to the south of Staryy Urgench. In the centre of the khanate of Khiva canals were dug to the north of the town of Kyat to irrigate the formerly arid region known as Shimamkent. Between 1822 and 1842 the Khan-Aryk was constructed in what is now the Tashkent *oblast*, and between 1868 and 1871 a main canal was dug in the Fergana Valley. Irrigation works completed and projected during the Soviet regime will be described in a later chapter.

To conclude this brief description of the natural conditions of Soviet Central Asia and Kazakhstan some mention must be made of the climate. This can broadly be described as continental with hot summers and cold winters. In the extreme south of the region, particularly at Ashkhabad and Termez the climate is subtropical with shade temperatures reaching 104° F (40° C). Termez has the reputation of being the hottest place in the Soviet Union. Winter is very severe in the semi-desert and desert regions, temperatures in the former falling to −42·1° F in the west and −49·6° F in the east. Precipitation is low throughout the whole area, but it varies very much in its incidence. In the semi-desert most of the rain falls in summer, while in the south of the desert region most rain falls in March. There have been years in Tashkent when no rain has fallen from the beginning of July until the end of September. Except in the mountain region heavy falls of snow are very uncommon. The Aral Sea freezes in the north for four–five months of the year, and so do the lower reaches of the Syr-Dar'ya. In some years the whole of Lake Balkhash also freezes. Very strong winds are a feature of the semi-desert and desert regions. In the Fergana basin and the Tashkent area these winds are hot and dry and cause premature growth of the crops. In southern Tadzhikistan a dry wind blows from Afghanistan, and is called 'the Afghan'; in winter it brings with it heavy falls of snow.

The People

Conquest and colonization have wrought great changes in the population of Central Asia and Kazakhstan. The original population of ancient Turkestan, and very likely of the Steppe Region also, was of the same Iranian stock as the Persians. In the fifth century southern Turkestan was conquered by the Ephthalites or White Huns who were also in all probability of Iranian descent. During the sixth century the whole region was overrun by the Turks, who are described by Barthold as forming 'the most extensive nomad empire ever known up to that date'. By the time of the Arab conquest in the eighth century the nomad Iranians had been dislodged from Central Asia, but the sedentary Central Asian Iranians, the Soghdians, remained. Thenceforward the process of Turkicization continued, particularly as regards language; but the effect of Iranian culture on Transoxania, the country lying between the Amu-Dar'ya and Syr-Dar'ya rivers, remained and still remains today, for as will be seen in the next chapter, the Arab Muslim conquests eventually resulted in the most populous part of the region coming under Persian domination. The physical and cultural effects of subsequent conquests and dominations by Asian peoples were relatively small. The Karakhanid and Seljuk invasions of the eleventh century carried Turkicization still further but do not appear to have resulted in any large-scale colonization. The picture of Central Asia as having been overrun by vast hordes of slit-eyed Mongol pagans is fallacious since the Mongol armies consisted mostly of Kypchak and other Turkish tribes recruited by Mongolian officers. Even the existence among the Uzbeks, Karakalpaks and Kazakhs of such Mongolian tribal names as Kungrat, Kiyat and Mangyt does not, in the opinion of Russian ethnographers, mean that these tribes were of Mongolian origin. Such Mongols as did settle in the region were quickly assimilated with the local population and adopted Turkic languages, Islam and the local culture.

After the establishment of the empire of the nomad Turks in the sixth century the main influences which affected the population of Central Asia were those of Islam and the Russian conquest. The effect of the first was deep and lasting. It was almost entirely cultural, although in the fourteenth century the urban population was to some extent affected by the introduction of architects, artisans, artists and captured slaves as a result of Timur's conquests in Mesopotamia, Syria, India and Persia. The Arab conquests did not penetrate the desert and Steppe Region where Islam was only established much later, and its effect on the culture and way of life of the nomads was much less than on the settled population. Very little is known of the way in which Islam was spread, but it was probably more the result of penetration by Muslim merchants than of forcible conversion at the point of the sword. Be that as it may, there can be no question but that Islam is the most prevalent, penetrating and lasting influence which has so far reached Central Asia and Kazakhstan.

With the possible exception of the Cossack settlements on the right bank of the Ural River, Russian influence did not begin to operate in the Steppe Region until the eighteenth century; and it did not make any considerable impact on Turkestan until the second half of the nineteenth century. It barely touched the way of life and culture of the population of the Khanates of Bukhara and Khiva until the independence of these states was finally liquidated in 1921. Consideration of the political, cultural and economic effects of the Russian conquest and subsequent domination is, however, reserved for later chapters; the concern of the present chapter is only with the physical presence of the Russians as an element in the population of the region. Statistics published by the Tsarist Government in 1914 showed the total of Russian (i.e. Slav) 'settlers' in the Steppe Region and Turkestan (excluding the vassal states of Bukhara and Khiva) as being approximately 2,000,000 in 1911. Of these approximately 1,800,000 were in the

Steppe Region and Semirech'ye and a maximum of 200,000 in the remaining four *oblasts* of Turkestan. There were said to have been not less than 50,000 Russians in the state of Bukhara, mostly frontier guards, employees on the railways and other establishments, and traders. No figures were given for Khiva, but the number is unlikely to have exceeded 10,000. Corresponding figures given in the 1959 Soviet census show a total of 7,408,000 Slavs (Russians, Ukrainians and Belorussians) in all five republics. Of these 4,884,000 were in Kazakhstan and 2,524,000 in the remaining four republics of Soviet Central Asia. Thus, while the number of Slav settlers in the more sparsely populated region of Kazakhstan has increased less than three times since 1911, the number of those in the more populous region of the four southern republics has increased nearly ten times.

The present position is that the population of the whole region is made up of three main elements, namely, Turkic (Uzbeks, Kazakhs, Karakalpaks, Kirgiz and Turkmens) – 12,112,000, Slav (Russians, Ukrainians and Belorussians) – 7,408,000, and Iranian (Tadzhiks) – 1,378,000.

The present more or less precise division of the indigenous peoples of Central Asia into six main nationalities – Uzbek, Kazakh, Turkmen, Kirgiz, Karakalpak and Tadzhik – is a recent and to some extent arbitrary one. Before the Revolution such a division was only dimly realized by the peoples themselves. Russian ethnographers and philologists were of course aware of ethnic and linguistic differences, but the Tsarist Government attached no political significance to them. History was mainly written on dynastic or regional lines and the intermingling and interlacing of peoples and cultures was generally accepted. The classic example of the Tsarist indifference to nationality was the tendency to refer to the Kazakhs as Kirgiz, partly in order to distinguish them from the Cossacks (in Russian *Kazak*). The real Kirgiz were called Kara-Kirgiz.

At the beginning of the Russian impact, and indeed up to the beginning of the Soviet regime, the distinction of the peoples of Central Asia was not as between nationalities, or even as between Turkic and Iranian groups, but as between nomad and sedentary peoples. At the time of the Russian conquest the nomads were exclusively Turkic, but sedentary peoples included both Iranian (Tadzhiks) and Turkic (Uzbeks, Karakalpaks, etc.) elements. In

7

accordance with long-established traditional practice Tsarist ethnographers classified the sedentary population as 'Sart', a word to which they attached an almost racial and even linguistic significance. They described the Sarts as 'after the Kirgiz (i.e. Kazakh) the second people of the Turkic group' and as 'by origin presenting a cross between the aboriginal Tadzhik (Iranian) inhabitants and their Uzbek (Turkic) conquerors'. Barthold, however, held that the name 'Sart' was given at first only to the Persians, then to the Persians and Turks, and finally only to the Turks. He also stated that 'the sedentary element in Central Asia regarded itself as being in the first place "Muslim" and then as inhabiting a town or definite region. Ethnic considerations had scarcely any importance in their eyes.' The word Sart is now no longer used.

The adoption or resuscitation of precise ethnic labels as a result or as a part of nationalist movements has been a common enough phenomenon during the past fifty years. For example, the people of Turkey did not officially describe themselves as Turks or their country as Turkey (Türkiye) until 1923. Before the culmination of the Turkish nationalist movement under Mustafa Kemal the word Turk as used in imperial society was a derogatory term reserved for 'Turcoman nomads' or ignorant peasants.[3] While, however, no one would dispute that the emergence of modern Turkey was the work of the people who now proudly call themselves Turks, the emergence of the nationalities of Central Asia is a much more controversial matter. Soviet historians claim that the creation of the Central Asian republics was the work of the various peoples themselves aided by the Russian people. In support of this claim they have traced the ethnogenesis of each people much farther back than had been done by Tsarist ethnographers and historians. At the same time they assert that ever since contact was first established between the Russian people (as distinct from the Tsarist Government) and the peoples of Central Asia, the former did everything they could to further the just national aspirations of the latter. Much of the evidence now adduced by Soviet historians is unacceptable to Western scholars, most of whom incline to the view that the Soviet nationalities policy was dictated by considerations of expediency rather than of altruism and that the creation of separate nations out of such peoples as the Kirgiz and Karakalpaks did not correspond with any national consciousness or yearnings on the part of those peoples. Nevertheless, just as elsewhere political identities imposed by colonial regimes have often gained lasting acceptance, so the idea of separate peoples with distinctive cultures was not necessarily repugnant to the peoples of Central Asia and has probably been to a large extent accepted by them. Quite recently the impartial historian has been presented with an additional complication in the shape of a new tendency on the part of the Soviet authorities to minimize the same differences of culture, language and even of origin on which they previously insisted, with the eventual object of achieving the fusion of all the nationalities of the Soviet Union.

The description of the peoples of Central Asia and Kazakhstan which follows has been largely derived from Soviet works on ethnography written during the past three years. Such works are usually informed by considerable scholarship and are based on careful research into source material not available to Western scholars. They must therefore in a sense be regarded as the most authoritative accounts available. It is, however, important to remember that just as they differ in some respects from Tsarist accounts and even from earlier Soviet accounts, so it may be expected that they will in the future be tailored to suit future political requirements. The Slav elements have been omitted from the description, since, unlike the Slav settlers in Siberia, their establishment is too recent for them to have developed a distinctive way of life.

Anthropologically the peoples of Central Asia may be grouped as follows. The Uzbeks and Tadzhiks belong to the Caucasoid race of the type known as Central Asian riverain; they are brachycephalic, of medium height and have dark hair and eyes. Mongoloid features are apparent among the Tadzhiks of the plains, and to a lesser extent among the mountaineers of Karategin and Darvaz, and also among the Uzbeks of northern Khorezm and the Kypchak Uzbeks of Fergana. Among the Tadzhiks of the western Pamir and the Uzbeks of southern Khorezm no Mongoloid features can be observed. The Kazakhs and Kirgiz belong to the South Siberian type formed as a result of the mingling of the Central Asian Mongoloids with the ancient Caucasoid population of Kazakhstan. Consequently, although the Mongoloid features of the Kazakhs, and even more of the Kirgiz, are more evident than those of the other peoples of Central Asia they are not typical representatives of the Mongoloid race. The Karakalpaks occupy a position midway between the Uzbeks and Kazakhs, somewhat closer to the latter. The Turkmens are in some respects in a different ethnic class. They have predominantly Caucasoid physical features, but unlike the Caucasoid Uzbeks and Tadzhiks, they are dolichocephalic and considerably taller. Their type, which is sometimes called the Khorasan type, is related to the Mediterranean group and includes a small but clearly distinguishable Mongoloid element.

The Uzbeks

According to present-day Soviet classification the Uzbeks are the largest Turkic group in the Soviet Union and the largest in the world after the Turks of Turkey. With a total number of over 6,000,000 they are the fourth most numerous nationality in the Soviet Union after the Russians. Their name was probably derived from Uzbek, one of the khans of the Golden Horde. Since Uzbek himself became a Muslim, his name came to be applied to the Muslim element of the Golden Horde which constituted its ruling class. During the fifteenth century after the defection from the Golden Horde of the Khanates of Kazan' and Crimea, the Uzbeks occupied the country between the Lower Volga and the Aral Sea. They first came into historical prominence when Shaibani Khan at the beginning of the sixteenth century conquered the settled regions of Bukhara and Samarkand, and later of Urgench and Tashkent, thus supplanting the Timurid empire. By this time the Uzbeks were no longer in any sense homogeneous: they had become mixed with the many nomadic groups who had at some earlier epoch settled in the valleys of the Amu-Dar'ya, Syr-Dar'ya and Zeravshan rivers and with the ancient Iranian population of Khorezm and Sogd. After the disappearance of the Shaibanid empire, from the sixteenth to the nineteenth century, the term Uzbek related primarily to the predominating element in the populations of the Bukhara, Khiva and Kokand khanates. In 1914, the Uzbeks were officially described as constituting the preponderant element in the Samarkand *oblast* and in certain parts of the Fergana and Syr-Dar'ya *oblasts*. They also accounted for about 65 per cent of the population of Khiva, and a third of the population of Bukhara. At the same time, the 1914 Tsarist estimate of the Sart population at 1,847,000 undoubtedly included a large proportion of Uzbeks. According to Soviet ethnographers the process of consolidating the Uzbek nation is continuing and traces of the old division of the Uzbeks into 97 tribes still remain. In the Fergana Valley there are still some groups such as the Kypchak and Turk, which remain aware of their distinct origin and preserve their own way of life with its tendency towards nomadism. The Kurama, on the banks of the Angren River south of Tashkent, are an intermediate group between the Kazakhs and Uzbeks. The Uzbeks of northern Khorezm still call themselves Mangyts, Kungrats and Kypchaks, and some Uzbek groups in South Tadzhikistan have preserved such tribal names as Turk, Karluk, Barlas, and Lokay. Outside the Soviet Union there are about 1,000,000 Uzbeks in Afghanistan and about 8,000 in the Sinkiang-Uygur Autonomous Region of China.

The Kazakhs

According to the 1959 Soviet census the total number of Kazakhs in the Soviet Union was 3,581,000, of whom 2,755,000 live in Kazakhstan and the remainder in the other eastern republics and in that part of the RSFSR bordering on Kazakhstan. The origin of the Kazakhs cannot be traced with any certainty beyond the fifteenth century. In Turkic language historical records the word Kazakh appears from the eleventh century onwards, but only as a general term meaning 'riders of the Steppe' and not to describe any particular people. In Russian writing the first mention of the Kazakhs as living in Central Asia appeared in 1534. After the Russians actually came into contact with the Kazakhs at the end of the seventeenth century, they always referred to them as Kirgiz or sometimes as Kaisak-Kirgiz. The Kazakhs had no ethnic relation whatever with the *Kazaki* or Cossacks, and Soviet ethnographers believe the notion that both words are derived from some Turkic word meaning 'marauder' or 'outlaw' is without foundation. The most reliable theory about the origin of the Kazakhs now seems to be that they were formed from the Kypchak tribes who were part of the Golden Horde. Barthold described them as 'Uzbeks who in the fifteenth century had

detached themselves from the bulk of their nation and consequently had not taken part in the conquest of the Timurid
kingdom'. At some time after the dissolution of the Golden
Horde in the fifteenth century, the Kazakh tribes formed themselves into three hordes spread over a large part of what is now
Kazakhstan: the Greater Horde was located round Lake Balkhash,
the Middle Horde in the northern and central part of Kazakhstan,
and the Lesser Horde in the western part nearer the Caspian and
the Ural River. A fourth Horde, called the Inner or Bukey Horde
(from the name of its khan), was later formed out of the Lesser
Horde, and occupied the country between the lower reaches of
the Ural River and the Volga. In 1723 the Greater Horde was
defeated by the Kalmyks coming from Dzhungaria in what is now
Sinkiang. This caused the Lesser and Middle Hordes to seek
Russian protection; but the Greater Horde did not recognize
Russian suzerainty until the middle of the nineteenth century.
During the twentieth century the total number of the Kazakhs in
Russian or Soviet territory has fluctuated considerably. In 1914,
the Tsarist Government, which regarded the Kirgiz (or Kara-
Kirgiz as they called them) to be merely a tribal offshoot of the
Kazakhs, estimated the total of both peoples to be $4\frac{1}{2}$ millions.
The Soviet census of 1926 found the total of both peoples to be
approximately the same as in 1914 (Kazakhs 3,968,289 and Kirgiz
762,736), but in the 1939 census the total of the Kazakhs had
dropped to 3,098,764. There are about 500,000 Kazakhs in the
Sinkiang-Uygur Autonomous Region and some thousands in the
Mongolian Peoples Republic.

The Kirgiz

In 1959, the total number of Kirgiz living in Soviet Asia was
officially given as 974,000, of whom 837,000 lived in the Kirgiz
SSR. Of the remainder, 92,000 were given as living in the Uzbek
SSR and 26,000 in the Tadzhik SSR. The origin of the Kirgiz has
not yet been fully established. Tsarist ethnographers regarded
them as closely allied to the Kazakhs in race and language, but
Soviet ethnographers make a very sharp distinction between the
two peoples. It is significant that whereas the 1959 census shows
20,000 Kazakhs as living in Kirgizia, no Kirgiz are shown as
living in Kazakhstan. Kirgiz are known to have inhabited the

upper reaches of the Yenisey River between the sixth and ninth centuries. They were encountered there by the Russians during the sixteenth century. It is these Kirgiz who are mentioned in the Orkhon inscriptions which date from the eighth century, and the language of those inscriptions bears a striking resemblance to the language of the present inhabitants of Kirgizia. What has not yet been fully established is how or when the latter arrived in their present habitat. Nothing was heard of the Yenisey Kirgiz after 1703, when a large part of them were said to have been expelled by the invading Kalmyks. It was formerly thought that they must have entered present-day Kirgizia at this time; but Soviet ethnographers now incline to the view supported by archaeological evidence, that the Kirgiz first appeared there during the twelfth century, having been brought from the Yenisey by the invading Karakitays. Barthold thought it possible that some Kirgiz may have entered their present home during the tenth century at the time of the Karakhanids. He notes, however, that if they had, they would have been converted to Islam, whereas 'they were still looked upon as heathen in the sixteenth century'. Outside the USSR there are some 70,000 Kirgiz living in Sinkiang to the north and west of Kashgar.

The Turkmens

The Turkmens are the most distinctive Turkic people in Central Asia, but there are various theories about their origin. One Turkmen tradition traces their origin to a legendary Oguz Khan, possibly a personification of the Oguz, a tribal union mentioned in the Orkhon inscriptions. Part of the Oguz moved west during the latter part of the tenth century and were the founders of the Seljuk dynasty which had its capital in Merv (now Mary). The Oguz probably became mixed with other tribes coming from the Mangyshlak Peninsula; but the Soviet ethnographer Tokarev considers it unlikely that the Turkmens were pure descendants of Turkic nomads. Their long-shaped heads suggest intermingling with some ancient non-Turkish stock. Their language belongs to the south-western group suggesting a closer connexion with the Osmanli or Azerbaydzhani Turks than with the other Turkic peoples of Central Asia. Of the total of 1,400,000 Turkmens in the USSR 924,000 live in Turkmenistan and the remainder in

Uzbekistan. There are 200,000 in Persia and some thousands in Afghanistan.

The Karakalpaks

The Karakalpaks are almost entirely concentrated in the Karakal-pak ASSR (part of Uzbekistan) and numbered 173,000 in 1959. Although they may have originated from the Oguz tribal union, they were probably largely absorbed by the Kypchaks during their invasion in the twelfth century. The first historical mention of the Karakalpaks as such dates from the end of the sixteenth century when they were living on the lower reaches of the Syr-Dar'ya River. In the seventeenth century another group is mentioned as living on the middle reaches of the Syr-Dar'ya, both groups being under the influence of the Kazakh hordes. During the eighteenth century, and possibly earlier, the southern group settled on the Zeravshan River and in Fergana, while the northern group moved to the delta of the Amu-Dar'ya.

The Tadzhiks

The Tadzhiks are the largest Iranian people in Central Asia. Of their total number in the USSR of 1,397,000, 1,051,000 live in Tadzhikistan, and this figure includes some smaller Iranian communities such as the Yagnobis and Shugnanis which still preserve a certain individuality. 312,000 Tadzhiks live in Uzbekistan. There is no doubt that the Tadzhiks constitute the oldest ethnic element in Central Asia, but apart from their language and the fact that they have always been sedentary, there now seems to be no real distinction between them and the Uzbeks other than that of language. A large number of the Tadzhiks in Uzbekistan are bilingual and are said to be becoming Turkicized. According to Barthold, the word Tadzhik is derived from Tay, the name of an Arab tribe. In the tenth century, Tazi, a corruption of Tay, was used locally as a generic term for all Muslims. In the eleventh century the nomad Turkic invaders called the settled population Tadzhik. Although there is no doubt that the Tadzhiks can fairly be called the descendants of the ancient Sogdian and Bactrian population of Central Asia, traces of ancient Iranian civilization do not seem to be any more marked among them than among the Uzbeks, except possibly among the so-called mountain Tadzhiks of the Gorno-Badakhshan Autonomous Oblast.

The total Tadzhik population of Soviet Central Asia is far exceeded by the number of Tadzhiks living outside it. There are estimated to be 2,100,000 Tadzhiks in Afghanistan where they represent descendants of its ancient agricultural people. They form compact national groups in the province of Badakhshan, the valley of the Hari Rud and regions on the southern slopes of the Hindu Kush. There are also considerable Tadzhik elements mixed with other peoples in nearly all parts of Afghanistan, there is a Tadzhik community living between Nishapur and Sabzavar in North Persia, and there are about 17,000 Tadzhiks in Sinkiang.

Apart from the Russians and Ukrainians the only other peoples mentioned in the General Outline of Ethnography (Asiatic part of the USSR)[4] as forming part of the population of Central Asia and Kazakhstan are the Uygurs, Dungans, Koreans, Jews and Baluchis (Beludzhis). The *Tatars*, whose number in the five republics now amounts to 780,000 and are thus the largest element after the Tadzhiks, are for some reason not mentioned. This figure marks a considerable increase over that of the 1939 census and no doubt includes almost the entire former Tatar population of the Crimean ASSR who were deported in 1944 for alleged co-operation with the Germans. The majority of the Crimean Tatars are now known to be in Uzbekistan.

The *Uygurs* were known to Tsarist ethnographers as Taranchis. They now total 95,000 (51,000 in 1939) and are mainly concentrated in the Alma-Ata *oblast* of Kazakhstan, and in the Fergana Valley in the neighbourhood of Andizhan. The Uygurs originate from the Ili district of what is now the Sinkiang-Uygur Autonomous Region of China, whence they emigrated at various times between 1828 and 1884, the largest migration being between 1881 and 1884, when some 45,000 people moved into Russian territory. It is not known whether the great increase in the number of Uygurs since 1939 is due to some further migration.

The *Dungans* are Chinese Muslims numbering in all 21,000 (15,000 in 1939). Most of them live in compact groups round Osh, Dzhambul and Przheval'sk, with a smaller group in the Fergana Valley. Most of the Dungans entered Russian territory in the 1870s, a smaller group entering with the Uygurs between

1881 and 1884. They are said to be descended from Turkic-speaking Muslim settlers in the Kansu, Shensi and Ningsia provinces of China, but they are of Mongol race and their language has evolved from the Kansu and Shensi dialects of Chinese.

The *Koreans* now number 213,000 (182,000 in 1939) and live in compact groups in the Tashkent and Khorezm *oblasts* of Uzbekistan, in the Fergana Valley, in Karakalpakia, and in the Kzyl-Orda and Alma-Ata *oblasts* of Kazakhstan. The Koreans were resettled by the Soviet Government in Central Asia from various parts of the Soviet Far East in the 1930s.

The number of *Jews* in Central Asia was not included in the 1939 census, but the 1926 census gave the total as 19,000. The 1959 census shows 94,000 Jews as living in Uzbekistan alone. The only details so far given for other republics are 9,000 in Kirgizia and 12,000 in Tadzhikistan.* Very little information is available about the history or distribution of the Jews. A part of the large increase since 1926 may be made up of refugees from Nazi Germany, but the majority are still indigenous.

Beludzhi (Baluchis)

There are 7,800 Baluchis in the USSR, the majority of whom live in the Mary *oblast* of Turkmenistan. There is a smaller number in Tadzhikistan. Most of these Baluchis emigrated from Afghanistan to Turkmenistan via Persia between 1923 and 1928.

Some other peoples inhabiting Central Asia and Kazakhstan are not considered by Soviet ethnographers to form a significant part of the population, possibly because of their wide dispersal or because they are being gradually absorbed by other peoples. This might apply to the Arab and Afghan elements.

Germans constitute another important element of the population. According to the 1959 census figures so far published there are 333,000 in the Tselinnyy Kray (New Lands Region) of Kazakhstan, 18,000 in Uzbekistan, 40,000 in Kirgizia and 33,000 in Tadzhikistan. These presumably are part of the residue of the Volga Germans whose republic was abolished in 1941.

The foregoing brief and somewhat staccato description of the peoples of Central Asia takes no account of their political or

* The total of Jews in the five republics is now known to be 147,495.

cultural history, these matters being reserved for later chapters. The treatment of the ethnogenesis and division of the peoples may be open to criticism on the grounds that it conforms too closely to the Soviet theory of nationalities; it can be argued that Soviet ethnography has been specially contrived in order to support the arbitrary alignment of national boundaries carried out in 1924. Many Western specialists as well as refugees from the area contend that left to themselves the peoples of Central Asia and Kazakhstan would have evolved an entirely different national grouping and that the present grouping is a purely artificial one informed by Soviet imperialist and economic considerations. This may well be true; but it is important to remember that history is concerned with facts in so far as they can be determined and that national frontiers and divisions and the writing of national history and the development of national traditions, even if they are artificially contrived by a foreign power, may – and often do – become accepted as facts by the peoples concerned. The creation and fostering of nationalist ideas and ideals where none existed before is a far easier matter than the removal of those ideas and ideals and the inculcation of an internationalist outlook. Thus, in dealing with the history of the peoples of Central Asia their present division into nations in some sort on the Western model cannot be ignored since it may, and in some instances has already, become real. In any event, whether permanent or transitory the present political status of the peoples of Central Asia and Kazakhstan is an important result of their impact with the West and it is with this impact that the present volume is largely concerned.

CHAPTER II

EARLY HISTORY

THE PRESENT chapter should ideally provide some clear historical background to the five so-called sovereign nation states of Central Asia as they exist today, that is to say, the Kazakh, Uzbek, Turkmen, Kirgiz and Tadzhik Soviet Socialist Republics. At first sight, it would seem reasonable to take as a basis for such a background study the voluminous Soviet histories of these republics, which trace the origins of the nations concerned back to the earliest times and without doubt contain much interesting and scholarly historical material. A study so based might be made to appear neat and schematic; but it would not accord with accepted Western historical theories and might moreover very soon find itself out of step with new trends in Marxist historiography. As was pointed out in the preceding chapter the tendency since 1960 has been to lay emphasis on the interresemblance and affinities of the various peoples of Central Asia rather than on their distinctiveness. An interesting indication of this tendency can be found in the recent decision to prepare a definitive edition of the works of V. V. Barthold, none of whose major works published before the Revolution had, up to 1962, been reprinted. On general grounds, therefore, Barthold seems to be the safest guide to follow, and more particularly his short history of Turkestan which, although published for the first time in Tashkent in 1922, was based fundamentally on his theses presented to the University of St Petersburg in 1900. Soviet historians have accepted many, if not most, of these theses, although they have frequently condemned Barthold's 'bourgeois' attitude in respect of Islam. It is interesting to note that they never seem to have queried the first sentence of his short history in which Turkestan is described as 'the southernmost region of Russia'. No Russian historian could use such an expression today, however much he might agree with it in his heart.

ring on Sinkiang – Kazakhstan, Kirgizia and Tadzhikistan –
nscious of this new development.

e end of the Omayyad Caliphate in 750 really marked the
ning of the end of direct Arab rule in Khorezm and
oxania. The Abbasid Caliphate which replaced it, in
ld's words, 'wished to create a state in which the provinces
Persian population would be included on the same footing
Arabs'.9 The development was a complex one but it
ally resulted in Transoxania, and in particular the cities
arkand and Bukhara, becoming part of the territory of the
id dynasty of Persia.

ough the Arab conquests and direct Arab rule may be said
come to an end in the middle of the eighth century, the
e of Islam and Islamic culture proceeded apace. Details
he conversion to Islam of the various Turkic and Iranian
of Central Asia and the Steppe Region are lacking and it
ject unlikely to be pursued by Soviet historians and
aphers. As stated in the preceding chapter there is little or
tance in the legend that conversion to Islam was carried
e point of the sword. It is much more likely that Islamic
and civilization were spread by Muslim traders who,
he eighth century, penetrated as far as Khorezm and
the banks of the Volga. These traders propagated Islam
a way of life than as a creed and, unlike Buddhism,
ity and Manichaeanism, Islam was at that time un-
by missionaries. This theory is borne out by the fact
any parts of the Steppe Region, where the Arabs never
, Islamic canon law (the *shariat*) and customary law
even the limited use of the Arabic script, came into
ong peoples who still retained shamanistic rites and
beliefs. At the end of the tenth century the Samanid
Persia was regarded as the north-eastern limit of the
am. Beyond lay the Turks, nomads who had not yet
lam but were beginning to enter into cultural relations
rsians.

Period

999, the Samanid dynasty was overthrown by the
s, a Turkic people whose khans eventually established

Even with Barthold's help it is by no means easy to present a coherent account of the early history of the Central Asian peoples. Sir Olaf Caroe, one of the most sympathetic and illuminating writers on the subject, thinks that 'the investigator of Turkish and Mongol history in this part of the world is like a man standing on an upper floor, watching the unpredictable and disordered movement of a crowd gathered on some great occasion. Groups meet and coalesce, groups melt and dissolve; a sudden interest draws a mass in one direction, only to split up again; a bidder or leader may for some moments gather a knot of adherents; political or personal causes lead to rioting; . . . there is slaughter and destruction, or even for a time a sense of purpose and direction of effort.'5 Few students of Central Asian history will dispute the aptness of this comparison and it may therefore, as an aid to clarity, be convenient, if not strictly scientific, to divide this brief survey of early history into the following five periods: the pre-Islamic period; the Arabo-Persian Islamic conquest and the rule of the Samanid dynasty (AD 700–999); the Turkic period (Kara-Khanids, Seljuks and Khorezmshahs) (AD 999–1200); the Mongols and the Timurid dynasty (AD 1200–1500); the Uzbek (Shaibanid) empire, the Persian Safavid dynasty, the formation of the Uzbek khanates and the appearance of the Russians in the Kazakh Steppe (AD 1500–1730). This 'periodization', as Soviet historians would call it, is merely intended as a guide and overlooks the many developments and foreign incursions which coincided with or straddled the different periods. Some of these, however, will be mentioned in what follows.

Pre-Islamic Period

Historical records relating to the period before the Islamic conquest at the beginning of the eighth century are extremely scanty. The most civilized part of the whole region about which there is any coherent information was Sogd or Sogdiana corresponding roughly with what was later known as Transoxania, a literal translation of the Arabic Mavarannahr – the land beyond the river. This was the area lying between the Amu-dar'ya and Syr-dar'ya rivers, as well as the adjacent area east of the middle course of the Syr-dar'ya. The people of Sogd were of Iranian origin but the nomad empire of the Turks held sway over the whole of Central Asia during the sixth century. This empire was divided into two parts: the eastern Turks who possessed the territory between the Urals and Mongolia; and the western Turks, known to the Chinese as the Tu-kiue, who were centred on Semirech'ye. Turkestan at this time was politically divided into a number of small states, the most powerful ruler being the Prince of Samarkand, who bore the title of *ikhshid*. The general term for the landowning noblemen of Turkestan was *dihqan* – a word which now merely has the meaning of peasant farmer. The dihqans lived in castles from which they dominated the surrounding country. The prevailing religions were Zoroastrianism and Manichaeanism, Buddhism having died out before the coming of Islam, except in Tokharistan, the country round present-day Termez. The dihqans owed allegiance to the Turkish khans and occasionally to the Chinese: but a part of what is now Turkmenistan belonged to the Sasanian dynasty of Persia.

The Islamic Conquest

The scarcity of historical records which obscures the earlier history of Central Asia ends with the beginning of the Arab invasion. Whereas earlier records are almost exclusively Chinese, from the latter part of the seventh century onwards, there is an abundance of Arabic material which has been carefully sifted by various scholars. The importance of the Arab conquest and of the subsequent establishment of Islam first among the settled population and later among the nomads can hardly be overestimated. It arrested what might have been the gradual absorption first of Semirech'ye and then of Transoxania by the Chinese; it outlasted the invasion of the Mongols, who were eventually assimilated by the civilization which they had come to destroy; and even today, although faced with an influx of foreign colonizers far greater than those of other post-Arab invaders (Seljuks, Karakhanids, Karakitays, Mongols and Kalmyks), it is still holding its own.

The history of the Arab conquests and of the rise of Islam under the Persian Samanid dynasty can be read elsewhere; only a very brief outline is necessary here. The Arab conquest of the Persian Sasanian empire had been achieved during the seventh century by the Omayyad Caliphate centred on Damascus. The northernmost province of this empire was Khorasan, which

stretched from the Caspian Sea to the capital at Merv. This province was used their invasion of Transoxania and Tokh Qutayba ibn Muslim arrived in Merv, oxania and Tokharistan had merely tak forays without any attempt at perman conquests, which lasted until his d Transoxania, Tokharistan and Khor domination, but as Gibb explains 'th were everywhere maintained as the quered peoples and vehicle of the civi administrative and financial authority passed to the Wali, or agent of the A Resistance to the Arab invasion was the largely Iranian population of 1 and of the Turks, mainly the 1 Semirech'ye. Turkish resistance w national spirit of the Iranians . . . the supremacy of the Arabs and dynasties in Islam'.[7] Of potent Iranian and Turkish resistance w the Chinese. 'The Arabs themselv Turkestan as a province wreste There are records of many emba Peking asking for help, and also to prevent Chinese intervention tion in the affairs of Western Ce defeat of the Chinese in 1751 although Gibb maintains tha tradition of Chinese overlord participation of Central Asia the emperor (of China) to his lands to whom China had see unconquerable empire now weaknesses that Chinese dif From this blow Chinese p statement remained true eve the Chinese empire in 1758 colonization of Sinkiang wl known to what extent the

bord
are c

Th
begin
Trans
Barth
with a
as the
eventu
of Sam
Saman

Alth
to have
advance
about t
peoples
is a su
ethnogr
no subs
out at th
culture
during
thence to
more as
Christian
supported
that in m
penetrated
('*adat*) an
vogue am
religious
dynasty o
land of Is
accepted Is
with the P

The Turkic

In the year
Karakhanid

themselves in Samarkand and virtually controlled the whole of Transoxania until the twelfth century. The year 999 is an historical landmark of considerable importance, for from that time onwards until the coming of the Russians, with two relatively brief intervals following the invasion by the Karakitays (1125–1210) and the Mongols, Central Asia remained under Turkic Muslim rulers.

The rule of the Karakhanids in Transoxania and Semirech'ye coincided with the rise of the Ghaznavid dynasty established by Mahmud Ghaznavi with its capital at Balkh. Mahmud's successors were dislodged from Persia and Northern Afghanistan by the Seljuks, whose empire, from the capital Merv, eventually extended its sway over the whole of Muslim Asia including Anatolia, Persia, Mesopotamia, Syria and Palestine, as well as to Khorezm and the lands along the lower course of the Syr-dar'ya.

By the beginning of the twelfth century, most of the area now occupied by the four southern Central Asian republics could be described as Muslim, although Islam lay, as it continues to lie today, somewhat lightly on the Kazakhs and Kirgiz. In about 1140, the Karakhanids, whose power was still paramount in Transoxania, were overthrown by the Kara-Kitays, who now established themselves in Transoxania and Semirech'ye. The Kara-Kitays were a new ethnic element in Central Asia: they were probably of Mongolian origin, but although nomads they had absorbed Chinese culture to a much greater extent than other nomad invaders. Unlike the Mongols, they never embraced Islam. They were at first successful in securing the submission of their Muslim vassals, but eventually they came into conflict with the rulers of Khorezm together with whom they were quickly overrun by the Mongols early in the thirteenth century. By the end of the thirteenth century, the Kara-Kitays had disappeared from history.

The Mongol Period and the Timurid Dynasty

One of the most remarkable features of the Mongol period was that a conquest so complete should not have left more trace. As has already been explained, the notion of 'Mongol hordes' pouring into Central Asia and settling there is quite mistaken. The vast majority of the Mongols remained in Mongolia, where Chingiz Khan himself returned after the military operations were over. According to Barthold, 'the Mongols took measures to restore the welfare of the conquered regions', and 'the opinion that the Mongols did not appreciate culture and would have turned all the land into grazing grounds is contradicted by the facts'.[10] Nevertheless, the Mongol conquest did, as it were, change the balance of power as between the nomad and settled regions, and the Turkic nomad element of the steppes began to some extent to encroach on the towns. The Turkicization of the Mongol rulers appears to have started very early after the Mongol state was established, a good deal earlier indeed than their adoption of Islam. Chingiz Khan's second son, Chaghatay, who succeeded to that part of the empire which included Transoxania, part of Kashgar, Badakhshan, Balkh and Ghazna, was a resolute enemy of Islam; but he gave his name to the literary Turkic language which was created in Central Asia at that time. It is probable that the Mongols adopted Muslim culture some time before they embraced the Islamic religion, which did not become *de rigueur* until about the middle of the fourteenth century, when the Mongol empire was already breaking up. The eventual acceptance not only of Muslim culture and law but of 'the idea of Islam' by the Mongol rulers of Central Asia, Persia and the Golden Horde could be regarded as a victory for religion, since in the national and administrative life of the Mongols – as indeed among all nomads – religion held only second place.

From the rise in 1360 of Timur, or Tamerlane as he is more generally known in the West, until the first decade of the sixteenth century paramount power in Central Asia was in the hands of the Timurid dynasty. The so-called Asian empire established by Timur himself was little more than a widespread though temporary military ascendancy resulting from plundering raids. His expeditions ranged over a huge area stretching from Yelets in Russia to Kucha in Sinkiang and from Izmir (Smyrna) to Delhi. These expeditions were not entirely destructive and included some positive achievements, for example, in irrigation; but Timur established no system of administration except in Transoxania itself, and even of this very little is known outside the cities. He brought all his booty, as well as scholars, artists, artisans and architects to Samarkand, which he intended should become the capital of the world. Soviet historians think that the splendour of the 'Golden Age' of Timur has been exaggerated, and this may well be true. Under the rule of his grandson, Ulugh Beg, however, there was a genuine flourishing of the arts and sciences in Samarkand and Bukhara.

Great and lasting as the effect of Islam on Central Asia was, the effect of the Mongol conquest and the Timurid dynasty which followed it, or rather of the combination of elements of the Turko-Mongolian political and military system with elements of Muslim, mainly Persian, culture should not be underestimated. Barthold discussed this matter in the opening chapter of his brilliant monograph on Ulugh Beg. He pointed out that the political organization created in the countries which they conquered by nomad empires like those of the Arabs and the Mongols had a far greater effect on the fate of those countries than in the Arabian peninsula and Mongolia. The Arab conquests had a kind of cathartic effect on the Middle East and on South and Central Asia, and the Mongol conquest which followed it resulted in the establishment of a more stable political order in China, Muslim Asia and in Russia. It is tempting to wonder whether the Communist principle may not similarly have a more lasting effect in Asia than in Europe where it had its origin.

The Uzbek Empire, the Uzbek Khanates and the Appearance of the Russians in the Kazakh Steppe

In the second half of the fifteenth century the cultural centre of Central Asia shifted to Herat and at the beginning of the sixteenth century the Uzbeks invading from the North-East under Shaibani Khan conquered all the Timurid possessions in Turkestan and Khorezm and also gained control of Khorezm, which by contrast with the high cultural level which it had attained in the fourteenth century was now quite barbaric. But although the Shaibanids may have been less cultured than the Timurids, they by no means arrested cultural progress: it was under them that a rich native historical literature was created, whereas the historians of the Timurids nearly all originated from Persia. Some of the buildings erected by the Shaibanids, too, are scarcely inferior to those built by Timur and Ulugh Beg.

Confused and scanty as are the historical records relating to the southern desert region of Central Asia, particularly from the Mongol conquests down to the formation of the khanates, those relating to the Steppe Region, or what is now Kazakhstan, are

25

much scantier. Indeed, until the end of the fifteenth century, the Kazakhs were merely part of the Uzbek confederation which had been formed at the beginning of the century. They do not seem to have developed any individuality as a people until part of the Uzbek confederation under Shaibani Khan moved south to establish the Uzbek empire. M. Vyatkin, one of the best authorities on Kazakh history, although recently somewhat discredited officially, says that 'by the beginning of the sixteenth century a distinction had already developed between the economic life of the Uzbeks and that of the Kazakhs. The Uzbeks had begun to change over to a settled, agricultural life, while the Kazakhs remained nomad cattle breeders.'[11] In the confused historical record relating to the first half of the sixteenth century the 'riders of the Kazakh Steppe' as well as their khans and sultans are still referred to as Uzbeks. The Steppe was now continually at war with the fringes of the settled regions, with the Uzbeks dominating Transoxania as well as Moghulistan. This was the name given to a kind of relic of the Mongol Empire under rulers whose sway extended over part of Eastern Turkestan and over that part of Semirech'ye south of Lake Issyk Kul. At times, too, the Steppe rulers made common cause with Moghulistan in attacks against Transoxania.

In the second half of the sixteenth century a so-called Kazakh Union or Confederation was formed under the Khan Haqq Nazar. He and his successors waged almost continual war against Moghulistan, the Shaibanid rulers in Bukhara, and also with the Siberian Khan Kuchum. For this reason he was regarded favourably by the Russians, whose trading operations were being interfered with both by Kuchum and Bukhara. Haqq Nazar's main habitat seems to have been in the Nogay country to the north of the Caspian Sea, and it was here, along the Yaik (now Ural) River that the Russians first established contact with the Kazakhs. With the conquest of the Astrakhan khanate in the second half of the sixteenth century, the Russians began to put out feelers into the Kazakh country from the west and from the north, and there are records of various Russian embassies to Kazakh rulers and from the latter to Russia.

The date at which the three Kazakh hordes were formed is not known. There is no record of the existence of any separate hordes before the end of the sixteenth century, but this is no proof that they were not already in existence. There is much speculation among Soviet historians about the 'political significance' of these hordes, but no very clear picture emerges from the considerable research which has been done on the subject. At various times after they are supposed to have been formed, the names of khans are mentioned without reference to any particular horde. The famous Khan Teuke who wielded something like paramount power among the Kazakhs between 1680 and 1718 is said to have reunited the hordes under one political control. A factor which certainly contributed towards the union of the Kazakhs during the seventeenth and first part of the eighteenth centuries was the war with the Kalmyks coming from Jungaria; but this union, if it ever took place, was again disrupted by the Lesser Horde submitting voluntarily to Russian rule, or being incorporated in the Russian empire – both formulas are used by Soviet historians at different times. As will be seen later, Soviet versions of Kazakh history during the whole of the eighteenth century are extremely contradictory.

The Kalmyk invasions of Semirech'ye and the Steppe Region during the first half of the eighteenth century were the last nomad invasions of Central Asia, and Nadir Shah's incursion in the 1740s was to be the last attack on Central Asia by an Asian ruler. Although the second half of the eighteenth century cannot be described as peaceful or secure from the point of view of the people of Central Asia except those living in the large cities, the relative freedom from outside interference made possible the formation of the Uzbek khanates in the southern part of the region.

The Shaibanid dynasty came to an end with the death of Abd ul-Mu'min in 1655. From then until the coming of the Russians it can hardly be said that any ruler or dynasty held paramount power in Central Asia, or even in a considerable part of it, except during the brief military domination of Nadir Shah (1740–7). In his 'Short History' Barthold dismisses the history of the eighteenth century in a few lines as 'a period of political, economic and cultural decadence'. This seems to have been due partly to the development of maritime routes controlled by Western Europe, which brought about the decline of the caravan trade, and partly to the renewed encroachment on the settled areas by the nomads of the steppes, the Turkmens in the west and the Kazakhs in the east. At the end of the eighteenth century, two new dynasties, both of them Uzbek in origin, were founded – the Mangit in Bukhara, and the Kungrad in Khorezm, which now came to be called Khiva. At about the same time a third khanate was formed in Kokand by the Begs of Fergana who had ruled there inter-mittently since the beginning of the eighteenth century.

The object of the foregoing greatly condensed and perhaps over-simplified historical introduction has been to show the kind of influences to which Central Asia had been subjected before contact was made with Western civilization. To pre-Soviet historians, whether Russian, Central Asian, Arab, Persian or Chinese, it appeared clear that the overriding, if not the only, cultural influence to which the peoples of Central Asia had been subjected since the dawn of history was Islam. By the beginning of the tenth century Islamic tradition and practice and Islamic canon and customary law had taken firm hold throughout the desert and oasis regions: all writing was in the Arabic character, whether the language written was Arabic or Persian; and the Arabic character was used for writing Chagatay, although it was quite incompatible with Turkic phonetics. All the Turkic languages, even those of the Steppe, adopted a large Islamic, that is to say, Arabic and Persian, loan vocabulary. The arts, including oral literature and music, and particularly architecture, were Islamic. All these marks of Islamic influence were to outlast the Kara-Kitay, Mongol and Kalmyk invasions so that the Russians when they arrived, were confronted with an unmistak-ably Muslim society. This is not to say, of course, that there were not many survivals of pre-Islamic traditions, customs and super-stitions particularly among the nomad Kazakhs and Kirgiz. But it is difficult even now after forty years of Soviet denigration of Islam and Islamic culture to discern anything which can be called specifically Central Asian, Turkic or Turanian culture. Soviet anthropologists dispute this: they contend that it was not Central Asian culture which was affected by the Arabs and Islam, but that the best of Arab and Islamic culture was derived from Central Asia. For Western, including pre-Soviet Russian historians, how-ever, it was Islam which, as it were, put Central Asia on the map as a region inhabited by peoples who had to some extent succeeded in organizing their society and were thus qualified to 'enter history'. How was it then that they never succeeded in entering history as one or more nations in the same way as the majority of Asian peoples?

Caroe writes that 'the curtain had fallen on Turkestan long before the days of Soviet rule, even before the Tsars'. By this he implies that Turkestan had become cut off from the rest of the Muslim world or rather from that part of it now known as the Middle East. This he attributes partly to the growth of Shiism in Safavid Persia which caused a theological rift between Sunni Transoxania and Shiah Persia, and partly to 'the fanatical exclusiveness of the Bukhara Emirs'. Another reason for the partial isolation of Turkestan from the south is to be found in the fact already referred to that the caravan routes which had connected Central Asia with the Middle and Far East since the second century BC had, during the Ilkhan dynasty established in Persia and Iraq during the thirteenth century, begun to give way to sea routes between the southern Chinese ports and the Persian Gulf. But, as Caroe emphasizes, there was no cultural barrier between Turkestan and Sunni Afghanistan, and even the old Silk Road which had connected China with the Roman Empire retained some importance until Russian domination in Siberia established a new west-east route far to the north of Central Asia.

Centuries of foreign invasion and domination had prevented the natural process of nation-forming among the peoples of Central Asia. From the middle of the eighteenth century Turkestan at least was to enjoy a period of immunity from invasion which lasted over a hundred years until the coming of the Russians, already by then masters of the Kazakh Steppe. Frontiers – an entirely new phenomenon – were established and these were based not on national but on imperial and military considerations. Even in Tsarist times, however, isolation was not complete. There were continued contacts with the outside Muslim world, and the natural process of nation-forming, although discouraged by the Russians, who now filled the political vacuum, did not entirely cease, just as it did not cease in British India. The Russian advance severed contact between the Central Asian and Ottoman Turks, but the total segregation of Central Asia from the Muslim Middle East and South Asia did not take place until the consolidation of the Soviet regime in 1927. Until that time even the Pathans in the North-West Frontier Province of India, and particularly in the city of Peshawar, could regard themselves as part of the

Bukhara-Samarkand cultural complex; and the Persians could think nostalgically of Khorasan as stretching to the Murgab River. In 1918, the then Persian Governor-General of Khorasan – none other than Ahmad Qavam as-saltane, later to become Prime Minister – hearing that British troops might be entering Merv, offered a British officer a valuable diamond ring if he would plant the Persian flag on the citadel there.

The possibility of the people of Central Asia eventually 'entering history' as one or as several nations cannot of course be excluded but, as will be seen in the following chapters, it has recently become more rather than less remote.

CHAPTER III

ON THE EVE OF THE
RUSSIAN CONQUEST

RUSSIA'S ADVANCE from Western Siberia to the frontiers of Sinkiang in the South East and of Persia and Afghanistan in the South was undertaken in two phases whose beginnings were separated by more than a hundred years. The first advance covered most of what is now Kazakhstan; the second moved over the territory now occupied by the four southern republics of Kirgizia, Uzbekistan, Tadzhikistan and Turkmenistan, with the partial exclusion of what were then the khanates of Bukhara and Khiva. It follows from this that any consideration of the state of the peoples of the region before the Western impact must necessarily be divided into separate descriptions of the Kazakh hordes and their nomadic society on the one hand and of the social and political structure of the khanates on the other.

The Kazakhs and Their Nomad Society

At the beginning of the eighteenth century the Kazakhs formed three so-called hordes whose approximate location can be seen on the map on page 250. The word 'horde' is hardly appropriate in English since it suggests vast numbers or at any rate concentrations, whereas the total Kazakh population was extremely sparse and the hordes ranged over wide areas. Although the word horde may be derived from the Turkic word *orda*, an army, or more precisely a striking force, the Kazakhs themselves used the word *zhuz*, which simply meant '100' or 'a considerable number'.

In attempting a description of the social and economic organization of the Kazakhs any Western writer will naturally try to produce something clear and schematic which will make the matter intelligible to Western readers. In fact, however, no such description is possible since there is no precise Kazakh terminology defining social units or status; even the division into hordes suggests a tribal grouping much more definite than actually existed. Barthold explains the formation of the three hordes as resulting from the conditions for cattle-rearing which prevailed in the different regions of the Kazakh Steppes. There were three such regions: in the west the Lesser Horde found suitable winter quarters along the Ural River and good summer grazing in the Aktyubinsk district; in the second region the Middle Horde had its winter habitat along the Sary-Su River on the lower reaches of the Syr-Dar'ya, while its summer grazing lands were along the Irtysh, Tobol and Ishim rivers; and in the third region the Greater Horde ranged over the lands of Semirech'ye (or Dzhetisu, as the Kazakhs called it) and the eastern course of the Syr-Dar'ya to the south of the River Chu. This seems a much more likely explanation than the notion that the hordes constituted some kind of political division.

In theory, each horde was ruled by a khan with a group of sultans owing allegiance to him; but it does not seem to be possible to determine who were the khans of the various hordes at any given period. The horde was loosely grouped into clans, the heads of which were styled *aksakals* (elders, literally 'greybeards') or *biis*, often with the additional title of *batyr* (from the same Altaic origin as the Persian *bahadur*). The khan was in theory elected by the sultans from one of their number, but usually the khanate was hereditary. On the death of the khan, however, there was often a dispute as to who should succeed him. If there was no son, some claimants to the throne would allege their close relationship to the former khan; others relied on friends and relatives or even on force of arms to press their claim. The Kazakh equivalent of an aristocracy was composed of those sultans who could claim to be descendants of Chingiz Khan; they were known as 'white-bone', that is, noble. 'Whitebone' was divided into 'pure' and 'mixed'. If both a man's parents came from a sultan's family he was 'pure white-bone'; but if the mother was of humble birth he could only claim to be 'mixed'. The rest of the population were known as 'black-bone'.

The basic unit of Kazakh society was the patriarchal or joint family. Such families combined together to form an *aul*, a term which is nowadays used for a village, but in Kazakh nomad society only had such an application during the winter when men and herds were stationary. The *aul*, which was sometimes called *taipa* (from the Arabic *ta'ifa*), could be considered as a sub-division of the clan (*uru* or *ru*); but none of these divisions and sub-divisions were at all clear-cut. The so-called clan system, which was originally based on the union of a number of families related to one another and sharing a communal economy, had begun to change by the seventeenth century with the increase in wealth resulting from the conquest by the Kazakhs of some of the southern cultivated areas and the partial introduction of agri-culture among them. The development of the clan system may be divided into three stages: the community, the community-family and the family-community. During this last stage a Kazakh's loyalties would be first to the family, and the community would take second place. It was probably at this point that economic inequalities began to appear and abuses of old customs to spring up. During the seventeenth century the gradual breaking up of the clans was accelerated, and in most cases the place of groups of families of the same clan was taken by *aymaks* or mixed com-munities made up of different clans. This was brought about partly by the needs of cattle-grazing, which forced the clans to break up in the summer for the lack of water, and partly by the frequent wars between the sultans. These intertribal wars in-creased with the growth of the population, the consequent closer contact of one tribe with another and the increased interest of individual families in the accumulation of wealth.

Before the coming of the Russians the gradual and somewhat haphazard infiltration of Islam had very little effect on the social structure of the Kazakhs or even on their legal system. A good deal is known about this legal system, thanks to the codification of laws carried out by the Khan Teuke (1680–1718). From this it appears that the borrowing from Muslim customary law (*'adat*) was mainly in order to give additional authority to existing traditional customs and procedure, particularly in respect of the rights of women, or rather of the absence of any such rights. Kazakh justice was to a large extent based on the principle of retribution or *qun* to the injured party. This retribution included death, mutilation and fines according to the offence. Kazakh customary law had three sources: custom, practice in the courts of the *biis* or magistrates, and resolutions taken at periodical meetings of the *biis*. In different regions and clans customary laws would vary superficially, although fundamentally they remained the same everywhere. Practice in the courts of the *biis* was an important element in the formation of customary law; Rudakov, a pre-revolutionary authority on Kazakh customary law, stated that 'common practice in the law courts was regarded as authoritative even where justice was administered according to written law; . . . and where the court was not bound by any defined law . . . legal practice could be a great creator of new forms'. Often the methods or maxims of a well-known *bii* would serve as an example and gradually acquire the force of law. The third source of customary law, resolutions taken at meetings of the *biis*, was known as *erezhe*. This consisted of a review and definition of the principles of customary law which was often resorted to before the judgement of more complicated cases.

The main effect of Islam among the Kazakhs was on their culture, and even here the effect was strictly limited by the conditions of nomadic life. Islam, however, brought the art of writing, and such education as there was was based on the Arabic script and on Arabic and Persian literature. There had always existed an oral literature in the Kazakh language and occasional attempts were made to transcribe it into the Arabic script. A considerable Arabic and Persian loan vocabulary began to find its way into the Kazakh language, mainly for the expression of abstract ideas.

At the beginning of the eighteenth century the Kazakh economy was still based on cattle-breeding. During the sixteenth century Kazakh encroachment on the semi-desert region lying to the south of the Steppe Region had resulted in some urban development and agriculture and also in a certain amount of trade with the settled population of Semirech'ye and Transoxania. In the north and west, too, there were the beginnings of commercial relations with the Russians. Wealth became increasingly concentrated in fewer hands; but it was wealth which consisted entirely of livestock. The whole of Kazakh life was regulated by the search for summer grazing grounds with adequate water, and winter pastures sheltered from the wind and cold and particularly from the dreaded *dzhut* – the freezing over of previously thawed snow which made it impossible for cattle to reach fodder. Most of the perpetual tribal wars were due to quarrels over winter pastures and the general condition of insecurity made life for the Kazakhs hard and precarious. But the Kazakh economy was exceedingly vigorous and had outlasted two other nomad economies – those of the Nogays and Kalmyks. Tolybekov, a Kazakh historian and writer on economic problems, gives two reasons for this: the first was that the Kazakhs made themselves much more mobile than the Nogays and Kalmyks by substituting camel pack-transport for the old-fashioned Mongol wheeled carts. They also confined their flocks to horses, camels, sheep and goats, and almost entirely abandoned the breeding of large horned cattle. They were thus able to move in relatively large bodies, which was better from the security point of view and resulted in their preserving the patriarchal family way of life. The second reason was the great extent of the territory over which they roamed and which afforded them a wide choice of summer and winter pastures.[12]

How long the Kazakhs would have persisted in their nomad way of life if they had been left to themselves and not been forcibly stabilized can only be conjectured. Even if the Russian eastward expansion had not turned southwards during the eighteenth century the Kazakhs would still have been affected by Russian trading operations in the north and by the lure of urban civilization in the south. There are no absolute standards by which the relative merits and demerits of nomad life and economy can be judged. Both were evidently considerable as far as the Kazakhs were concerned. They seem to have reacted more or less favourably to the relatively mild campaign of stabilization instituted by the Tsarist Government, but most unfavourably to the much more rigorous measures brought in during the Soviet regime. Before the coming of the Russians the principal bane of Kazakh existence was insecurity, and this was largely removed during the Tsarist regime.

The Russian advance into the Steppe Region was for the most part such a gradual process that it is difficult to say exactly when it began. While a map in the 1957 official history of the Kazakh SSR (*Kazakhstan on the Eve of its Annexation to Russia*)[13] shows the Russian fortified posts established along the Irtysh River up to 1720, it does not show what the Asian frontiers of the Russian state were thought to be at that time. Indeed, no Russian maps show a definite frontier in this region as existing before the end of the eighteenth century. On the other hand, Tsarist sources say that shortly after 1731 the territories of both Lesser and Middle hordes, that is, what later became the *oblasts* of Ural, Turgay and part of Akmolinsk, 'became an integral part of Russia'. Western maps showing the chronology of the Russian southward advance from Western Siberia also give the line of Russian fortified posts in 1734 as coinciding almost exactly with the accepted frontier line at the end of the eighteenth century. The fact is that before the submission of the Lesser Horde to the Russians in 1730, which is usually taken as the date when the Kazakh Steppe began to be incorporated in the Russian empire, the Russians had already encroached deeply into Kazakh lands in the north-east up to the Irtysh, and in the west up to the Ural River. The dates of the founding of some of the towns in west and north-east Kazakhstan give a clear indication of this: Yaitsk (now Ural'sk) – 1520, Gur'yev – 1645, Zhelezinskaya and Yamyshevskaya (on the Irtysh north and south of present-day Pavlodar) – 1717, and Ust'-Kamenogorsk – 1720. Other details entered in the map in the 1957 history, and evidently regarded as significant by the compilers, are the route followed by the ill-fated expedition of Bekovich-Cherkasskiy through Kazakh territory to Khiva in 1715–7 and the existence of various caravan routes passing through Kazakh territory between Western Siberia and Transoxania. Bekovich-Cherkasskiy's expedition was, however, a complete failure and the caravan routes seemed to have been used more by Central Asian merchants than by Russians.

It can be said with a fair degree of certainty that although by 1730 the Russians had formulated no definite plans for the overrunning of the Steppe Region, the fate of the Kazakhs was sealed in the sense that henceforward their future was to be bound up with Russia. Peter the Great, who died in 1725, had had grandiose plans for the development of trade with Bukhara, and thence with India, but he seems to have had in mind the establishment of a defended line of communications rather than the conquest of the whole region. In what is probably the last official Tsarist statement on the conquest of Central Asia[14] the impression is given that the Tsarist Government decided to bring the Steppe Region completely under its control only at the beginning of the nineteenth century. It is indeed probable that up to that time the Government still considered the three khanates of Bukhara, Khiva and Kokand to be 'properly constituted states' at the frontiers of which the Russian advance might reasonably be expected to end. The period between 1730 until 1800 was therefore an interim one when the Western impact was in the offing, but its practical effects – colonization, the building of towns and the establishment of communications and Western administrative institutions – were not yet felt.

The impartial student who aims at 'getting at the significant facts' of Kazakh history during the eighteenth century is confronted with an almost impossible task. This is because there is a fundamental difference not only between the very scanty Tsarist version of Kazakh history and that written since the Revolution, but between the versions which have been published during the Soviet regime. In respect of the Russian advance there seems to be general agreement on one fact only, namely, that at the end of the eighteenth century the frontier of the Russian state was as shown on the map on page 250. Even this must be subject to some qualification, for the last Soviet map which shows such a frontier is dated 1955; the 1957 history of the Kazakh SSR does not commit itself on the point. The same map, which appeared in the June 1955 issue of the Bulletin of the Kazakhstan Academy of Sciences, shows a large area south of the frontier line as having come under Russian suzerainty between 1731 and 1740. The description by all Soviet sources of the movements inside this area towards the end of the eighteenth century s 'revolts', and of Russian punitive expeditions by both Tsarist and Soviet sources suggests that Russia regarded this area as coming within her jurisdiction long before the end of the eighteenth century. The truth probably is that the Russian Government had no very clear idea of what was happening in this remote region and particularly about the forces which were behind the various movements of the Kazakhs beyond the line of fortified posts.

The main point of divergence which emerges from a comparison of two official Soviet histories of 1943 and 1957 concerns the significance which each history attributes to the incorporation of Kazakhstan into the Russian empire. In the earlier work emphasis is laid on the fact that the Kazakhs lost their freedom and independence on becoming Russian subjects and entered the 'prison of the peoples', i.e. Tsarist Russia. Comparison of the sub-sections in the two histories describing the significance of the annexation reveals the difference in attitude. The sub-section in the first is headed 'The Significance of the colonization of Kazakhstan' and begins: 'The turning of Kazakhstan into a colony meant the end of the independent existence of the Kazakh people, and their inclusion in the system of military-feudal exploitation created by the Tsarist rule . . . this was the worst result of the colonization of Kazakhstan, against which the Kazakh people struggled for almost a whole century.' In the second history the sub-section is entitled 'The Historical Significance of the Union of Kazakhstan with Russia' and starts: 'The union of Kazakhstan with Russia was caused by important economic and political factors. It had a progressive significance for the historical fate of the Kazakh people and was a turning point in their history.' Just as the first work admits that the colonization of Kazakhstan also exercised a beneficial influence, the second admits that annexation also subjected the Kazakhs to exploitation by the Tsarist regime; but it is implied that this was outweighed by Russia's progressive influence on the economic and social life of the people. The first history stresses the evils of colonization, while the second stresses the benefits of annexation. According to which aspect each history emphasizes, the masses of the people either fought against or submitted to Russian domination. Subjection to Russia, according to the earlier work, was only desired by the ruling class who hoped in this way to consolidate their power and gain support against the invasion of neighbouring peoples; the bulk of the Kazakh people were against a union which would deprive them of their independence; 'subjection was accepted against the will of the popular masses. The Kazakh people fought against it.' Yet the struggle of the Kazakhs against Russian domination which is stressed so much in the first history is not mentioned at all in the second; and such formerly common expressions as 'the rising of the Kazakhs against the Tsarist colonizers' or 'the battle of the Kazakhs for independence' have been entirely eliminated. It is not union with Russia that the Kazakhs struggled against, according to the later work, but feudal and colonial oppression.

The 1957 history does not contain any reasoned explanation why it differs so fundamentally from the 1943 history. The conclusions drawn in the latter work have been criticized in various articles and discussions, but usually by the simple process of flat contradiction. For example, Tolybekov in his article quoted above strongly attacks M. Vyatkin, one of the collaborators in the earlier history and author of a number of other works on Kazakh history, for stating that 'the acceptance of Russian subjection by Khan Abulkhair in the 1730s facilitated the attack by feudal Russia on the Kazakh Steppes'. But all he can say in refutation of this seemingly obvious statement is that 'in the first place, the Kazakh Steppes were not conquered by the Russian state, since the incorporation of the Lesser and later of the Middle and Greater Kazakh hordes was carried out of their own free will. In the second place, the union of the Lesser Horde with the Russian empire did not involve the restriction of its territory or of its nomadic practices. The isolated punitive expeditions carried out by Russian frontier troops in reply to the marauding expeditions of the Kazakh batyrs in the course of which many innocent Kazakh villages also suffered, cannot be regarded as a general campaign of conquest against the Kazakhs carried out by the Russian state.' The fact that Tolybekov is himself a Kazakh does not make his arguments any more convincing. Indeed, he gives the impression that he is leaning over backwards in order to please the authorities. This, however, he does not always succeed in doing. For example, the 1957 history does not agree with Vyatkin's theory that the 'revolt' organized by Batyr Srym in 1737 resulted from the Russian threat to turn the Lesser Horde into a colony and that it therefore bore the character of 'a struggle for freedom', but it does seem to agree that Srym had the backing of the Kazakh people and was not merely a reactionary 'in touch with Turkish official bodies' who aimed at transferring the power of the Lesser Horde from the hands of the progressive dynasty of Abulkhair into those of such reactionary sultans as Kaip, the Khan of Khiva.

The most realistic picture of the situation in the area of Batyr Srym's revolt, that is, to the east of the Ural River, is that painted by Vyatkin. He describes how much of the oppression exercised by the Khan on the various tribes and clans was carried out at the real or alleged instance of the Russian military forces and that the Kazakh 'black-bone' naturally turned against the Russians as well as against the Khan. Such a situation is, of course, not unfamiliar in frontier territories in many other parts of the world. It is a natural, if unpleasant, feature of imperialist expansion and hardly seems to require any elaborate explanation or justification. To sum up, in spite of spirited Soviet attempts to prove the contrary, it seems highly improbable that at the end of the eighteenth century the Kazakhs were at all favourably impressed with the 'beneficial effect' of their partial incorporation in the Russian empire, nor were they by any means unanimously decided to submit tamely to Russian rule.

Turkestan

The Russian conquest of Turkestan – as the region now occupied by the four republics of Turkmenistan, Uzbekistan, Kirgizia and Tadzhikistan may now conveniently be called – was conceived and achieved in a much shorter space of time than that of the Steppe Region lying to the north of it. The use of the expression 'on the eve of the Russian conquest' is therefore much more intelligible in respect of Turkestan. During the first half of the nineteenth century the three khanates of Bukhara, Khiva and Kokand, among which the territory of Turkestan was, generally speaking, divided, were virtually untouched by Western influence. During the second half of the century, or it can even be said during the third quarter, Russian influence spread over the whole region and Russia constituted herself the paramount power. The khanate of Kokand disappeared and Bukhara and Khiva descended to the level of vassal states.

During the second half of the eighteenth century, Turkestan gradually assumed a state of relative stability. Nadir Khan's incursion had fizzled out; the Kalmyks had been finally defeated by the Chinese; and apart from occasional forays into Turkmen territory, Persia had ceased to aspire to Transoxania. As can be seen from the map on page 251 the frontiers and jurisdiction of the three khanates were by no means well defined, but the power which they enjoyed was sufficient for the Russians to suppose for a time that they were states as properly constituted as those of Persia and Afghanistan. In fact, they were in no sense and at no time 'nation states': their peoples had no national consciousness in the modern sense and, it seems, no feeling of allegiance, with the exception of those who made up the immediate entourage of the rulers. In these respects, however, they differed little from medieval principalities in other parts of the world, which eventually developed into fully-fledged nations. Had the Russian advance stopped short at the Aral Sea-Orenburg-Irtysh River line, it is reasonable to suppose that with the passage of time the three khanates would have formed normal nation states, or would perhaps have merged into one. Their populations were scarcely more heterogeneous than those of the present-day republics and in some instances less so; and there were, as there are today, strong interresemblances of race and culture both within the khanates and among all three of them.

The Russian invasion of Turkestan began when the ruling dynasties of the khanates had been in power for little more than fifty years. Quite apart from their exceedingly tenuous national existence, they were all at war with each other and were therefore in no position to face what was for them a common enemy. The Soviet contention, that the absence of any united resistance to the Russian advance was due to the people (as distinct from their rulers) welcoming the Russians as saviours from the age-long oppression of tyrannical Muslim potentates who were in some mysterious way in league with the British imperialists, cannot be sustained by any historical evidence and seems on the face of it highly improbable.

Before giving a brief account of the political structure and history of the khanates during the first half of the nineteenth century, a few words must be said about the population of the region as a whole. A more detailed description of the culture and social structure of the people will be given in a later chapter. The bulk of the people were settled and concerned with agriculture and to a smaller extent with trade. Exceptions were the Turkmens who, apart from those living in the khanate of Khiva, were for the most part nomadic and depended for their livelihood on stockbreeding, and the Kirgiz, seasonal nomads who moved up and down the slopes of the Tien-Shan Mountains. The population of the Pamirs was also nomadic, but it was extremely sparse. Elsewhere, in the oases, the population was mainly Uzbek and Tadzhik, often inextricably intermingled, especially in the towns. The term *Sart*, already mentioned in the first chapter, was applied to Uzbeks and Tadzhiks alike and broadly speaking meant a town-dweller. The ideas of 'nationality' and 'frontier' had no meaning whatever for the people of Turkestan, the only group with some notion of ethnic cohesion being the Turkmens. The adjoining countries of Persia, Afghanistan and China also had no firm frontiers, although Persia could perhaps be described as a nation state. The absence of any proper or recognized frontiers meant that the khanates were more or less perpetually at war not only with each other, but with Persia, Afghanistan and China. Khiva disputed part of the Turkmen territory with Persia and Afghanistan; Balkh, Hissar, Kulyab, Badakhshan and the Pamir vilayets were claimed by both Bukhara and Afghanistan, and the Pamir vilayets by Bukhara and the Chinese rulers of Kashgar; both Afghanistan and Kokand often supported Muslim risings in Chinese Turkestan. The areas of internal conflict among the khanates are shown on the map; in addition the Kazakh and Turkmen nomads, who acknowledged no suzerainty, continually raided the settled areas.

The Emirate of Bukhara

It can be said that the principality of Bukhara was founded by the Mangit dynasty in 1753. The early Mangit rulers styled themselves as Khan, the first ruler to describe himself as Emir being Haidar (1800–26). During the nineteenth century the Mangits aimed at re-establishing the ascendancy of Transoxania throughout Turkestan and this resulted in clashes with Khiva and Kokand. Haidar, however, did not pursue this aggressive policy and during his reign it was Khiva which attacked Bukhara and captured Merv. Haidar's successor, Nasrullah, was much more ambitious and pursued an expansionist policy which resulted in his partial triumph over Kokand, and the sack and recapture of Merv. Although a tyrannical despot of great cruelty he did something in the way of state-building: he established a professional army with some kind of officer *élite* owing allegiance to his person; and he carried through some irrigation schemes and a measure of administrative reform. Although he from time to time received envoys from Russia, he did not come into conflict with her because, as Mary Holdsworth has pointed out,[15] 'the immediate cause of Russia's first conflicts with both Khiva and Kokand was rivalry for the control of the nomad and semi-nomad population who straddled both the path of Russia's expansion along the Steppe and the territories within those two khanates between the valleys'.

The administrative system of Bukhara – as well as that of Kokand – was to some extent a legacy of the Perso-Arab administration of Transoxania under the Abbasid caliphate and the Timurids: most of the terms relating to finance, land-tenure, justice and taxation were Arabic in origin; those relating to the army were mainly Persian. The system was at once simple and loose, being based largely on taxation and tribute. The Emirate was sub-divided into *vilayets*, or provinces, ruled over by *hakims* or *begs*. These again were sub-divided into *tumens* and finally into smaller units known variously as *kent* or *amlakadari* whose principal function was the collection of taxes and the administration of water for irrigation purposes. The hakims farmed the taxes, retaining a portion for their own maintenance and paying a prescribed amount to the Emir. There were two main taxes – *zekat* (from the Arabic *zakat*, alms) on merchandise, movable property and cattle, and *tanap* (a measurement) a tax on land property. There were also additional taxes levied by the Emir for special purposes such as wars. The land tax formed the bulk of the Emir's revenue and, although sometimes calculated as a percentage of the harvest, it was generally paid in cash. Throughout the Emirate, land was the pre-eminent commodity and sign of wealth. The system of land tenure was extremely complicated and a detailed description of it is outside the scope of this brief account. Broadly speaking, land was divided into *waqf* or religious foundations, and *mulk* (freehold) and *tankhwah*, or 'gift' lands, a large part of the latter being exempt from taxation.

The system of justice was essentially Muslim, being based on the *shariat* (canon) and *'adat* (customary) laws. The chief judicial official was the *kazi* assisted by the *aglian* (probably from the Perso-Arabic *'aqlian*) who were lawyers. The muftis were the exponents of the law, the chief mufti being the Emir's chief counsellor.

As already stated, Nasrullah created something in the way of a regular army consisting mainly of infantry (*sarbaz*) and artillery (*topchi*). The cavalry (*sipah*) was raised locally by the hakims to whom it owed personal allegiance. The army was very poorly equipped and its fighting qualities were low since, apart from the absence of any national feeling, the Turkestanis, except for the Turkmens, were unwarlike by nature.

In spite of what would nowadays be considered a low standard of productivity, the commercial life of Bukhara was exceedingly brisk. From time to time Soviet historians have tended to deny this and to describe the economic condition of Turkestan before the coming of the Russians as miserably low. In 1956, however, an article by O. Chekhovich[16] appeared which took an entirely different line and painted a picture of Central Asian economy closely according with the conclusions drawn by contemporary Western and Russian travellers and historians. The picture was one of a flourishing, albeit feudal, economy: quoting from Barthold's *History of Irrigation in Turkestan*, the author describes the great progress made in constructing irrigation canals; she then gives a glowing account of the building of new towns to replace old ones which had lost their significance, and of the buildings in Bukhara and other cities devoted to commerce; finally, she describes the trade conducted with Russia and other countries, pointing out that Turkestan textiles were in demand all over Russia long before the conquest, the value of exports to Russia between 1827 and 1837 exceeding that of imports by 2,000,000 roubles. The exports consisted principally of raw cotton, cotton textiles, silk, dyes and fruit, while from Russia were exported pottery, hardware, sugar, paper, tin, fur, mercury, candles, and later paraffin and manufactured goods and textiles. Although trade was conducted direct with foreign countries by other towns, Bukhara was by far the most important commercial centre. It was in particular the centre of the regional silk industry and to some extent of the valuable *karakul* trade. Apart from foreign trade, there was a well-developed internal trade which embraced the whole region and even extended to the nomad communities on its fringes.

The Khanate of Kokand

The khanate of Kokand came into existence in 1798 and by 1850 it had already begun to collapse under the Russian impact. Originally centred on the fertile Fergana Valley, its khans aimed at expanding the territory of the khanate into Tashkent, Khojent (now Leninabad) and Ura-Tyube, and then into the Steppe Region along the north bank of the Syr-Dar'ya River. This led to a series of wars with Bukhara and the Kazakh rulers, and after the capture and sack of the city of Kokand by Bukhara in 1842 the khanate virtually passed under the control of the Mangit dynasty. The Min dynasty of Kokand was re-established under Sher Ali Khan, but during his reign (1842–5) there developed a serious rivalry between the Persianized town population of the Fergana Valley and the Kypchak Uzbeks occupying the northern part of the valley. It was this internecine rivalry between the nomads on the edge of the Steppe and the town dwellers which precipitated the downfall of Kokand.

As already stated the administrative system of Kokand differed little from that of Bukhara, except that the sub-divisions of the vilayets were known as *beklik* instead of *tumen*. In spite of continual wars and feuds trade was almost as prosperous as in Bukhara.

The Khanate of Khiva

The khanate of Khiva was in a sense the descendant of the old kingdom of Khorezm by which name it was known until the nineteenth century. During the eighteenth century it had been ruled by the Uzbek *inaqs* or powerful nobles who had held administrative power under shadow khans descended from Chingiz Khan. At the beginning of the nineteenth century Inaq Iltuzer declared himself Khan and established a dynasty which ruled until 1920. The town of Khiva had become the capital in the late sixteenth century, when a change in the course of the Amu-Dar'ya had deprived the old capital Urgench of its water supply. The extent of the khanate's real and potential jurisdiction can be seen from the map. The population amounted to about 700,000, some 40,000 Uzbeks forming the ruling classes and providing the administration. In addition, there was a large Persian slave element, mostly in the towns. These slaves had been captured during Turkmen raids into Persia, some of which had extended as far as Isfahan. They seem to have had an important effect on the culture of the khanate.

Conditions in Khiva were very different from those in Bukhara and Kokand. In a sense it was a much more compact state since it did not consist of principalities with strong local traditions and a tendency towards separatism. On the other hand, the towns developed a kind of local patriotism amounting at times to autonomy; and the Karakalpaks living round Kungrad on the Amu-Dar'ya delta frequently gave trouble. Another problem which the rulers had to face was the fact that the khanate bordered on desert areas lying to the north and south-west, where roamed Kazakh and Turkmen nomads. Throughout the eighteenth century there had been no established dynasty, and when in 1804 the Inaq Iltuzer assumed power, he had to establish his authority by organizing punitive expeditions against the nomads and the Karakalpaks. The khanate's external operations were conducted against Bukhara from whom Merv was captured on two occasions. Relations with Russia in the first half of the century were confined to the reception of occasional envoys, a certain amount of trade, and the abortive Russian military expedition under Perovskiy in 1839. At about the time of the Russian expedition Khiva was also visited by at least two British officers, one of whom was Captain Richmond Shakespear. These visits have been interpreted by Soviet historians as clear proof of Britain's intention to turn Central Asia into a colony.[17] The fact that the visits of British officers were not followed by British colonization, but that the visits of Russian officers were the prelude to conquest and annexation is, of course, never mentioned by Russian writers.

The system of land tenure in Khiva was similar to that in Bukhara and Kokand, but the proportion of 'gift' lands handed over by the Khan to his entourage free of tax was exceptionally high. Soviet historians claim that as much as half the agricultural land belonged to the Khan and to his beneficiaries and that 45 per cent of all the irrigated land belonged to the waqf. Artificial irrigation was extensive, the canals which were maintained by forced labour being fed from the Amu-Dar'ya. There were six main canals from 70 to 100 kilometres in length. About 75 per cent of the population was settled and carried on irrigated cultivation in which the rotation of crops was extensively practised. The northern districts grew wheat and millet; the southern wheat, cotton and fruit, including melons of various kinds.

Both internal and external trade was fairly well developed, although not so extensively as in Bukhara and Kokand. Foreign trade was with Afghanistan, Persia and Russia, and the Amu-Dar'ya was much used for the conveyance of goods.

A great deal of interesting information on the state of Khiva in the middle of the century is available from an account written by a Persian envoy, Reza Qoli, who visited the khanate in 1851 in order to negotiate for the liberation of the Persian slaves.[18] In general, he found the oasis country prosperous and he described the palaces and gardens in Khiva as equal to anything in Persia. He was, however, very scornful of the Khivan army which he found bore no comparison with that of the Shah of Persia.

By contemporary Western European standards the levels of government, sustenance, morals, literacy and public health in the Central Asian khanates in the mid-nineteenth century must have seemed deplorably low, especially to the more favoured members of Western society who had an opportunity of observing them. In some, but not in all, respects they were also low by Russian standards and all Russian travellers to the region before the Russian conquest testified to the rapacity, cruelty and viciousness of the local rulers and even of religious dignitaries, and to the prevailing poverty, hunger, dirt and disease among the population. The general picture presented is not, perhaps, wholly accurate: disparagement of existing conditions is a well-known prelude to and concomitant of imperialist aggression. There were many aspects of nomad and rural life in Central Asia which were deserving of admiration and even of envy; and the rulers were not all inhuman monsters. Besides, it is by no means certain that the standards of ruling and living in Central Asia were much lower than in medieval Europe where large-scale foreign invasion, pillage and devastation virtually came to an end some two hundred years earlier than they did in Central Asia. It seems equally possible that the peoples of Central Asia would have been able to work out their own salvation without the superimposition of non-Asian notions of civilization.

CHAPTER IV

THE RUSSIAN CONQUEST
OF CENTRAL ASIA

THE PRESENT study is concerned more with the effects of the Russian conquest and subsequent administration of Central Asia than with its causes. Nevertheless, some brief consideration of these causes is necessary if the special circumstances of Russian domination of the region and the differences between Russian and other kinds of colonialism are to be understood.

Russia's association with Asia and with the Muslim world has from the beginning been different from that of other European imperial powers. The geographical difference is obvious enough, although it is often overlooked: Russia is herself part of the Eurasian land mass and although it was formerly customary to distinguish between Russia in Europe and Russia in Asia, there were no distinct geographical barriers between the two, except perhaps in the Caucasus, where the Caucasus Mountains were considered as marking the frontier between the two continents.* In the second place, Russia was herself under the domination of an Asian people, the Mongols, for 250 years, and some 70 years after the collapse of this domination, two of its relics, the Tatar khanates of Kazan' and Astrakhan, were conquered by the Russians and became integral parts of Russia. During the eighteenth century Russia had close and mostly hostile contacts with Turkey and Persia and, as has been noticed in an earlier chapter, with the Kazakhs of the Steppe Region. Thus, although from a cultural, and particularly from a religious, point of view, the Muslim peoples may have seemed barbaric to the Russians, they did not have for them the same feelings of biological superiority which existed elsewhere.

* It is significant that in 1958 Soviet geographers decided that in future the whole of the Caucasus would be regarded as part of Asia.

Russia's expansion into Asia began in the sixteenth century. It was in no sense a co-ordinated expansion, but rather an irrepressible urge partly touched off by the removal of Mongol rule and restrictions. The predatory spirit of the Cossacks, the merchant-adventurer tradition of the Novgorod traders, and the sense of mission implanted in the Russians by the feeling that they were heirs to the Byzantine imperial tradition all played their part. The first movement was due East along the line of least resistance, and the Pacific was reached at the end of the seventeenth century. During this phase the Russians encountered only primitive tribes, who were soon outnumbered by Russian settlers. The southward movement from Siberia which began in the eighteenth century first into the Steppe Region and later into Turkestan, was what has elsewhere been called 'manifest destiny'. In Lord Curzon's words, 'Russia was as much compelled to go forward as the earth is to go round the sun'. In retrospect, a number of logical reasons – economic, political and military – have been advanced, but it is still not clear how far and in what proportion these reasons weighed with the Russian Government, confronted as it often was with situations created by decisions taken on the spot by local military commanders or governors. Among the reasons cited by Russian, Soviet and other historians have been Russia's need to establish new markets for her trade, British designs on Central Asia, and Russian designs on India. All these, even if the last two were exaggerated or altogether imaginary, certainly served as a stimulus to and justification of the expansion. Soviet treatment of it has varied considerably: while fairly consistent in condemning the imperialism of the Tsarist Government and the oppressive nature of the subsequent administration of Central Asia, Soviet historians have at times contrived to give the impression that although the Tsarist Government may not have been actuated by the purest motives, the Russian conquest was not in fact a conquest at all, but a process of 'voluntary incorporation' in the Russian empire of peoples oppressed by their native rulers or threatened with colonialist absorption by other imperialist powers, notably by Britain. In most Soviet history written during the last ten years the word 'conquest' (*zavoyevaniye*) has been dropped and the expression 'voluntary incorporation' (*dobrovol'noye prisoyedineniye*) substituted: but in a recent book by N. A. Khalfin,[1] one of the most objective which has so far appeared in the Soviet

Union, the preparations for the actual conduct of the final military campaign in Central Asia have been described in such a way as to leave no doubt that it was an operation typical of nineteenth-century imperialism. As if, however, to correct any unfortunate impression which this novel and matter-of-fact approach might have on Soviet readers the book ends with a lengthy Conclusion whose general tenor is so different from that of the rest of the work that it might well have been written by another hand. To this Conclusion further reference will be made later.

On balance the motives and methods of the nineteenth-century Russian imperialists were probably no more and no less reprehensible than those of other imperialists of the period. But, stemming from the fundamental geographical and historical differences alluded to earlier, there were certain other differences between Russian and other forms of colonialism the effects of which are still felt today. In serving temporarily or settling in the Muslim lands of Russia the Russian peasant, soldier or civil servant did not have the same sensation of leaving his homeland either temporarily or permanently as did their counterparts leaving, for example, England to serve or settle in India. The standard of living of the Russian peasant was not noticeably higher than that of the Central Asian, and in some cases a good deal lower. The Russian soldiers, most of whom were themselves of peasant stock, could see this at a glance, and so eventually could the Russian peasant colonists, although settlement on a large scale did not start until the beginning of the twentieth century. Secondly, although the Russians adopted an extremely intolerant attitude towards non-orthodox forms of Christianity and Judaism, they exhibited a genuine tolerance towards entirely different creeds such as Islam and Buddhism. Thirdly, the slave traffic never played any part in the history of the Russian empire, except, paradoxically, in the presence of Russian slaves in the Khivan and to a smaller extent Bukharan khanates. Finally, spreading overland as they did from their own country the Russians were from the beginning obsessed with the idea of reaching a definite frontier. This meant that they developed an entirely different idea of frontier policy from that adopted by the British in India. In dealing with the redoubtable Teke Turkmens, a people every whit as brave and warlike as the Pathans of the North West Frontier of India, the Russians adopted a policy of hitting them as hard as they could so as to finish with resistance once and for all. Great though they were, the hardship and loss of life thus caused to the people in a battle like that of Geok Tepe (1881) were probably no more than those resulting from innumerable smaller actions engaged in by British forces on the North West Frontier of India.

As already indicated the subjugation and eventual annexation of what are today Kazakhstan and Soviet Central Asia fell broadly speaking into two phases: the subjugation of the Steppe Region, that is to say, northern and north-western Kazakhstan, and the consolidation of the so-called Syr-Dar'ya line; and the advance from this line into Turkestan until the frontiers of the Russian empire eventually ran with those of Persia, Afghanistan and China. Historically speaking the first of these phases was the more important since it marked the beginning of the imposition of Russian rule over territories inhabited by people with some kind of organized society and at least some elements of Islamic culture. The establishment of Russian administration in Siberia had been preceded by what Barthold called 'an elemental up-heaval of the popular masses', that is to say, the unorganized influx of millions of pioneer settlers into a vast territory only sparsely inhabited by primitive tribes. The problem of administering Siberia was in essence a Russian problem, since the vast majority of the inhabitants were Russians; but it was complicated by the fact that many of the original settlers were fugitives from, if not actually rebels against, Russian official authority. By contrast, the occupation of the Steppe Region and Turkestan was from the beginning carried out under official auspices, with the possible exception of the Cossack colony on the banks of the River Yaik. The armed resistance encountered by Russian forces was negligible by comparison, for instance, with that which obstructed the extension of British power in India. The tergiversation and inconsequence which characterized the whole of the first and part of the second phase of Russian expansion into the Muslim lands of Central Asia were the result of insufficient acquaintance with the way of life and past history of the local population.

I have assumed in an earlier chapter that Russia's expansion into the Steppe Region, with its inevitable extension into the desert region of Turkestan, began with the so-called acceptance of Russian subjection in 1730 by Abulkhair, the Khan of the

Lesser Horde. Whatever may have been assumed since by Soviet historians, there seems no doubt that the Russian Government believed that this submission of the Khan would be followed by the submission of the people, and it was in consequence ready to support the Khan's authority. The Khan for his part regarded the fort built by the Russians at the mouth of the River Or' as somewhere where he could take refuge in the event of trouble among his people, and he expected that the Russians would support him indefinitely. Eventually the Russians realized that the Khan's voluntary submission meant nothing whatever: it brought neither peace nor security for the Russian caravans passing through the Khan's territory to the trading marts of Turkestan; and the Khan's descendants, as well as the khans of other hordes, kept on taking equally meaningless oaths of submission or allegiance not only to the Russians but to China and to other Central Asian states. During the second half of the eighteenth century the Russians gradually came to understand that their road to the rich trading prospects of Central Asia and beyond was barred by an intractable people who resented their presence and only pretended to treat with them in the hope of gaining support in their own internecine quarrels. What might nowadays seem to be the correct ethical course of leaving the people of the Steppe to their own devices simply did not occur to the Russians any more than it occurred to the contemporary imperialist powers faced with similar situations.

Although the bare facts of the Russian conquest of the Steppe Region and Turkestan are not in dispute the motives and conflicting aspirations from which they resulted have been the subject of lively controversy. The Tsarist presentation of the case as stated in 1914 in *Aziatskaya Rossiya** may have been reactionary and unethical, but it was at least consistent and relatively honest. The Russian Government and local military commanders knew and admitted that the Kazakhs resented their presence and wanted to continue their wild and independent existence without interference from outside. They may have realized that the khans and sultans were oppressive rulers, but their only object in destroying their power was to further their own ends.

The concepts of the nation state or even of nationalism barely

* See Appendix.

penetrated either the Steppe Region or Turkestan until after the abrupt ending of the Tsarist regime in 1917. Consequently, the Tsarist Government was never confronted by the need for compromising with nationalist movements, for granting real or synthetic self-determination to the non-Russian nationalities, or for justifying the retention of imperial domination in the face of world opinion. The establishment of the Soviet regime, on the other hand, coincided almost exactly with the rise of nationalism all over Asia and Africa, which drastically reduced the extent of the British and French empires and resulted in the total disappearance of the Ottoman Empire. Soviet historians have therefore been faced with the seemingly impossible task of glossing over the fact that the Soviet Asia of today preserves, with two slight additions in the Far East, precisely the same frontiers as the Asian empire of the Tsars. Since the subjugation of the Kazakh steppe was the decisive move which eventually led to the Russian acquisition of the whole of Muslim Central Asia, and the establishment of the Russian frontiers to march with those of Afghanistan and Persia, it is on new and special interpretations of this first phase of the Russian conquest that Soviet historians have concentrated.

In the last chapter a brief description was given of the discrepancies in the treatment accorded by the official 1943 and 1957 histories of the Kazakh SSR to the development of Russian expansion in the Steppe Region during the eighteenth century. The discrepancy between the two histories is much more apparent in their treatment of the nineteenth century since by this time the Russians had to some extent taken the measure of the Kazakhs and had decided to bring the whole region under their control. As the Kazakhs realized this, their resistance to Russian encroachment became stiffer and took the form of a number of risings of which by far the most serious was that of Kenesary Kasim, which lasted from 1837 to 1847. These revolts are described in the 1943 history under the heading of 'The struggle of the Kazakh hordes to preserve their independence', and Kenesary Kasim's movement is given a whole chapter to itself. While it is acknowledged that the leaders of the rebellions before that of Kasim had acted in their own interests and desired only to gain power, it is maintained that the movements had the backing of the population and were commendable in that they attempted to preserve the political freedom of the Kazakhs. 'All these risings of the Kazakh peoples in the twenties and thirties of the nineteenth century showed how great was their indignation, and how courageously they fought for the independence of their country.' In the 1957 history the risings are treated very shortly and Kenesary Kasim is given barely two pages. The section dealing with the subject is headed 'Feudal-Monarchical Movements in the first half of the Nineteenth Century' and the rebellions are attributed to the discontent of the sultans who had been deprived of much of their power by the Russians; 'the Kazakh pseudo-aristocracy strove to regain their lost privileges'. There is no mention whatever of a desire for independence or a struggle for freedom on the part of the people. Kasim's revolt is no longer found to be as in the 1943 history 'the culminating point and synthesis of all the succeeding movements' revealing 'the freedom loving and fighting spirit of the Kazakh people, who were not easily to be parted from their national independence'. Instead, the rising is characterized as 'a reactionary feudal-monarchical movement which dragged the Kazakh people back to the consolidation of patriarchal and feudal conditions, to the restoration of the medieval rule of the Khan, and to the isolation of Kazakhstan from Russia and the Russian people'. Comparatively little space is devoted to the revolt itself, and only the briefest outline of Kasim's activities is given, revealing him for the most part in an unfavourable light. He is no longer described as in the 1943 history as a 'hero of the people', enjoying considerable authority and popularity, a talented statesman and general. Instead, he is depicted as rapacious and cruel, imposing burdens and taxes on the people and caring little for their well-being. 'Kasim was barbarously cruel to the peaceable population. At his command hundreds of people were put to death . . . as a result of his raids, whole regions were laid waste.' A considerable part of the Kazakh peasantry, the second history maintains, dissatisfied with the land limitations of the Tsarist Government, supported Kasim's movement at first; but they soon began to protest against his despotism and cruelty and to rise against him, and he was left with only his feudal retinue and bodyguard. His demands to the Russians to withdraw from Kazakh territory, his protests against their fortifications and raids, the details of his battles, the various stages and fluctuations of his movement, his activities as a statesman, his military prowess, his war with Kokand and his election as Khan, all of which are described in detail in the first history, are ignored entirely in the second. And no mention is made of the widespread popularity of his movement in which, according to the earlier work, there participated the popular masses of all three Kazakh hordes. The final war in Kirgizia and Kasim's ultimate defeat are related by the two works in characteristic manner. According to the first, Kasim suggested to the Ala-Tau Kirgiz that they should join forces with him against the Tsarist colonizers and Kokand. This offer was rejected by the Kirgiz *manaps*, who had long been under the influence of the khans of Kokand and who in any case had established relations with the Russian administration; instead, the leaders started to incite their people to raid the Kazakh *auls*. Kasim sent a conciliatory note and freed a number of Kirgiz prisoners taken during these raids in order to prove his peaceful intentions, but neither measure produced the desired effect. The Kirgiz *manaps* began to spread the false rumour amongst their people that Kasim intended to use force in order to gain the alliance of the Kirgiz in his struggle against Russia and Kokand. He then held a meeting of representatives of the Greater Horde and it was decided to punish the Kirgiz *manaps*. So began the war against the Kirgiz which ended in Kasim's defeat. In the second history the subject is dismissed in a short paragraph: 'In 1846 Kenesary was forced to leave the Middle Horde for the South of Kazakhstan, whence, in 1847, he attempted to seize northern Kirgizia. He cruelly punished the peaceable population and robbed and destroyed the Kirgiz auls. The Kirgiz people, defending their land, offered stern resistance to the invader. The whole population of northern Kirgizia rose against Kenesary, and his forces were crushed. In one of the battles with the Kirgiz popular volunteer army Kenesary was surrounded, taken prisoner and put to death.'

No attempt is made to attribute this remarkable *volte-face* to the discovery of any new source of material, or indeed to conceal the fact that the change was due to a fundamental change in the Soviet attitude towards Tsarist imperialism which took place between 1943 and 1951, when the 1943 history was first subjected to criticism. This change will be described more fully in a later chapter. Here it need only be said that during the Second World War it became necessary to re-establish the mystique of Russian superiority and infallibility and this inevitably resulted in the retrospective denigration of early attempts by Asian peoples to resist Russian conquest and annexation. Since Stalin's death in 1953 there has been some reversion to Lenin's stigmatization of 'great power chauvinism'. Although it is admitted that the Asian peoples suffered under Tsarist oppression, no mention is now made of resistance to incorporation with Russia; whereas before it was held that subjection to Russia was only desired by the ruling classes who hoped in this way to maintain their position, it is now considered that the ruling class, on the contrary, led the reactionary struggles against subjection to Russia in an attempt to retain or regain their former privileges.

The second phase of the Russian conquest of Central Asia, subjection of the khanates and the establishment of the Governorate-General of Turkestan, has been described in detail by many Western writers, the most recent and probably the best account being that by Richard Pierce in his *Russian Central Asia, 1867–1917*. The actual military operations were of no particular significance and reflect little credit on the Russians. Although they were sometimes able to concentrate numerically superior forces against the invaders, the Central Asians had no experience of modern warfare and were only armed with primitive weapons. Moreover, their resistance was sporadic and unco-ordinated; they were unable to forget their internecine feuds and unite in order to face a common enemy. Some idea of the relative ease with which the Russian conquest was carried out can be gained from the fact reported by Maksheyev[20] that in all the operations in Central Asia between 1847 and 1873 Russian casualties only amounted to 400 killed and about 1,600 wounded. The main problem was that of supply and this became progressively easier as the Russians were able to establish advanced bases. The casualties suffered by the Central Asians, on the other hand, certainly ran into many tens of thousands, though no precise figures are available.

Instead of recapitulating the Russian advance to the frontiers of Afghanistan and Persia which took place between the years 1857 and 1884, I have thought it appropriate to include in the Appendix the relevant part of the historical section of *Aziatskaya Rossiya* (Asiatic Russia), a voluminous official handbook published in 1914 by the Directorate of Land Exploitation and Agriculture. Besides providing a convenient summary of events within the compass of the present volume, this constitutes what is probably the last Tsarist official account of the Russian advance published before the 1917 Revolution. It sets forth the Russian imperial point of view which has been lost sight of, if not deliberately obscured, by the regime which inherited the Russian empire without restoring the smallest portion of it to its former owners, the peoples of Central Asia.

The impression which the Tsarist account endeavours to give of deliberate planning for the destruction of the power of the khanates hardly corresponds with the facts. During the crucial period 1857 to 1868 there were many different opinions on how the khanates should be brought to heel. In 1858, Count N. P. Ignat'yev, who had previously been Russian Military Attaché in London, set out on a mission to the khanates of Khiva and Bukhara in the course of which he submitted various proposals to Kovalevskiy, Head of the Asian Department. The object of these proposals was to gain the co-operation of these two khanates against the khanate of Kokand, the reduction of which was generally considered to be the first strategic objective. Ignat'yev seems to have thought that something was to be gained by the signing of formal treaties with Khiva and Bukhara, but eventually he became completely disillusioned. 'The information obtained by our mission,' he wrote, 'and the consequent dispersal of the former mirage, brought about a sharp change in our relations with these treacherous and crafty neighbours, and induced a more correct view of the significance and foundation of their power, of the real strength and particularly of the position which we must and can occupy in Central Asia . . . as well as of the objectives we must pursue for a more real and powerful protection of our essential interests.' Ignat'yev's proposals for treaties directed against Kokand were not accepted by the Russian Government partly because they did not consider the Emir of Bukhara in particular a reliable ally, and partly because they were not unanimous in wishing to extend Russia's Asian possessions by force of arms. The principal advocate of vigorous action against Kokand with or without assistance from the other khanates was Milyutin, the Minister for War, acting on advice from the Governorate-General of Orenburg, a post which was occupied from 1860 to 1865 by General A. P. Bezak. Bezak visited the Syr-Dar'ya line in 1861 and formed the opinion that Tashkent should be captured as soon as possible. 'From there,' he wrote, 'a convenient direct road runs through the fortress of Auliye-ata (now Dzhambul) to Kuldja and Chuguchak and I imagine it will be quite easy for the Siberian Corps to build a fort at Pishpek (now Frunze) and join up with the troops of the Orenburg force near Tashkent. They (the Orenburg force) can, together with the Siberian Corps, proceed to capture Tashkent, having first built a fort on the Syr at a suitable spot near Tashkent; this would give protection to the ships and all food and military supplies would be stored there.' In this way, Russia would secure a convenient frontier with the khanate of Kokand, while her control of Tashkent would considerably promote her trade. Trade routes from Bukhara, China and Russia passed through it and 'with Tashkent in our hands we shall not only dominate completely the Kokand khanate but we shall strengthen our influence on Bukhara which will greatly increase our trade with those countries and particularly with the populous Chinese towns of Kashgar and Yarkand'.

The Ministry of Foreign Affairs feared that too active a Russian policy in Central Asia would annoy Britain. To this Bezak answered that Russian expansion up to the Syr-dar'ya would be less objectionable to Britain than up to the Amu-dar'ya, which would bring Russia nearer to India. He added that he did not believe that the British reckoned seriously with a Russian attack on India. The Tsar approved Bezak's views, but another four years were to elapse before Tashkent was finally captured. Indeed, had it not been for the prompt and largely unauthorized action of the local commander, General Chernyayev, the final decision might never have been taken.

There can, of course, be no doubt that the conviction of the military and economic authorities of Russia about the importance of Tashkent was soundly based. The city and surrounding district constituted a kind of semi-independent principality; although nominally under what today would be called the suzerainty of Kokand, it was not regarded and did not regard itself as a part of the Kokand khanate. Apart from the intrinsic commercial importance of the city, it lay at the junction of the Steppe and oasis regions and was coveted alike by the nomad Kazakhs and the Emir of Bukhara: its climate was good, it offered unlimited scope for expansion, and it was in almost every way suitable for what it eventually became and now is, a great Russian political and cultural centre in the heart of Asia. It seems probable that these considerations were well understood by the whole Russian Government and by the Tsar; but in a series of four memoranda presented by the Ministry of Foreign Affairs to the Tsar in October 1864, the very month in which Chernyayev made his first unsuccessful attempt to capture Tashkent, the expediency of such a step was categorically rejected on the ground that it would inevitably involve the Russian empire in all the Central Asian discords. 'It would not set a limit to our advance into the heart of Central Asia' but on the contrary would lead to 'an advance on Kokand, then on Bukhara and finally, even further afield'. While, however, the memoranda noted that the Russian Government had no desire 'to extend the limits of its influence by conquest', it also in the same breath noted that the Russian empire 'influenced by the insistent demands of our trade, and some mysterious but irresistible urge towards the East, was steadily moving into the heart of the Steppe'. The same kind of equivocation appeared, according to Khalfin, in a plan of operations in Central Asia approved by the Tsar in November 1864. 'In preparing this document for "internal use", the Tsarist statesmen emphasized the necessity of refraining from further advances in Central Asia. But the statement contained in it about the "inevitability" of capturing the whole of the Kokand khanate makes nonsense of the words about the inexpediency of "the further extension of the imperial domains".'[21]

When, in June 1865, Chernyayev once more decided to attack and capture Tashkent, he was, again according to Khalfin, taking action 'which in fact fully corresponded with the ideas both of the government and the military-feudal aristocracy of the Russian empire, and of commercial and industrial circles. He understood perfectly well that the repeated appeals by the diplomatic department for the cessation of further advance in Central Asia were a special kind of manoeuvre, a smoke screen, resulting from fears of undesirable protests from Britain. Chernyayev took advantage of the strong support of expansionist elements in the capital . . . and among his own close associates; he knew that not only would he not be taken to task for his "independent" action, but that, on the contrary, he could count on receiving decorations and promotion.'

Whether intended or merely connived at by the Russian

Government, the capture of Tashkent by Chernyayev with a total Russian loss of 25 killed and 89 wounded quickly produced results which exceeded the most sanguine expectations of the Orenburg Governorate-General as well as the hopes more discreetly cherished in St Petersburg. At first, the Ministry of Foreign Affairs continued to deny any intention of including Tashkent in the Russian empire. It considered it 'more expedient to turn Tashkent and the territory surrounding it into a separate khanate which would have to be under the full control of Tsarism and play the role of a buffer state between Russian domains and the Emirate of Bukhara'.[22] This view was strongly opposed by Chernyayev as being totally impracticable; but it was supported by Kryzhanovskiy, the newly appointed Governor-General of Orenburg, who thought it was better 'to have under one's thumb a militarily weak but commercially well-developed state as a vassal, rather than to acquire that state for the empire and establish in it Russian officials'. Accordingly, the inhabitants of Tashkent were called upon to elect their own khan. This, however, as they declared in an address presented to General Chernyayev, they had no wish to do. They preferred that the civil government of Tashkent should be in the hands of Chernyayev, while the religious and judicial administration would remain vested in the person of the Kazi Kalan, or supreme judge of the Canon Law, subject to confirmation by Chernyayev. It is of some interest to note that according to Barthold, this address was submitted before the inhabitants of Tashkent were told to elect their own khan, and there is a suggestion that the address was engineered by Chernyayev himself. Be that as it may, Kryzhanovskiy began to change his tactics and to declare that it was quite natural for the people of Tashkent to want 'to become part of a strong state, able to protect them from external enemies and to rid them of age-long internal disturbances and disputes'. In August 1866, Tashkent was declared part of Russia and its inhabitants Russian subjects.

In 1867 the Governorate-General of Turkestan was established with its headquarters at Tashkent and General Kaufman as the first incumbent. In dealing with the further stages of the Russian conquest of Central Asia which followed, some Western writers speak of Russian commanders and administrators 'yielding to the temptation' to continue the advance. In fact, however, there was no question of stopping. Bukhara was humbled by the capture in 1868 of Samarkand and the imposition of a treaty which reduced the khanate to a state of vassalage. The same procedure was followed with Khiva in 1873. The whole of the khanate of Kokand was gradually overrun and came to an end in 1876. The Transcaspian region had still to be subdued but fighting was concluded witht he battle of Geok Tepe in 1881 and the conquest of the whole region was by then complete.

Russia's advance in Central Asia naturally gave some cause for alarm to the states bordering on the region and particularly in British India. Of the other states – China, Afghanistan and Persia – none was in a position to take any effective action against Russia, and two of them, Persia and Afghanistan, were not displeased at the appearance of a rival to British power. The Russian Government took so little account of Chinese power and protests that in order to guard against the effects of the rebellion which broke out in Sinkiang in 1867 and the temporary establishment there of Yaqub Beg, who was thought to be on friendly terms with the British, they ordered the military occupation of the upper Ili Valley and did not relinquish control of it until 1883. In so far as the Afghans could be said to exist as a state at all, their foreign policy was under the control of the British Government of India: but the Russian Government does not seem to have been apprehensive of any effective interference in their advance either from Afghanistan or from Persia. From Persia, indeed, they were able to derive considerable advantage by obtaining supplies from the northern province of Khorasan during the operations against the Teke Turkmens in 1881-2. Russia's relations with Britain as a great power were much more complicated. During the second phase of the operations in Central Asia, that is, the advance from the Syr-dar'ya line to the frontiers of Persia and Afghanistan, she was partially affected by two apparently contradictory considerations. She wished on the one hand to avoid antagonizing Britain and thus prejudicing her position in Europe; on the other hand, she was conscious of British sensitivity on the subject of India and was not averse to creating the impression that India constituted her ultimate objective. There was of course a good deal of misunderstanding on both sides about their respective intentions. Broadly speaking, it may be said that Russian policy was expansionist, but not beyond the frontiers of what the Ministry of Foreign Affairs described as 'properly organized states', and only in so far as the risk of war with a major European power could be avoided. British policy was mainly concerned with the defence of India; it aimed at keeping Russian influence out of Persia and Afghanistan, but steered clear of going to war with Russia over Russian aspirations in the Central Asian states. This is not to say that there were no individual Russians who wished to attack India, or individual Englishmen who wished to advance into Central Asia. It is, for instance, true that suggestions for the extension of British support to the states of Central Asia were occasionally put forward by such well-known Russophobes as Lord Lytton and McNeill; but they were hardly taken seriously by the British Government and certainly never acted upon. The Indian intelligence organizations were naturally concerned not so much with blocking Russia's expansion in Central Asia as with surveying the routes and logistics of a possible Russian advance against India. Russian historians, both Tsarist and Soviet, have always been obsessed with the sinister intentions and vast influence wielded by British agents, many of whom appeared long before the Russian advance into Turkestan began. It was equally natural that the Russian advance from the Steppe into the oasis region of Central Asia should be preceded by a careful reconnaissance of the terrain, the tribal situation and the trade possibilities. All such activities, as well as Russian attempts to establish direct trade relations with Kashmir and the Punjab – states adjacent to but not then part of British India – can be seen in retrospect as quite normal on the part of a rapidly expanding nation intent on extending its political and commercial influences in Asia. But Soviet historians, while continuing to condemn British intelligence activities, find it necessary to describe Russian military reconnaissances as 'scientific investigation' and intelligence officers as 'explorers'. The theme of British plans said to have formulated in the first half of the nineteenth century for the annexation and colonization of an area then under independent rulers and hitherto untouched by any imperialist expansion is still a favourite one with Soviet historians. The fact that in the event the area was colonized not by the British but by the Russians is now attributed to the desire of the population to become incorporated in the Russian empire.

British expressions of alarm at the Russian advance were a feature of the second half of the nineteenth century and reached their culmination in 1884 with the annexation of the Merv oasis. After the Panjdeh incident of 1885 and the subsequent delimitation of the Afghanistan frontier in 1887, British apprehension to some extent died down since it was felt that the Russians were unlikely to encroach any further into Afghan territory. But 'the Russian threat to India' continued to exist in the minds of many British statesmen and soldiers until the signing of the Anglo-Russian Convention of 1907, which defined Russian and British spheres of influence in Persia, Afghanistan and Tibet.

The historical significance of the Russian conquest and annexation of Central Asia is a subject which has severely taxed the ingenuity of Soviet historians. They have to explain why the vast and valuable territories acquired by the Tsarist Government by a process of naked imperialist aggression still remain an integral part of what is simply the Tsarist empire under its new name of the Soviet Union. Most of the devices used for this purpose appear in the conclusion to N. A. Khalfin's book to which a reference was made earlier in this chapter. 'Soviet historians', he writes with a *naïveté* which is almost engaging, 'are of the definite opinion that for Central Asia to have become part of the British dominions would have been the greatest possible disaster for its peoples.' In comparing the respective Russian and British conquests and administrations of Central Asia and India, he mentions the unquestionable fact that in India the people only came into contact with the British in the unrepresentative guise of officials and self-seeking traders, whereas the Central Asians were able to get to know the Russian peasants who were as poor and as much oppressed by the Russian Government as themselves. Attempts made by 'bourgeois nationalists and reactionaries' to blame the Russian people for the sufferings which fell to the lot of the people of Central Asia were, according to Khalfin, 'a palpable juggling with facts, a distortion of historical truth'. He does not mention the fact that, whereas India and Pakistan are now independent with no British element in their population apart from a business community, Central Asia is not independent and contains over seven million non-Asian settlers and officials out of a total population of some twenty-three millions. There is, of course, no reason to dispute Khalfin's contention that in many instances 'the local population, exasperated by the cruel, feudal exploitation and by every kind of taxation and extortion' exercised by the local authorities, often operated openly on the side of the invading forces. This was equally true in India.

Perhaps a more objective assessment of the historical significance of the Russian conquest of Central Asia would be the following: once Russia had established herself in the vast expanse of virtually uninhabited territory between the Urals and the Pacific, it was inevitable that she should expand southward to the frontiers of properly constituted states. When the Russians appeared on the scene, the peoples of Central Asia were just beginning to recover from long centuries of foreign invasion, massacre and enslavement. Russia was the only power on the Asiatic mainland with the necessary military strength, dynamism and economic urge to take over responsibility for the Central Asian steppes, deserts and mountainous regions. There is no doubt that by doing so she enormously improved her strategic, political and economic position. Nor is there any doubt that from a material point of view, that is, according to Western standards, the lot and prospects of the local population also improved. That each of the nationalities which later emerged under the Soviet regime could have formed an independent and economically viable nation state seems doubtful, but they might have formed two or more states, or have been grouped together in some kind of federation.

CHAPTER V

THE TSARIST ADMINISTRATION
OF CENTRAL ASIA

DURING THE century and a half which ended with the battle of Geok Tepe in 1881, Russia had acquired a vast territory rather larger than the Indian sub-continent in area but with a population of less than nine millions. In the Steppe Region the advance had been slow and hesitant and Russian control was not fully established until the middle of the century. But once Tashkent had been captured in 1865 the conquest of the more populous oasis region and the final curbing of the power and influence of the khanates of Kokand, Khiva and Bukhara were very rapid.

It is not easy to assess the reaction of the peoples of Central Asia to the Russian conquest. Since the population was relatively small and the inhabited areas restricted, the presence of the Russians was known to all classes of the people. This was entirely different from the situation in India where up to the gaining of independence in 1947, millions of people had never seen, much less spoken to an Englishman, and if they had heard of the British, were not aware that they exercised paramount control in the country. It cannot be too strongly emphasized that in Central Asia there was nothing whatever in the way of national sentiment or state loyalty. Even in the heyday of the khanates no one thought of himself as a Bukharan, a Khivan or a Kokandi. There were no closely knit communities like the Sikhs and Mahrattas in India. Nationality was a barely understood concept even among a comparatively distinctive people such as the Turkmens. A man would think of himself more as a Yomut, Salor or Teke than as a Turkmen and in such areas with a mixed and largely bilingual population as the Zeravshan Valley, the people often had no idea whether they were Uzbeks or Tadzhiks. The loyalty that did exist, and exist strongly, was that to tribe, clan and joint family.

The Russian Government did not seriously consider the question of administrative divisions until 1865, by which time Kazakhstan had ceased to be a border region and the limit of the Russian conquests had reached Tashkent, some 1400 miles from Orenburg. Hitherto the new territories had been administered by the Governorates-General of Orenburg and Western Siberia. The Steppe Commission of 1865 initiated among other things the Governorate-General of Turkestan, which included a large part of what is now southern Kazakhstan, the northern part remaining under Orenburg and Western Siberia. The later acquisition in 1868 and 1873 of part of the territories of Bukhara and Khiva and the overrunning of Transcaspia, brought further changes in 1882. The arrangement made in that year, which lasted until 1917, was that the whole region with the exception of the western *oblasts* (provinces) of Turgay and Ural'sk (corresponding roughly to the present *oblasts* of Aktyubinsk, West-Kazakhstan and Gur'-yev) was divided into two Governorates-General, those of the Steppe Region and Turkestan. The Turgay and Ural'sk *oblasts* were administered separately and were directly responsible to the Ministry of the Interior. This arrangement seems to have been intended to make a broad separation between the nomad and settled peoples. Since, however, the northern part of Turkestan included about one and a half million nomad Kazakhs and Kirgiz, General Kaufman had proposed in 1880 that Turkestan itself should be subdivided into two zones, the northern being nomad and the southern settled. Kaufman died before this proposal could be implemented or even formally presented; there is no doubt, however, that it was soundly based, as he himself said, 'not so much on the external or temporary conditions determined by the military and political situations of the past epoch of conquests and annexations, as on the requirements of the civil organization of our occupied territories'.

It is quite untrue, as has been stated by Soviet historians and dutifully repeated by some Western writers, that the provincial division of the Governorates-General was carried out with the express purpose of breaking down national formations, which did not in point of fact exist. *Oblast* and even *uyezd* (county) boundaries were to some extent contrived with the object of breaking up tribal and clan combinations, but this was not at all the same thing and was a process which from the beginning has had the warm approval of the Soviet regime. The 1957 history of the Kazakh SSR does not repeat the accusations of the 1943 history in respect of Kazakhstan but as regards the other parts of Central Asia the charge of *razdrobleniye* or parcelling out is still maintained.

The system of administration established by the Tsarist Government in Central Asia as military operations came to an end was probably the best that could have been expected in the circumstances. In Russia itself serfdom had only just been abolished and government was still despotic, unrepresentative and semi-military in character. Corruption was rife in the army and in all government departments, and the standard of living and literacy was deplorably low. With such a background it was hardly surprising that there was no cadre of experienced civil administrators and officials to whom the government of the newly acquired territories could be entrusted. In the event, the administration of the Steppe Region and Turkestan was from the beginning of the advance up to the Revolution of 1917 an essentially military one. Apart from a few liberal-minded reformers – many of them of foreign extraction, such as Count Pahlen – military government seemed perfectly natural to the Russians. Writing as late as 1912, A. Krivosheyn, head of the Agricultural Administration, felt that Turkestan was 'still a Russian military camp, a temporary halting place during the victorious march of Russia into Central Asia. The Russian military might speaks to the subject mass of the natives a more comprehensible and impressive language than the civil administration.' Krivosheyn saw Turkestan as 'an endless sea of natives' and the Russian settlements as 'still only islands in this sea, although they are, thank God, firm bases for the further settlement of Russians'. (These settlements, it may be noted, amounted at the time to about two million in the whole of the Steppe Region and Turkestan, excluding Khiva and Bukhara.) He was probably right when he added that 'the military administration has not hindered the economic development of Turkestan so far', but his statement that 'the administration is in general well prepared for its immediate task' was very wide of the mark.

The military character of the administration was particularly marked in the Turkestan Governorate-General. The Governor-General himself was always a serving general officer who was responsible to the Ministry of War for the entire administration of Turkestan. All the *oblast* (provincial) governors and so-called '*uyezd* (county) commandants' were, according to *Aziatskaya Rossiya*, serving army officers and constituted 'a so-called military administration, which enjoys great respect and influence'. The status of all the *oblasts* was the same except for that of Transcaspia which enjoyed a certain degree of independence largely owing to the patriarchal regime inaugurated by General Kuropatkin, who was Governor there from 1890 to 1898. The Governor of Transcaspia was empowered to deal directly with the Russian Ambassador in Tehran and the Consul General in Meshed, and also with the Russian Political Agent in Bokhara; but not with the khans of Bukhara or Khiva.

The administration of the so-called Steppe *oblasts* was somewhat different. All of them except Semirech'ye, which was called a Steppe *oblast* although it was included in the Turkestan Governorate-General, came under the Ministry of the Interior. Only two, Akmolinsk and Semipalatinsk, made up the Governorate-General of the Steppe Region; Ural'sk and Turgay being directly responsible to the Ministry. Ural'sk was described as a military governorate, but most, if not all, of the *oblast* and *uyezd* commandants seem to have been military officers.

In both Turkestan and the Steppe Region local government was allowed to continue on more or less traditional lines, although it was to some extent regularized by the Russians and locally elected elders and water inspectors were liable to summary removal by the *uyezd* commandants. Much the same applied to the lower judicial courts which were conducted according to Muslim customary law (*'adat*) with occasional recourse to the Muslim canon law (*shariat*). It was also possible to appeal against both the customary and canon law to the *uyezd* commandant and this was sometimes done in cases of matrimonial disputes. For instance, there was often objection to the Kazakh nomad custom by which a widow automatically became the wife of her husband's nearest relative. The Russian administration was opposed to such customs and usually supported resistance to them, but otherwise those who had recourse to the *uyezd* commandant or to higher Russian courts for the settlement of civil disputes seldom got any more satisfaction than they got in their own courts.

As can readily be imagined the standard of the military administrators was not on the whole high. There were certainly in the higher ranks some efficient and enlightened administrators such as General Kaufman and General Kolpakovskiy, and there were colourful personalities such as Chernyayev and Skobelev who caught the imagination of the local population, although they were unequal to the task of day-to-day administration. Chernyayev in particular was positively venerated by the population of Tashkent after its capture in 1865 but was a total failure as Governor-General of Turkestan in 1882. But the general average of *oblast* and *uyezd* commandants seems to have been low. Armies do not as a rule release their best officers for administrative posts and those sent specially for the purpose from European Russia were often men who had got into financial or some other trouble there. Bribery and corruption were widespread and in spite of frequent enquiries and exposures it seems to have been just as bad at the time of the Pahlen commission in 1908–9 as it was at the beginning of the annexation.

With its obvious shortcomings in principle and personnel the Russian administration of Central Asia did provide in Richard Pierce's words 'an effective system for peopling and developing the region'. The Russians were honest in their aims and in their opinion of the extent to which the local population could help in attaining them: they intended to exploit the region economically and militarily to the best of their ability; they did not think the local population could help them much in these respects except by keeping quiet and providing a certain amount of labour. With a few notable exceptions, they were not interested in the people and did not like them; nor did they pretend as did their Soviet successors that the Central Asians liked and even loved them. They did not make them liable for military service, partly because they doubted their usefulness as soldiers, but mainly because they did not want to teach them the use of modern weapons. The Russians therefore concentrated their efforts on making the region a fit country for Russians to live in. This is not to say, however, that in so doing they did not contribute greatly to the material welfare and security of the local population.

The Russian conviction that the region could not be exploited to the full or made militarily secure without extensive Russian colonization was accompanied by the belief in the minds of their more far-seeing administrators that colonization could not be made to work unless the native population was reasonably content. In addition, therefore, to making arrangements for the extensive settlement of Russian peasants and to engaging in public works and urban development to suit Russian requirements, they also made considerable efforts to regularize the systems of land tenure and taxation. Crude and reactionary as the military system of government may have been, it certainly enabled reforms to be pushed through much more effectively and quickly than would have been possible under a civil administration. It should be mentioned here that the strength of the Russian armed forces in the Steppe Region and Turkestan never fell below the total of British Service forces in India, and was often much greater, although the Central Asian local population only amounted to one-thirtieth of that of the Indian sub-continent.

Probably the most spectacular achievement of the Tsarist regime in Central Asia was in town planning and urban development. The policy was not to develop existing native cities but to create entirely European cities adjoining or within a few miles of them. These European cities were properly planned with long straight radial streets lined with trees. In modern amenities such as shops, theatres, public gardens and water supplies they kept pace with and were in some cases ahead of corresponding European Russian cities. They were certainly ahead of all but a few cities in India, where the counterpart of the adjacent European city consisted of a straggling cantonment. By 1914 most of the cities of Central Asia were equipped with electric current; whereas many Indian cities, for example, Quetta, the second largest garrison in the British empire, were not lighted by electricity until the late 1920s. On the other hand, little or nothing was done by the Russians to improve living conditions in the native cities which remained rabbit warrens of narrow lanes lined with flat-roofed mud houses.

When the Russians arrived, the region was without communications of any kind and their first step was to create a system of post roads with stations provided with relief horses at intervals of fifteen to twenty miles. This system continued to operate until 1917 but was useful only for the transport of passengers and mail. No improvement in the transport of goods was effected until the building of railways, and, much later, the introduction of motor roads and transport. (It is in fact by the latter method that the majority of goods are moved in Central Asia today.) The first railway was built from Uzun Ada on the Caspian to Kizyl-Arvat in 1881. From there it was extended to the Amu-Dar'ya in 1885 and thence to Samarkand in 1888. The line reached Tashkent in 1898, but Tashkent itself was not connected with Orenburg and thus to European Russia until 1906. Apart from the extension of the line to Andizhan in 1899 and the building of a branch line from Merv (now Mary) to Kushka on the Afghan frontier in 1898, this was the sum total of railway construction during the Tsarist regime. Several important projects, including the famous Turkestan-Siberia railway linking the Central Asian system with the Trans-Siberian line, were planned, but were not carried out until the Soviet regime.

Vast plans were laid down for the improvement of irrigation but very little was actually achieved. An elaborate system of irrigation had existed in Central Asia in ancient times, but many of its more important works had been destroyed by the Mongols. Some attempt to repair the damage was made during the Timurid dynasty and again in the first half of the nineteenth century in the Uzbek khanates. But it was not until the Russian conquest brought security to the region that reconstruction on a large scale became possible. Although the Russians looked askance at the seemingly primitive but ingenious and enduring native irrigation works, their own efforts to better them were largely unsuccessful. The only large-scale works which were created were the Murgab and Golodnaya Step' (Hungry steppe) projects, but the Russians were fully alive to the need for extending artificial irrigation and there is no reason to suppose that the vast scheme put forward in 1912 by Krivosheyn for the irrigation of 12,500 square miles of new land and the resettlement there of one and a half million Russian peasants, would not have been realized. During the Tsarist regime a great many small irrigation schemes were carried out under native initiative, which was in itself a tribute to the more stable and secure conditions introduced by the Russians.

One of the most difficult and pressing problems which confronted the Tsarist administration was the collection of revenue and its channelling into a central treasury. Since the economy was almost entirely agricultural, land was the main source of revenue and the system of land tenure was a complicated one which had been inherited from pre-Islamic times, although to some extent regularized by the Arab conquerors. With Islam, too, came an additional complication – the establishment of *Waqf* lands, or religious foundations which in general were not subject to taxation, but whose revenues were devoted to religious or charitable purposes. Since all revenues were collected by the authority of the khans or other local rulers, none of whose domains were in any way precisely defined, the ramifications, to say nothing of the abuses, involved in the collection of revenue, were extensive before the arrival of the Russians. As the authority of the local rulers was removed from the whole of Kokand and from parts of the khanates of Bukhara and Khiva, the Russians were clearly obliged to institute some kind of uniform system both of land tenure and taxation in order to pay for the cost of administration and for the upkeep of the armed forces.

'It is unfortunate', writes Pierce (*Russian Central Asia, 1867–1917*, page 148), 'that Soviet historical literature has not yet provided any detailed description of this land reform, one of the most progressive steps taken by the colonial regime.' In fact, what purports to be such a study has since appeared.* However, the object of this article is merely to paint as black a picture as possible of Tsarist administration and, since the bulk of the source material used is not available for scrutiny by Western scholars, it is difficult to say how far the picture drawn is an objective one. Kaufman, who as originator of the land and tax reforms is roundly castigated in the Soviet article, was, like all imperialist administrators, including those of the Soviet regime, concerned primarily with promoting the interests of the Russian state. But he was also aware of the need to improve the living conditions of the local population and to equalize the burden of taxation. There can be little doubt that the reforms did have this result, although it was inevitable that they should evoke complaints that whereas the people had previously been chastised with whips they were now being chastised with scorpions. It is complaints of this kind which are used to support the indictment contained in the Soviet article.

In the khanates all land was in theory the property of the ruler.

* See *Central Asian Review*, 1961, No. 4, for an analysis of this study which appeared in *Istoricheskiye Zapiski* No. 66, 1960.

Part of it remained at his personal disposal, part was known as gift land, that is, it was leased in perpetuity to those who used it for agriculture or other purposes; and a part was *waqf* land. Of the gift land a part was tax free, having been granted to the original owners by special charter, and the remainder paid taxes. These were the *kharaj*, in practice one-fifth of the value of the harvest, and *tanap*, a tax based on the actual extent of the land. There were several different kinds of *waqf* land but all of it was administered in some way or another by the clergy with whom the khan was seldom able to interfere. In order to evade taxes some land holders bequeathed or made over a part of their land to the *waqf* on the understanding that in exchange for a sum of money, they would in fact continue to own the land. When the Russian Government became the rulers of the khanate of Kokand and of those parts of the khanates of Khiva and Bukhara which it annexed, it *ipso facto* became the prescriptive owner of all the land in these territories, and this was accepted as a normal procedure by the local population. But the Russians went much further than this: they expropriated all the land except that owned by the *waqfs* and declared it to be the property of the existing tenants, that is, of those who actually worked it as distinct from absentee landlords. The *kharaj* and *tanap* taxes were retained for a time, the former being reduced to its original one-tenth. Later, in 1870, the two taxes were combined into a land tax based on the yield from the collection of both taxes in 1869, which was a good harvest year. Many other taxes had been in existence from time immemorial and some of these were maintained by the Russians in a somewhat simplified form with a view both to lightening the burden on the poor and to reducing the expenses of collection. The *zekat* tax on cattle, manufactures and finance capital was abolished in 1875. Before the Russian conquest the nomads had only paid taxes when they came under the influence of one or other of the khanates. The Russians now instituted the so-called *kibitka* or tent tax, which was in reality a tax on each household.

In practice, of course, the simplified systems of land tenure and taxation introduced by the Russians were open to strong criticism. There was widespread abuse and corruption both on the part of the native tax collectors and of Russian officials. Probably the greatest defect of the reforms was that they were introduced too abruptly. This was in great part due to the military form of government; under a civil administration changes could only have been introduced gradually. The greatest single cause for complaint, and the underlying cause of the 1916 revolt, resulted from the wholesale settlement of Russians on the so-called unoccupied lands and on lands used by the nomads for grazing purposes. Looked at from a political point of view the expropriation of the land had the important effect of reducing the power of the local aristocracy: had this been able to retain its former hold on the peasant population revolts against Tsarist authority would have been on a much more serious scale. The need for further reforms and safeguards for the local population, particularly in respect of water rights, was recognized and various proposals for improvement were put forward, particularly by the Pahlen commission of 1908. There was, however, strong opposition to reform by conservative and reactionary elements both in Tashkent and in St Petersburg, and nothing had been done by the outbreak of the First World War in 1914.

Colonization, or resettlement as the Russians have always preferred to call it, by Russians and other non-Asians from Russia has had more material effect on the life of the peoples of Central Asia than any other circumstance. As already explained in an earlier chapter, the colonization which followed other foreign invasions of the region was minimal by comparison with that which followed the Russian conquest. It was not only that the rapid introduction of large numbers of European settlers greatly speeded up the process of westernization; it was the presence in 1917 of two million well-established settlers in the Steppe Region and Turkestan which made possible the association of these regions with the Revolution and their retention in the Russian empire under its new name of the Soviet Union. Had the Russian occupation been confined to a military force and a handful of officials and traders this could hardly have happened.

When the Russians began their colonization of Central Asia the ethical questions raised by colonization had scarcely been given any serious consideration in the West. These questions are outside the scope of the present chapter, which is concerned rather with what the Russians actually did than with what they ought or ought not to have done; some brief mention of them, however, is necessary in order to avoid giving the impression that they have been overlooked. How far can the people actually living in a country be said to own it? If a people is unwilling or unable to exploit to the full the resources of the country in which it lives, has another people with better facilities for such exploitation the right to undertake it by force if by so doing it not only raises the standard of the native people but provides a livelihood for its own surplus population? To what extent is it incumbent on the colonizing power to train the indigenous population in the art of government with a view to the ultimate return to them of their own country? Although there have from time to time been high-sounding international declarations on these problems, no uniform line of conduct or action has so far been agreed upon by all the imperialist powers concerned.

After the capture of Tashkent in 1865, the Russian Government soon realized that the extension of Russian dominions to the frontiers of Afghanistan and Persia was inevitable and they made little concealment of their views and intentions about the future of the newly acquired territories. Here was a region rich in natural resources of great potential economic and strategic importance to Russia. The local population was too sparse and too backward to exploit to the full the agricultural and mineral wealth of the country. It must therefore be supplemented by Russians who would serve the double purpose of increasing productivity and achieving security against the possibility of revolt. Further, the drawing off of a part of the surplus population of Western Russia would reduce distress and discontent there and thus the possibilities of internal revolution. These views and intentions predominated over but were not necessarily incompatible with more liberal sentiments and plans for bettering the lot of the natives: there were just as many Tsarist as there have since been Soviet statesmen and administrators who had the interests and welfare of the local population at heart, and it is interesting to recall that even before the 1905 Revolution, the ideas of 'coming together' (i.e. with the Russians), and of the Russians as the 'elder brother' of the Central Asian peoples were in current use. Great play has been and still is made under the Soviet regime with these notions although, as will be seen later, a different slant has been given to the first of them.

Whether or not the Tsarist policy of colonizing Central Asia was justifiable on practical or ethical grounds is a matter of opinion; but there can be no doubt that it was carried out most inefficiently and in such a way as to antagonize the local population quite unnecessarily. The most objective view on this subject is probably that given by Barthold in his *History of the Cultural Life of Turkestan*. This remarkable book, to which extensive reference will be made later, was published in 1927 when Soviet views on the iniquity of Tsarist imperial administration were at their height; but it takes an entirely dispassionate view of Tsarist aims, policy and methods. There is none of the violence and unqualified condemnation of the Tsarist regime characteristic of all other history written during the Soviet regime up to that time and for many years afterwards; but while it gives credit wherever Barthold thought it due, it also does not hesitate to criticize. In particular, Barthold does not give any support to the view so constantly expressed by Soviet writers that although the Central Asians abhorred Russian officialdom they conceived and cherished an abiding affection for the Russian people as personified in the peasant settlers, even when those same settlers were occupying some of their best land and depriving them of their water rights.

Attempts have been made to represent the great influx of Russian settlers into the Kazakh Steppe as a kind of saga not unlike that associated with the moving frontier of the United States. No analogy could be less accurate. At no time was the settlement properly organized and as often as not it was not organized at all, no proper arrangements being made either for the transportation of the peasants or for their establishment in their new home. Even during the Soviet regime, when much better arrangements were made to cope with the even larger-scale emigration, there has been much hardship and discontent.

The settlement of Russian peasants in the Kazakh Steppe does not seem to have been contemplated by the Russian Government before the subjugation of the Steppe had been completed. Earlier, the Cossacks had been used to consolidate the territorial gains, first along the Ural River, then to the south of Orenburg and finally in Semirech'ye, and it was in this last comparatively fertile area that peasant colonization was first started in 1868, largely with the object of establishing a permanent Russian population on the Chinese border. The *oblast* of Semirech'ye consisted of what are now the Alma-Ata *oblast* (including the former *oblast* of Taldy-Kurgan, abolished in 1961) and the whole of the eastern half of Kirgizia, and its population was classed as nomadic, although many of the Kirgiz in the southern part had begun to adopt a settled existence and to take to agriculture. By 1867, there were already fourteen settlements of Cossacks who in many cases had appropriated the winter pastures of the nomads and the best lands of the settled Kirgiz and Kazakhs. Kaufman felt that Cossack settlement had had its day and strongly advocated that the Cossacks should be replaced by peasants from Western Russia. Accordingly, by 1881 some thirty thousand persons had been settled in Semirech'ye of whom rather less than half formed new settlements while the remainder joined the existing Cossack settlements. While Kaufman was opposed to Russian colonization in the fully settled regions of Turkestan, he considered that it was an urgent requirement in the adjoining Steppe areas, where the improved state of security was encouraging the settlement of Muslim settlers from the oases. With his constant fear of Islam as an anti-Russian influence, Kaufman thought that such settlers might result in a stiffening of Islamic, and therefore of anti-Russian, feeling among the nomads.

Meanwhile peasant colonization of the eastern Steppe *oblasts* of Akmolinsk and Semipalatinsk was proceeding apace, although it was not extended to the western *oblasts* of Turgay and Ural'sk until the 1880s. Attempts to control colonization by means of legislation, mainly by the Resettlement Act of 1889, were fruitless and during the 1890s it got completely out of control. The creation in 1896 of the Resettlement Administration (Pereselencheskoye Upravleniye) did little to improve matters. Pahlen was strongly critical of its operations in 1908, particularly in Semirech'ye; but little heed was taken of his objections and proposals and, after Stolypin and Krivosheyn's visit to the Steppe Region in 1910, settlement was continued with even less regard to the interests of the local population than before. It was now argued that since the Kazakhs were beginning to settle on the land and abandon stock breeding for agriculture, they needed less land than formerly and accordingly more would be available for settlers. In addition, the article in the 1891 Statute for the Government of the Turkestan Region, which virtually prohibited Russian peasant colonization in the Samarkand, Syr-Dar'ya and Fergana *oblasts*, was considerably modified so as to permit of such settlement. By 1911 the position was that the Russian settlers made up 40 per cent of the population in the Ural'sk, Turgay, Akmolinsk and Semipalatinsk *oblasts*, a total of 1,544,000 persons. In Turkestan, on the other hand, settlers only amounted to 407,000, or 6 per cent of the total population. Of these, moreover, over 204,000 were in Semirech'ye, leaving only just over 200,000 in the remaining four *oblasts*. What effect Krivosheyn's ambitious irrigation projects would have had on the settler population of Turkestan can only be conjectured; but it is worth noting that according to the 1959 census the settler population of the territory formerly occupied by Turkestan and the khanates of Bukhara and Khiva was certainly not less than one and a half millions and has probably since risen to at least two million. There were, of course, no Russian peasant settlers in the khanates before 1921.

In the last chapter a very brief description was given of the conditions prevailing in the three khanates of Kokand, Bukhara and Khiva up to the middle of the nineteenth century, that is to say, before the Russian impact had been seriously felt except in the outlying parts of Kokand. Some account must now be given of the final break-up of the Kokand khanate and its passing under direct Russian rule, and of Russia's relations with the khanates of Bukhara and Khiva from the creation of the Turkestan Governorate-General in 1867 up to the 1917 Revolution. There is little doubt that the Russian Government originally favoured the creation of a relationship with all three khanates similar to that which subsisted between the British Government and the Indian princely states. This, however, proved impossible in the case of Kokand once Russian rule had been established over Tashkent; and after the capture of Samarkand in 1868, it seemed probable that Bukhara, too, would be incorporated in the Russian empire. Indeed, this was proposed by the Emir, but declined by the Russians, who, as in the case of Tashkent, considered turning Samarkand into a semi-independent state. This project, too, was abandoned.

The final overrunning of Kokand and its incorporation into the Governorate-General of Turkestan does not merit any very detailed description. By the end of 1866, the Russians had taken not only Auliye Ata (now Dzhambul), Turkestan, Chimkent and Tashkent, but also Ura-Tyube and Khodzhent (now Leninabad) and had defeated the Bukharan army at Irdzhar. As a result, the Fergana Valley, the heart of the Kokand khanate, was now cut off from Bukhara and could not expect any support from it. The ruler, Khudayar Khan, continued to administer his greatly reduced domain from the town of Kokand, and he was still recognized by the Russians, who signed a commercial treaty with him in 1872. In spite of much internal intrigue and sporadic fighting, the economic situation of the khanate was still quite prosperous. Khoroshkin, one of Skobelev's officers, who carried out a reconnaissance in 1867, gave a glowing description of the city of Kokand. According to his report, the city had a population of 80,000 with 600 mosques and 15 madrasahs where about 15,000 students were taught. There were good buildings and a spacious and clean bazaar, built by Madali Khan (1821–42). The khanate exported wool, fruit, hides, silk, opium and indigo, silk and other textile factories being established at Namangan, Kokand, Margelan and Khodzhent. Khudayar was, however, highly unpopular with his subjects and when a revolt broke out in 1875 he was obliged to take refuge with the Russians in Tashkent. His son and heir, Nasir ud-Din, who had visited Tashkent in 1872 and, according to Barthold, had learnt Russian and also how to drink wine and vodka, now joined the insurgents and was nominated by the Russians as Khudayar's successor. A period of confusion followed during which Nasir ud-Din fought alternately with and against the Russians. For example, he does not seem to have been involved in the battle of Makhram, where the Russian forces totally routed a Kokandi army of 50,000 men with a total Russian loss of 6 killed and 8 wounded. A week after this battle Kaufman met Nasir ud-Din outside Kokand, recognized him as Khan and with him made a triumphal entry into the city. During the next few months the Russians were plainly baffled by the complexity of the revolts and counter revolts and by the many rival claimants to the throne of Kokand. Eventually, in January 1876, the Russian Government declared that the existence of the khanate of Kokand was at an end and that it would thenceforward form part of the Russian empire as the *oblast* of Fergana. General Skobelev was given the task of suppressing all elements which opposed Russian authority, and this he did with characteristic efficiency and ruthlessness.

The pacification of Kokand was particularly important for the Russians on account of its proximity to the so-called khanate of Kashgar which, although nominally a part of China, had since

1867 been ruled by Yaqub Beg, himself a Kokandi who had fought against the Russians at the taking of Ak-Mechet (now Kzyl-Orda) in 1853. Yaqub Beg's friendly relations with Britain had led to the Russian occupation of Kuldja in the Ili Valley in 1871 and Russia's relations with Kashgar had remained hostile. In 1876, after the subjugation of Kokand, it was decided to send Captain (later General) Kuropatkin on a special mission to Kashgar with a view to delimiting the frontier between the khanate and the new *oblast* of Fergana. Kuropatkin found Yaqub Beg's power to be far less than had been anticipated and he strongly pressed his demands for the surrender to the Russians of the forts which Yaqub Beg had built in the frontier strip with the Kokand khanate from Irkeshtam to Ulughchat. Yaqub Beg countered by sending an envoy to Tashkent to discuss the matter with Kaufman, and eventually it was decided that Ulughchat should remain in the Kashgar khanate. In 1877, however, the Chinese army recaptured the whole of the region and Yaqub Beg himself was killed. After the re-establishment of Chinese power, negotiations began for the evacuation of the Kuldja district and this was finally completed in 1883. The previous year a Russian consul had been appointed to Kashgar and a Russian colony began to build up there, thus laying the foundation of Russian influence which was to last until the seizure of power by the Chinese Communists in 1949. 'The strong position of the Russian Consul', wrote Barthold, 'was of particular advantage to the Muslim Russian subjects, whose rights were much better looked after than the Muslim subjects of China. In general, the Kashgar cultivators and town dwellers had grounds for envying their co-religionists living under Russian rule, while the nomads, of whom there were not a great number in Kashgar, preferred Chinese rule to Russian.'[23]

The question of what relations the Russian Government should establish with Bukhara was one which presented various complications. In the first place, Russia began by greatly overestimating the political and religious significance of the Emir of Bukhara in relation to the rest of Central Asia. They described him as the 'head of the Muslim world in Central Asia', and even as 'the leader of the Muslim clergy'. Secondly, the Emir's dominions bordered on Afghanistan where British influence was paramount. For the Russians to incorporate Bukhara in the Russian empire in the same way as they eventually incorporated Kokand would be certain to bring them into direct conflict with Britain, which was already gravely alarmed at Russia's advance towards the Persian and Afghan frontiers. Lastly, the Russian Government rightly regarded Bukhara as the principal trade mart in Central Asia and since exploitation of Central Asia's economic possibilities was one of their main objectives, they were most anxious to establish law and order as soon as possible. Chernyayev in particular was under a complete misapprehension about Bukhara's claim to be a stable state. Even before his capture of Tashkent in June 1865, he had written to the Emir to say that he had orders from the Tsar 'not to cross the Syr-Dar'ya river', and he left it to the Emir to establish order 'in the remaining part of the Kokand khanate, which would not, in the circumstances, be incorporated with Russia'.[24] After the capture of the city, he proposed to Kryzhanovskiy that the Russian frontier should run along the Syr-Dar'ya and Naryn rivers. When, however, the Emir began to make extravagant demands including one for the immediate evacuation of Tashkent by Russian forces, Chernyayev changed his line and in January 1866 crossed the Syr-Dar'ya with the object of capturing Dzhizak which, although not properly speaking in Bukharan territory, was occupied by Bukharan troops. The operation was a failure, and Chernyayev was replaced by General Romanovskiy who, continuing Chernyayev's original programme in the spring, defeated a large Bukharan army at Irdzhar on the road to Samarkand. Instead of advancing to Samarkand itself he drove on to Nau and Khodzhent thus driving a wedge between Bukhara and Kokand and forestalling any further attempt by the Emir to encroach on Kokandian territory. Operations against Bukhara were continued in the autumn of 1866 by General Kryzhanovskiy who captured Ura-Tyube and Dzhizak. Apart from a few skirmishes operations were then suspended until Kaufman's arrival in Tashkent in November 1867 to take over the newly constituted Governor-Generalship of Turkestan.

Kaufman's most urgent task was to reach some accommodation with Bukhara which would enable normal trading operations to be resumed. Further complications now became apparent: the Emir wished to deal direct with the Russian Government rather than with local officials and commanders. Relying perhaps on reports of the gullibility of the Russians in their dealings with the Kazakhs, he seems to have thought that his best policy was to gain time by giving various verbal assurances to the Russians without any intention of carrying them out. At the same time, he made desperate but abortive attempts to gain support not only from the khanate of Khiva, but from Turkey, Afghanistan, and even India. He himself was reluctant to resume military operations, but his hand was eventually forced by the clergy who, with some popular support, declared a jihad or Holy War against the Russians. Kaufman was therefore obliged to continue military operations in the spring of 1868. He marched against Samarkand but before actually attacking the city made various attempts to persuade the Emir to sign a treaty. The first draft treaty presented by Najm-ad-Din Hoja, who had acted as the Emir's Ambassador for a number of years, was rejected by the Russians on the grounds that it could not be understood owing to the 'large number of Arabic words used in the Persian drafting'; but enough of it was deciphered to show that it did not comply with Russian demands. After the capture of Samarkand on May 2, Kaufman made various other proposals to the Emir then residing at Kermine. During these negotiations, which were complicated by the Emir's tendency to behead the messengers bringing Kaufman's letters, the Governor-General considered a proposal to constitute Samarkand as a separate beklik or principality under the Emir's nephew Seyyid Abdullah. Indeed, in spite of the economic and political objections mentioned earlier, there would, from the Russian point of view, have been a strong case for taking over the whole of Bukhara. Kaufman's decision not to press on to the city of Bukhara and to sign a treaty with the Emir, which handed over the whole of the Samarkand and Katta-Kurgan districts to Russian administration while allowing the Emirate of Bukhara to remain independent, did not mean the end of military operations which in fact continued until 1870. Kaufman even refused to allow the abdication of the Emir, who was detested by his subjects and declared his wish to retire to Mecca. Later, however, with Russian support he managed to reassert his authority and even to extend his dominions to Karshi, Hisar (Gissar) and Kulab (Kulyab).

Apart from the matter of territory, the Russian Government showed a degree of indulgence towards Bukhara which in some respects exceeded that extended by Britain to the Indian states. Various barbarous Bukharan practices were allowed to continue; even slavery, although nominally prohibited, went on very much as before; and fugitives from so-called Bukharan justice, which usually meant the personal displeasure of the Emir, were often sent back from Russian-administered territory to Bukhara. More important than this, the Russian Government seems to have connived at the Emir's palpable intrigues in support of Khiva and Kokand during the Russian campaigns against those khanates. Russia's indulgence towards Bukhara was due in great part to its proximity to Afghanistan, particularly when in 1870 Abdurrahman, later to become Emir of Afghanistan, took refuge in Bukhara. He was at that time a bitter opponent of Britain and for that reason was sedulously cultivated by the Russian Government.

Kaufman insisted from the beginning that Bukhara's relations with Russia should be conducted through him as Governor-General of Turkestan. This was made difficult partly by the fact that the Emir considered that as monarch he should be in direct communication with the Tsar, and partly because there was in St Petersburg no Ministry concerned with Central Asian or Colonial affairs, but simply the Asiatic Department of the Ministry of Foreign Affairs. In the 1870s, the Russian Government encouraged the ceremonial visits to the capital of potentates and princes from the Asian dominions, since these gave a good impression of the importance of Russia's new conquests. Kaufman approved of this principle but at the same time he strongly deprecated the political consequences of such visits. For instance, in 1869, the heir apparent of Bukhara, Seyyid Abdullah Fatteh Khan, appeared in St Petersburg with a petition to the Tsar containing, among other things, a completely apocryphal account of the battle of Irdzhar and a request for the return to Bukhara of the forts captured by the Russians on that occasion. This and other similar attempts to circumvent the Governor-General's authority were unsuccessful, but Kaufman always had the feeling that the Court and the Central Government were apt to be taken in by the glamorous appearance and often engaging personality of Central Asian rulers, whom he personally regarded as little more than barbarians.

Until the late 1880s, Bukhara did indeed maintain some

semblance of independence. But the beginning of railway construction in 1886 and the creation of the Amu-Dar'ya flotilla in 1887 resulted in a considerable increase in Russian influence largely owing to the presence of Russian railway workers and other technicians. Nevertheless, the Russian political agent in Bukhara occupied a position which corresponded more to that of a High Commissioner than of a Political Agent in the Indian States. Until 1917 he remained directly responsible to the Ministry of Foreign Affairs in St Petersburg and various proposals that he should exercise control over the Bukharan economy and finances were never put into effect.

In 1888, Russia signed a treaty with Bukhara 'on the creation of settlements (i.e. Russian settlements) at the railway stations and river landing stages in the khanate of Bukhara'. In fact, however, such settlements seem only to have been created at Bukhara and Charjui (now Chardzhou) where separate 'European' cities were built on the lines of those existing in Russian-administered territory. In addition, the Customs union which came into force in 1894 resulted in a number of Russian garrisons being placed along the southern frontier of the khanate. The most important of these garrisons was at Kerki, and being in Turkmen territory, it facilitated the collection of taxes by the Emir from his recalcitrant subjects. Except along the railway and the river, Russian influence was not great. Although the import of Russian goods increased very sharply after the Customs union, trade remained largely in the hands of Bukharan and Tatar traders. The way of life remained medieval; although the Emir introduced some Western amenities into his household his general conduct and morals were barbarous in the extreme. He maintained, for example, a vast harem to which hundreds of women were recruited every year. As late as 1907, and probably much later, his vassal beks and princes were forced to approach him on all fours.

'To what extent', wrote Barthold in 1927,[25] 'the despotic government reflected on the well-being of the khanate, and to what extent the material and cultural level of its population was lower or higher than that which could be observed at the same time in other areas of Central Asia, is a matter which has never been made the subject of impartial investigation. In one of the panegyrics of Seyyid Abd-ul-Ahad (Emir from 1885 to 1910) the well-being of the subjects of the Emir is contrasted with the wretched life of the subjects of the Anglo-Indian administration: "At the very time when the peoples of India ruled over by the arrogant British are dying of hunger and complaining and rebelling against their oppressors, happy Bukhara, protected by Russia, lives in bliss and blesses its good fortune".' Barthold does not give the author of these panegyrics, but he makes it quite clear that he himself did not subscribe to them. After quoting D. N. Logofet's caustic comment that 'it can be assumed that if Britain ruled Bukhara, Bukhara would in a short time have completely changed its appearance and have been turned into a civilized country',[26] Barthold goes on to say that 'it would be difficult to adduce factual evidence in support of the opinion that the despotism of the Emir and the Beks could "in future turn a flourishing country into a lifeless desert" '.[27] On the other hand, he quotes a number of accounts from Russian officials and foreign travellers, including the well-known German explorer Rikmer-Rikmers, relating to the situation between 1872 and 1908, which bear testimony to the prosperous state of agriculture in the khanate. In commenting on reports about the flight of Bukharans into Russian and even into Afghan territory in order to escape the oppression of the Emir, Barthold shows that there were also cases of migrations from Russian and Afghan territory into Bukhara, and he quotes particularly the movement of Kirgiz (Kazakhs?) from Russian-administered territory into the principalities of Gissar, Kulyab and Kurgan-Tyube, 'from which it appears', he adds, 'that the Kirgiz at least did not always prefer Russian to Bukharan rule'.[28]

In respect of roads and urban development, Bukhara lagged far behind Russian-administered territory. Very little progress was made in irrigation projects, but no less than in Russian Turkestan. Barthold made no attempt to minimize the tyrannical and barbarous character of the Emir's rule, but even writing ten years after the Revolution, he seems to have remained convinced that in spite of widespread corruption and oppression the essentially Asian system of government was in many ways more suited to local conditions and better understood by the people than the materially more efficient and 'enlightened' methods introduced from the West.

Of the three khanates, Khiva was much the most inaccessible

to Russian penetration owing to its being virtually surrounded by deserts, in which two military expeditions (Bekovich-Cherkasskiy in 1717 and Perovskiy in 1839) had foundered. The Khivans therefore felt safe in contemptuously rejecting the Russian offer of negotiations made shortly after the establishment of the Governorate-Generalship of Turkestan in 1867. After Kokand and Bukhara had been brought to heel, Kaufman turned his attention to Khiva, whose intransigence was regarded as the main obstacle to the achievement of a stable situation in Transcaspia. As justification of a punitive expedition were advanced Khiva's refusal to negotiate about navigation on the Amu-dar'ya, her inability to control the Yomut Turkmens and the continued presence in the khanates of large numbers of Persian and some Russian slaves. Some historians and contemporary observers find other reasons for the campaign organized by Kaufman in 1873: the jingoistic spirit which had been aroused in Russian ruling and commercial circles; the professional desire of Russian officers in Turkestan to embark on new military operations; and the need to divert public attention from the growing rumours about corruption and maladministration in Turkestan. Be that as it may, there is no doubt that Russia could never have pacified the Turkmens, probably the most turbulent element in the whole of Turkestan, without first reducing the power of their main source of internal support, the khanate of Khiva.

The expedition consisted of four separate columns converging on the city of Khiva from Tashkent, Krasnovodsk, Mangyshlak and Orenburg. The crossing of the deserts involved great hardship, but once they had been successfully negotiated the defeat of the Khivan forces and the capture of the capital presented little difficulty. A treaty was signed according to which all Khivan territory on the right bank of the Amu-dar'ya, inhabited mainly by Turkmens and Kazakhs, was ceded to Russia and incorporated in the Syr-Dar'ya *oblast*, Russian vessels were accorded the exclusive right of navigation on the Amu-dar'ya, and slavery was abolished. Strict instructions were issued from St Petersburg that Khiva was to maintain its independent status. A kind of advisory Council was constituted consisting of seven members, four of whom were appointed by the Governor-General of Turkestan, and three by the khan. This Council only continued to function as long as Russian troops remained in the khanate, but

General Ivanov, the most effective member of the Council, continued to exercise almost complete control over Khivan affairs from the town of Petro-Aleksandrovsk (now Turtkul'), the headquarters of the Amu-dar'ya sector. According to Barthold Ivanov, generally known as 'yellow beard' and afterwards to become Governor-General of Turkestan, had to deal with Kaufman's 'most serious mistake', his decision virtually to annihilate the Yomut Turkmens. Ivanov advised clemency towards the Yomuts as future Russian subjects, and when in 1877 they applied to be received as Russian subjects, he strongly recommended that their plea should be granted and that the whole khanate of Khiva should be incorporated in the Russian empire. The Russian Government, however, refused and Ivanov was relieved of his duties. The Yomuts continued to remain nominally under Khivan rule and until 1916 Russian troops were used to keep them under control. After the subjugation of Khiva, the Russian Government decided to bring the whole of the Teke country lying along the Persian border under its dominion. The Tekes, however, proved even more truculent and warlike than the Yomuts and they were not finally defeated until the battle of Geok Tepe in 1881.

In spite of its more remote position, Khiva did not retain anything like the same degree of independence as Bukhara: the khan was not allowed to distribute medals and presents; and he remained under the direct orders of the Governor-General, and even of the Commandant of the Amu-dar'ya sector. The Russians played a much more important part in the khanate's trade, and Urgench, the commercial centre of the khanate, boasted a post and telegraph office, a treasury, transport offices and some cotton-ginning factories. Nevertheless, the administration maintained its medieval character, and it was only in 1888 to mark the escape of the royal family in the Borki railway accident that the abolition of torture was announced. It is not, however, known how far this reform was actually carried out.

'Though tempered by caution and vacillation, and relatively ineffective, the Russian encroachments on the Central Asian way of life were clear enough in intent. Acquiescence in the Russian design of "drawing closer" would have meant eventual loss of ethnic and cultural identity for steppe- and oasis-dweller alike. On the other hand, the futility of physical resistance had been impressed repeatedly on the native mind by the crushing defeats inflicted on the levies of the Central Asian states during the conquest. Though not extinguished, the spirit of opposition was at least lulled by fatalism and acceptance of material benefits during the occupation that followed.'[29] This aptly sums up the attitude of the Muslim peoples of Central Asia towards their Russian rulers between 1881 and the Revolution; *mutatis mutandis* it can be said to apply to their attitude today. Some Western commentators have attributed the relative passivity of Central Asia towards Russian rule to the prevalence of the Muslim doctrine of *takiya* or *ketman* which permitted, and indeed advocated, a superficial submission to the will of a conqueror. It seems probable, however, that it was due to more prosaic causes such as the absence of any national grouping and the fact that the Russians decided as a matter of policy not to permit the creation of any territorial military formations or even the conscription of the people of Central Asia into the Russian armed forces. Nevertheless, the Russians always had, and to some extent still have, an almost morbid dread of revolt on the part of their Muslim subjects. In 1900, for example, they considered that the Russian military garrison in Turkestan, amounting to 45,000 men, was barely sufficient to deal with a possible revolt by the local population which did not then exceed five million, none of whom had been trained in the use of modern weapons. By contrast, it is perhaps worth recalling that in India, with its population at that period of nearly three hundred million, the British garrison did not exceed 70,000 men, of whom a large part were permanently stationed on the Afghan frontier.

Whatever the underlying causes, the fact remains that once the power and influence of the three khanates had been broken and the Turkmens subjugated, that is, by 1881, no revolts against Russian authority of any importance took place until 1916. Russian and other historians are, however, accustomed to describe as 'revolts' local disturbances which were little more than riots resulting either from opposition to Russian administrative measures, or provoked by religious fanatics. An example of the first were the disorders incident on the cholera epidemic in Tashkent in 1892. The Russians tried to introduce sanitary measures which took no account of local custom regarding the seclusion of women and the washing of the dead. It was a small affair of no political significance and its handling reflected no credit on the Russian authorities. Of greater importance was the outbreak of religious fanaticism in the Andizhan uyezd in 1898. The prime mover in this outbreak was Muhammad Ali, an Ishan or Sufi preceptor, who enjoyed a great reputation for piety, good works and magical practices. He was credited by the Russians with a plan to seize the *oblast* of Fergana, and even the whole of Turkestan. From the fact, however, that the total of his followers did not exceed 2,000 and that in spite of the unpreparedness of the Russian authorities, the revolt was completely put down in two days, it seems probable that its dimensions and importance were greatly exaggerated. There is no doubt that this incident greatly alarmed the Russians. It suggested to them that the Central Asian peoples' resentment at their presence was far deeper than they had suspected, and that this resentment was mainly due to Muslim fanaticism possibly exploited by British and Turkish agents. The Russians have always been reluctant to believe that what they consider to be their cultural and material superiority could be held in question by people with an entirely different way of life. Accordingly, they have always been intent on discovering some underlying cause for any sign of resistance to their plans for administrative reform and cultural regimentation. Reports of British and Turkish interference were not at the time taken seriously by the Russian authorities, but they have since been inflated to great proportions by Soviet writers.

General Dukhovskoy, who was appointed Governor-General of Turkestan shortly after the Andizhan incident, reported in 1899 that he had been 'forced to the conclusion that this area is far from peaceful; that the embers of religious and national hatred for their conquerors, skilfully concealed by gratitude for the material benefits brought to the area, were ready at the first opportunity to burst into flames; and that for this reason, the native Muslim population should be kept under the most watchful and unremitting surveillance. . . . Our continued absolute non-interference in this sphere of native life and our widespread lack of interest in Islam which is a very stable and certainly hostile force should be considered harmful to Russian interests in the Muslim area . . .'* An enquiry which followed the Andizhan

* Quoted by A. P. Savitskiy in an article in the Journal of the Central Asian University, *Vypusk*, LXXVIII, 1956.

incident and a census of Islamic institutions carried out in 1900 together revealed a situation which came as a complete surprise to the Russian authorities. The Russians seemed, and to some extent still seem, unable to realize that a culture which had been established in the settled regions of Turkestan for upwards of a thousand years would inevitably obtain a hold on the lives and minds of the people, which could not be expected to relax after a few years of foreign rule, however enlightened, well-meaning and beneficial that rule might be. Savitskiy* says that 'For the first time, the Tsarist authorities came face to face with an astounding indication of their own ideological impotence', and that in his report General Dukhovskoy referred directly to 'the paltriness of the cultural means in the hands of the administration for combating Islam'.

In the Steppe Region the situation was different. The practice of Islam had not become at all widespread among the Kazakhs until the fourteenth century and in the absence of large cities or settled communities which could become strongholds of theocracy, Islam never exercised the same influence. In the early stages of their annexation, the Russians, so far from opposing Islam, had actually encouraged it; in 1787 Baron Igelstrom had formed a project for building mosques and Muslim schools, and a number of Tatar mullas had been introduced in order to staff them. This action was strongly criticized by later Tsarist administrators, who attributed the numerous revolts against Russian authority which took place in the first half of the nineteenth century to the same religious fanaticism which they were to condemn afterwards in Turkestan. In fact, however, the revolts of Kenesary Kasim (1837–47), Jan Hoja (1856) and the disturbances which broke out in the Turgay and Ural'sk *oblasts* in protest against the Statute of 1868 seem to have been the nearest approach to national opposition which the Russians encountered, and to have had little or nothing to do with Islam. After 1869, no disturbances of any consequence occurred in the Steppe Region till 1916.

The Revolution of 1905 had important repercussions on the by then considerable Russian element in Turkestan and the Steppe Region. But the mutinies which broke out in the Russian garrisons and the strikes and disturbances among factory workers, and more particularly among railway personnel, had no immediate effect

* Savitskiy, *op. cit.*

on the local population. Russian political affairs were quite beyond the comprehension of all but a few intellectuals, who on the whole were disposed to support rather than oppose the Tsarist regime. This is not to say, however, that they were not affected by what seemed to them to be the growth of liberal rather than revolutionary ideas. They gradually became interested in the initiative shown by the politically more advanced Tatars who were responsible for convening the first All-Russia-Muslim Congress which met secretly in Nizhniy Novgorod in August 1905 and in Muslim representation in the state Duma or parliament. Thirty-six Muslim deputies were allotted to the first Duma, but owing to an administrative muddle no deputies from the Steppe Region or Turkestan actually took their seats. The second Duma which met in March 1907 included four deputies from the Steppe and six from Turkestan; but after the dissolution of the second Duma the number of Muslim deputies in the third was reduced to ten and did not include any from the Steppe Region or Turkestan. This naturally caused considerable dissatisfaction among the intelligentsia but it is important here to emphasize a point which is often obscured by Soviet historians, namely, that at this stage the demands, and even the aspirations, of the Muslims of Central Asia did not include political independence or self-determination but were confined to such matters as the cessation of peasant colonization, freedom of religious teaching, freedom to publish books and newspapers, and the right to elect deputies. The same applies to the so-called Jadid movement (*usul-i-jadid* – new method) which, although it is sometimes represented as a revolutionary organization and was at first accepted as such by the Soviet regime, was in fact merely a Muslim reformist movement with no specific separatist aims. Political comprehension was, if anything, more advanced in the Steppe Region than in Turkestan. Culturally, the Kazakhs were less advanced than the Uzbeks and other peoples of the settled regions, and the Jadid movement made little progress there; but they were racially and linguistically much more homogenous and therefore susceptible to the idea of national consciousness. Something approaching a nationalist press began to appear in 1907 with the newspaper *Qazaq* published in Troitsk. Another version of this newspaper appeared in Orenburg in 1912 under the control of Baytursun, Dulat and Bukeykhan, who were later regarded as nationalist leaders, although they were eventually discredited by the Soviet authorities. This newspaper attacked the government for its policy of russification and colonization, but it also attacked reactionary pan-Islamism and nomadism. It did not, however, advocate separation from Russia and even went so far as to urge the extension of compulsory service in the Russian armed forces to Kazakhs.

The immediate cause of the great rebellion of 1916 was the Imperial Decree of June 25 calling up non-Russians for labour duties in rear of the Russian forces engaged in the First World War. The quotas set were 250,000 workers from Turkestan and 243,000 from the four *oblasts* of the Steppe Region. Hitherto, the population of both regions had been entirely exempt from military service and people of all classes were therefore shocked and angered by this departure from what they regarded as established Russian policy. The measure was conceived in desperation and in ignorance of the practical possibilities and probable consequences. In addition to practical objections (the Decree arrived at the height of the most important period of the cotton season) the people were affronted by the suggestion that they were not required to fight but only to dig. Nevertheless, the Decree was only the final puff of wind which fanned the smouldering embers of discontent into a blaze. The underlying cause was deep-seated resentment at the presence of the Russians, a resentment which the rapacious colonization policy of the Government and the blundering operations of the Resettlement Directorate had turned into hatred. There was also no doubt a partly subconscious feeling that Russia's embarrassment in the war and the possibility of her defeat were good reasons for striking a blow for freedom.

The best account of the revolt is that given by Pierce.[30] The facts need only be given briefly here. The revolt began early in July in the Samarkand *oblast*, the worst outbreak being at Dzhizak where, according to Willfort, an Austrian prisoner of war there, 1000 Central Asians were killed in the fighting around the town. Throughout July there were serious disturbances in the Samarkand, Syr-Dar'ya and Fergana *oblasts* and by the beginning of August these had spread to Semirech'ye. Here the Russian population was relatively dense and the worst excesses were perpetrated by both sides. Large numbers of Russian peasants were murdered by the Kirgiz, and the peasants as well as the troops carried out bloody reprisals on the local population irrespective of the part which they had played in the revolt. 'Official reports and testimony later given in the Court concerning these events paint an ugly picture of alarm, mistrust, mob violence, shirking of duty by those able to bear arms, and official incompetence.'[31]

The rebellion did not spread to the Steppe Region until the autumn of 1916. It was most violent in the Turgay *oblast*, outbreaks in the other three *oblasts* being more widely spread and less serious. The smaller importance of the revolt in the Steppe Region was mainly due to the fact that of the population of some 3,800,000, 1,500,000 were Russians. On the other hand, the vast expanse of the Steppe made its pacification much less easy than in the more restricted populated areas of Turkestan.

In Transcaspia the warlike Tekes were appeased by the decision that as some of their number were actually on active service with a volunteer regiment, they would only be used for guard duties over prisoners, railways and forests. The Yomuts, on the other hand, gave considerable trouble at Chikishliar on the shores of the Caspian near the Persian frontier, and also at Tedzhen.

By the end of 1916 the rebellion had been suppressed. On the spot reprisals had been savage and uncontrolled, but owing to the comparative clemency of General Kuropatkin, who had been appointed Governor-General in July, a large number of the sentences passed on those arrested were quashed or commuted. As the Revolution broke out the following year, no considered official report was ever published, the most reliable official Tsarist version being that contained in General Kuropatkin's report, which is now available in Soviet archives. In this he gives the Russian civilian losses in Turkestan alone as 2,325 killed and 1,384 missing. Apart from this, 24 Russian and 55 native officials were killed while, in the military operations from July 13, 1916, until January 25, 1917, 97 Russians were killed, 86 wounded and 76 listed as missing. In the Steppe Region Russian losses were much smaller. In Turgay, for example, only 45 Russian civilians, 3 Russian and 6 native officials were killed up to February 1917. No reliable estimate exists of casualties among the Muslims, but there is no doubt that they were extremely high, particularly in Semirech'ye. Soviet estimates are confined to a period when the Soviet Government was intent on denigrating the Tsarist regime as much as possible, but since they are the only ones in existence they may be worth quoting. Ryskulov, a Kirgiz writing in 1937, said that the population of Semirech'ye dropped by 275,000 between January 1915 and January 1917, and a Soviet demographer quoted by Lorimer[32] estimated an absolute loss of 1,230,000 persons in the population of Turkestan between 1914 and 1918. Another Soviet writer estimated that during the revolt 300,000 persons fled into Chinese territory.[33] No figures appear ever to have been published of Muslim casualties in the Steppe Region.

The significance of the 1916 revolt has been the subject of much controversy in the Soviet Union, controversy, however, resulting more from changes in Soviet policy and the Communist party line than from a genuine difference of opinion on the part of individual historians, or from the production of any new evidence. Broadly speaking, the tendency until about ten years ago was to find the revolt 'progressive' in the sense that it was anti-feudal and anti-Tsarist. Since 1953, however, a certain wariness is observable in Soviet writing on the subject of revolts against the Tsarist regime. The anti-Russian character of the revolts of Shamil in the Caucasus, and of Kenesary Kasim in Kazakhstan, which had hitherto been applauded, was now scouted. It was explained that in the 1916 revolt, the venom of the people had been directed not against ordinary Russians who sympathized with their complaints, but only against Tsarist officials, many of whom were said to have been in the pay of Germany and Turkey. Even Britain was, and still is, said to have been treacherously plotting the downfall of her Russian ally by encouraging the rebels. Although Soviet writers often speak of indisputable evidence and of the existence of 'masses of documents' proving that the revolt was supported, if not originated, by foreign agents, they have never disclosed the nature of this evidence and its existence is highly improbable. While, however, there is still a tendency to shift at least some of the responsibility for the revolt onto outside agencies, the present official line is that the revolt had a 'progressive' character in some areas, but not in others. It is still insisted that violence was only directed against officials and not against the settlers, and in the voluminous collection of documents published in 1960* a few very unconvincing cases are quoted to support this.

* *The 1916 Revolt in Central Asia and Kazakhstan.* 794 pp. Moscow, 1960.

On balance, the available evidence – as well as the tergiversation displayed by the Soviet official historians – strongly suggests that in fact the 1916 revolt was just as anti-Russian as the Indian Mutiny of 1857 was anti-British. 'Desirable as it might be from the Soviet standpoint,' writes Pierce,[34] 'to explain the uprisings of 1916 away, they indicate clearly the failure not only of the Imperial Government but of the Russian people to win the friendship and trust of the peoples of central Asia.' A similar judgement could be passed on the British Government and people and it must also be admitted that most contemporary accounts of the Mutiny do not state the Indian case at all fairly or describe at all fully the extent of the vengeance wreaked by the troops on the, in many cases, innocent and uncomprehending Indian populace. There was the same tendency to quote instances where Indian servants had saved their masters from the wrath of the mutineers at the imminent risk of their own lives. There is, however, nothing in these accounts to suggest that the mutineers or those that helped them were able or willing to discriminate between Government officials and innocent women and children. Perhaps the most significant thing about the 1916 revolt is that today the Russians still consider it necessary to whitewash its plainly anti-Russian character.

The Tsarist conquest, annexation and administration of the Steppe Region and Turkestan constituted the first phase of the Russian domination of the whole region which has persisted up to the present time; for in spite of the description of the republics as 'fully sovereign', every intelligent person knows that the destinies of the people of Soviet Central Asia and Kazakhstan are controlled by Moscow and by Moscow alone. Although the period of Russian administration is usually taken as beginning with the capture of Tashkent in 1865, Russian writ did not run throughout the whole region until 1884 and even then did not extend to the khanates of Bukhara and Khiva. If these facts are borne in mind it will be seen that the Tsarist Government only had at its disposal a period of forty years in which to advance the material and spiritual welfare of the people. During this period it was harassed not only by serious internal troubles which culminated in the 1905 revolution, but also by the disastrous war with Japan. In retrospect, of course, it is possible to note many shortcomings in imagination and achievement, much corruption, neglect and oppression during the Tsarist regime just as it is possible to point to many similar defects during the twenty-nine years of Stalin's rule. But on balance, the Tsarist record in Central Asia is by no means discreditable, if only in the sense that it prepared the ground and laid the foundations for the many material improvements for which the Soviet regime claims full and undivided credit. Quite apart from the initial tasks of conquest and pacification and of performing the first introduction to the people of Central Asia and of Western methods and know-how, the Tsarist administrators did much of the preliminary work on projects since realized by the Soviet regime. The Soviets did not scruple to do away with the nominal independence of Khiva and Bukhara, and whether or not this independence was preserved by the Tsarist regime from liberal motives, its final liquidation in 1921 certainly made the administration and economic unification of the region very much easier than they had been in Tsarist times.

Looked at from the point of view of the various Muslim peoples it is difficult to say whether the Tsarist conquest and the imposition of Russian rule were more a curse or a blessing. The exchange of the haphazard, ruthless and mainly selfish rule of the khans and local princelings for the more orderly and civilized but scarcely less ruthless and selfish rule of the Russians was materially speaking for the better. Since the peoples of Central Asia had not yet been affected by national consciousness and had not drunk the heady wine of genuine or synthetic nationalism, they were not offended by the phenomenon of alien rule. Nor did they feel any particular sense of shame at being conquered and ruled by infidels, although the ignorant masses were often susceptible to agitation by the Muslim clergy whose motives were not always of the purest. But whether they realized it or not, the indigenous cultural development of the peoples of Central Asia was seriously retarded, if not indefinitely postponed by the impact of Westernization. This was probably truer of the Steppe Region and Turkestan than of the other Muslim lands which came under Western domination. No other Western people is more convinced of its cultural superiority than the Russians and in no other Muslim country has non-Muslim colonization been carried out on such a wide scale. The nearest analogy is with the French who have a similar conviction but whose dominion over North Africa has now ended.

CHAPTER VI

THE REVOLUTION AND THE CIVIL WAR

THE SITUATION prevailing in Turkestan and the Steppe Region at the beginning of 1917 seemed conducive to the rapid success of a revolution designed to overthrow the Tsarist regime. The vacillating and inconsistent policies towards the Muslims followed by the Tsarist Government since the death of Kaufman in 1882 and the enormous increase in Russian and Ukrainian settlement in Muslim lands since the turn of the century had engendered widespread resentment against Russian rule, which culminated in the 1916 Revolt. In so far as the people as a whole were able to grasp the significance of the Revolution, they supposed it to mean the breakdown of Russian rule, which would eventually result in their lands and water rights being restored to them. But political comprehension of any kind was almost non-existent: it was not simply that 97 or 98 per cent of the population was illiterate; except for a very small group among the Kazakhs, there was not even an 'intelligentsia' in the sense in which this word was used in Russia at the time, that is to say, an element which aspired to independent or radical thinking. As it has several times been emphasized in these pages, the idea of a nation or even of nationality had barely penetrated among the people of Turkestan – it was just beginning to germinate only among the Kazakhs and the Turkmens – and there were in consequence no recognized national leaders. The only real bond of union was Islam, and this, besides being extremely tenuous among the nomad peoples, was dependent for its effectiveness on the clergy, who were themselves unorganized and hardly capable of exercising any sustained leadership. Finally, the people of Turkestan and the Steppe Region, never having performed any military service, were unskilled in the use of modern weapons and did not in fact possess any.

In examining the course of the Revolution and the Civil War in Central Asia and the part played in them by the local population, all the factors just mentioned should be borne constantly in mind. There was also another set of circumstances to which enough attention is not always paid. At the end of 1917, the Turkish empire, with its immense prestige throughout the Islamic world, was on the point of collapsing, and within a year was finally to do so. Persia was in a state bordering on anarchy; Afghanistan was hardly better off and was shortly to be engaged in a war with Britain. Only a few years had elapsed since the downfall of the Manchu dynasty in China and Chinese Government control over Sinkiang was of the slightest. The effective involvement of adjoining countries in the affairs of Central Asia during the years following the Revolution was, therefore, out of the question. Any large-scale intervention by Britain was equally impracticable, even if she had been disposed to undertake it. One last circumstance must be mentioned which was to prove of great importance: this was the presence in Turkestan of at least 40,000 German, Austrian and Hungarian prisoners-of-war taken by the Russians on the Eastern Front.

The Soviet official account of the Revolution and Civil War in Central Asia differs in many respects from that which Western historians have been able to construct from the evidence provided by Central Asian and Russian participants and by a few neutral observers. The main difference between the two accounts is that whereas Soviet historians assert that, apart from a relatively small minority acting either under the influence of religious or 'bourgeois nationalist' elements, or at the instigation of the imperialist powers, the peoples of Central Asia welcomed the Revolution and gave it their wholehearted and active support, most non-Soviet historians claim that the Muslim attitude towards the Revolution varied from sullen indifference to violent opposition and that the new regime was only established by force in the absence of any co-ordinated resistance. The impartial historian who examines all the available evidence is hard put to it to arrive at the facts: he realizes that there is prejudice, *suppressio veri* and exaggeration on both sides; and he notices that while recent Soviet histories ignore the circumstantial Soviet accounts published in the early 1920s and which are now exceedingly difficult to obtain, most of the conclusions reached by refugees and other participants are based on experiences in a limited area. He realizes in fact, that although the Soviet historian must always interpret past history in the light of the present, the truth about events in Central Asia between 1916 and 1924, in so far as it can be discovered at all, can best be pieced together by the combined study of *contemporary* Soviet publications and the more reliable accounts by refugees and others. This is the method which I have adopted in the following narrative.

Even before 1917, Lenin and other architects of the Revolution had violently denounced Tsarist imperialism and the Tsarist treatment of subject peoples, and the 'October' Revolution was quickly followed by promises of entirely different treatment based on racial equality and national self-determination. The problem presented to the Soviet leaders by their sudden inheritance of the Tsarist empire was formidable and many-sided. In the first place, although the whole concept of empire ran counter to Communist theory, the Russian Asiatic empire happened to contain natural resources vital to the continued existence of the Russian or Soviet state. Secondly, renunciation of the empire, or at any rate of the southern part of it which was relatively thickly populated by Asian peoples, would, according to Soviet reckoning, have laid Central Asia and Transcaucasia open to attacks by Britain and thus have jeopardized Russia's security. Thirdly, there were in Turkestan and the Steppe Region alone nearly two million Russian settlers who, whether they supported the Russian Revolution or not, considered this area to be an integral part of Russia which should not be lightly handed over to the backward indigenous population.

Definite Soviet action in respect of the Muslims of Russia was postponed until after the 'October' Revolution of November 7, 1917; but since the 'February' Revolution the Muslims had, entirely on their own initiative, moved some way towards unity on the broad basis of their common culture. The establishment of the Provisional Government was followed by the convening of various Muslim Congresses throughout the empire. The Kazakhs, having suffered particularly heavily at the hands of the Russians during the suppression of the 1916 Revolt, were probably more eager than any of the other Asian peoples to be rid of Russian rule and colonization, and the idea of territorial autonomy was apparently first expressed at the so-called Kazakh-Kirgiz Congress held in Orenburg in April 1917. Shortly after, at the first all-Russian Muslim Congress convened at Moscow on May 1, 1917, it was agreed that the form of government most capable of protecting the interests of the Muslim peoples was a democratic republic based on national, territorial and federal principles, with national-cultural autonomy for the nationalities which lacked a distinct territory. The participants in this and subsequent Muslim congresses were mainly Russian-educated intellectuals who were more concerned with cultural than with political matters, were not necessarily in favour of separation from Russia, and were prepared to leave their political future to an all-Russian Constituent Assembly. It is significant that at the National Assembly (*Milli Majlis*) convened in Ufa on November 20, 1917, only three Ministries were created, those of Religion, Education and Finance, these being the only spheres in which the Muslim peoples seemed at that stage to be seeking autonomy.

Before attempting to follow the course of events in the Steppe Region and Turkestan, a few words must be said about the general Soviet approach to the Muslim problem. Whatever may be the official Soviet version of the circumstances in which the Muslim republics came to be created, there can be little doubt that the first solution of the problem which occurred to the Soviet leaders was the plan of treating the Muslims as a cultural and even as a political entity. Shortly after the 'October' Revolution, the Commissariat of Nationalities, of which Stalin was the first Chairman, proceeded to approach the various all-Russian Muslim organizations which had been created since March 1917. So far as is known, no prominent position in these organizations was held by a Communist, the Chairman of the Executive Council being an Ossetin Menshevik, Ahmad Tsalikov, to whom Stalin offered the chairmanship of a new body to be called the Commissariat of Muslim Affairs. On his refusal, the post was given to Mulla Nur Vakhitov, a Kazan' Tatar, who under Stalin's direction rapidly formed bureaux and committees throughout the Muslim areas, which superseded the organs of the all-Russian Muslim movement. In June 1918, Vakhitov formed the 'Russian Party of Muslim Communists'. This seems to have had the cautious blessing of Stalin, but when, shortly after, Vakhitov was executed by the Czechs in Kazan', it was dissolved, and the functions of its Central Committee were taken over by the Central Bureau of

Muslim Organizations of the Russian Communist Party. In March 1919 the words 'Muslim Organizations' were changed to 'Organizations of the Peoples of the East'. Shortly afterwards the Muslim Commissariat itself disappeared, and thus the whole concept of Islam was removed from the Soviet political fabric never to return.

This gradual whittling away and eventual abolition of the corporate Muslim status in the new regime resulted from Soviet realization that if the Muslims were allowed to unite they would soon become uncontrollable.

The Steppe Region (Kazakhstan)

Immediately following the 'February' Revolution, the small number of Kazakh intellectuals associated with the newspaper *Qazaq* formed a moderate national party called Alash Orda, or Alash Host, Alash being the name of the mythical founder of the Kazakh people. The early deliberations of this party were concerned with agrarian rather than political problems, but resolutions were passed demanding the end of colonization and the redistribution of confiscated lands to the Kazakhs. Except in the matter of colonization, however, the Alash Orda did not express any anti-Russian views; it supported the provisional government and favoured the continuation of the war against Germany. Its leaders, who included Baytursunov, a moderate nationalist, were perfectly able to appreciate the nature of Communism and were strongly opposed to it. They were not, it appears, particularly interested in pan-Islam or pan-Turkism and since they rejected the idea of Tatar cultural hegemony they found themselves in disagreement with the Tatar-sponsored all-Russian Muslim Congress. The Alash Orda's attitude in these matters quickly brought it into conflict with the Kazakhs of the Syr-Dar'ya *oblast*, who were much more anti-Russian and much less anti-Tatar.

The 'October' Revolution was not immediately followed by Bolshevik penetration of the Kazakh steppe. The Ural, Orenburg and Semirech'ye Cossacks took the government of these regions into their own hands and the Kazakh steppe was for a time sealed off from the Bolsheviks. The Third all-Kirgiz (Kazakh) Congress, convened in Orenburg in December 1917, proclaimed an autonomous Kazakh region under the Alash Orda. This autonomous region had two centres, one at Semipalatinsk and the other at Dzhambeyty in the Ural *oblast*. The declared purpose of this autonomy was not apparently to create a Kazakh state, but merely to prevent the spread of Communism into the Kazakh steppe. Having no proper arms or organization, and rent as they were by internal feuds and rivalry, their attempts to do this were doomed to ultimate failure.

The first Bolshevik occupation of Kazakhstan was only temporary; between January and March 1918 they occupied the cities of Kustanay, Aktyubinsk, Orenburg, Semipalatinsk and Vernyy (now Alma-Ata), but by the summer of the same year, the tables had been turned on them by the Ural and Orenburg Cossacks, who had joined Ataman Dutov's forces operating in Siberia, and almost the whole of the Kazakh steppe was cleared of Bolshevik forces. The situation, however, was far from stable and during the ensuing year a state of almost complete anarchy reigned. Although the Red Army had been expelled, groups of pro-Bolshevik partisans continued to operate in the west and east. In the Turgay *oblast* their leader was Amangeldi Imanov, one of the leaders of the 1916 Revolt, who managed to cut off all communications between the Western Alash Orda government in Dzhambeyty and the Eastern in Semipalatinsk, while another group operated in the Mangyshlak and Buzachi Peninsulas on the Caspian Sea. The most serious opposition to the Alash Orda was still offered by the Kazakhs of the Syr-Dar'ya *oblast*, in what is now the South Kazakhstan *kray*. But most of the guerilla fighting which went on in these regions resulted more from long-standing feuds than from any genuine affiliation to Reds or Whites; it was in fact only incidental to the Civil War in Kazakhstan, which was mainly waged between rival Russian forces. In Zenkovsky's words, 'only the cities were controlled by Reds or Whites. The Steppe and its villages remained remote, occasionally raided by White, Red or Green (uncommitted peasants) partisans. The new settlers fought against the Kazakhs; Cossacks and 'older' settlers against the new; and various tribes with each other. The Alash Orda government was less than nominal.'[35] The fate of the Alash Orda was sealed when the anti-Bolshevik government in Omsk declared in November 1918 that it would no longer support Kazakh autonomy. Completely discouraged by this, the Kazakh leaders began to join forces with the Bolsheviks.

Baytursunov defected to them in March 1919, and both the Eastern and Western Alash Orda governments decided to recognize the new regime during the following November. By May 1919 Admiral Kolchak's forces had suffered final defeat in Siberia, and by March 1920 all resistance to the Bolshevik forces had faded away. The Civil War in Kazakhstan was over, and in August 1920 the creation of the Kirgiz (Kazakh) Autonomous Soviet Socialist Republic was announced.

Turkestan

As in the Steppe Region so in Turkestan the main participants in the Revolution and the Civil War were Russians and other non-Asians from the western part of Russia rather than the local population. In other respects, however, the situation prevailing in 1917 and the course followed by the Revolution were quite different. To begin with, in spite of the existence of large cities, a mainly settled population, and a higher standard of Islamic culture, there was among the peoples of Turkestan little in the way of an intelligentsia with enough political comprehension to form a government on the lines of the Alash Orda, ineffectual as this eventually proved to be. On the other hand, the Russian and Ukrainian settler population of Turkestan was much smaller, barely exceeding 400,000 as against the 1½ million in the Steppe Region. Again, there were in Turkestan the two semi-independent khanates of Bukhara and Khiva in which there were no settlers at all but only small Russian communities of railway workers and the like. Finally, there was the phenomenon, absent in the Steppe Region, of the presence of 40,000 European prisoners-of-war.

Relatively small though it was, the Russian element in Turkestan played a dominant part there. According to official statistics compiled in 1914, the Russians, who made up only one-fifth of the industrial workers in Turkestan, held three-quarters of the jobs requiring skilled labour. It was not therefore surprising that from the creation after the 'February' Revolution of the Turkestan Committee representing the provisional government, administrative power in Turkestan, such as it was, remained exclusively in the hands of Russian and other non-Asians. This situation continued until the new constitution for the Turkestan SSR was promulgated by the Ninth Regional Congress of Soviets in 1920, and, in effect, for some time after that.

During 1917, all political activity in Turkestan was concentrated in Tashkent. The Turkestan Committee created by the provisional government was made up of former Tsarist officials and it was opposed by a Soviet of workers and peasants' deputies, both bodies being entirely non-Muslim in composition. The Tashkent Soviet made an abortive attempt to seize power in September 1917 and both sides continued virtually to ignore the Muslim population which at first remained silent spectators of what seemed to be a political rivalry which barely concerned them. Very soon, however, national as distinct from tribal consciousness began to stir for the first time and an Extraordinary all-Muslim Conference convened in Tashkent demanded Muslim autonomy for Turkestan within a Russian federated republic. The Conference and its demands were ignored by the Russians and when, at the end of October, the Tashkent Soviet overturned the Turkestan Committee it made no attempt to enlist the support of the Muslims but concentrated on winning over the Russian military forces stationed in the district. At the Third Congress of Soviets convened in November with the object of laying the foundation of Soviet power in Turkestan, a special resolution was overwhelmingly adopted which entirely excluded Muslims from all Government posts. This resolution coupled with the wholesale plundering of the native population by the so-called 'Revolutionary Soldiers' which went on throughout 1917, particularly in Semirech'ye, changed the attitude of the Muslims, who now felt that their hopes of the Revolution involving the disappearance of Russian rule were completely unfounded. Even while the Third Congress of Soviets was still in session, a Third All-Muslim Congress convened in another part of Tashkent, passed with an overwhelming majority a resolution expressing hostility to the 'October' Revolution.[36] Events now moved rapidly, so rapidly indeed, that corporate Muslim opposition had hardly begun to take shape before it was struck a crippling blow from which it was hardly able to recover.

In early December the Fourth Extraordinary Regional Muslim Congress met in the town of Kokand and, in the presence of delegates from all the provinces of Turkestan except Semirech'ye, declared the autonomy of Turkestan. Almost simultaneously a vast demonstration of Muslims was held in Tashkent in favour of autonomy, but, contrary to the expectation of the Soviet authorities, it dispersed peaceably. At first, the demands of the Kokand government under its leader Mustafa Chokayev, were moderate, since it was rightly considered that the Tashkent Soviet was acting without the authority of the revolutionary leaders in Petrograd. To the latter the Muslims now appealed, only to receive from Stalin a reply rejecting their demand for intervention from the centre, but stating that if the Tashkent Soviet was, in the opinion of the Muslims, 'leaning upon the non-Muslim army elements, they should themselves dissolve it by force, if such force is available to the native proletarians and peasants'.[37] It is highly probable that Lenin, if he was fully informed of the situation in Turkestan, strongly disapproved of the Tashkent Soviet's attitude on grounds of expediency, if on no other. But he was powerless to intervene effectively, and so far as is known, did not attempt to do so. The Tashkent Soviet, for its part, quickly realized that the Kokand government was a serious challenge to its existence, since however 'bourgeois' its content, there was not the slightest doubt that it represented the will of the great mass of the Muslim population. At the Fourth Regional Congress of Soviets held in Tashkent at the end of January 1919, Kolesov, President of the Turkestan Council of Peoples' Commissars, pronounced the Kokand government to be 'counter-revolutionary' and as representing class rather than national interests. The Congress concluded with a resolution declaring war on the Kokand government. This was quickly put into effect, and in the middle of February Red Army forces surrounded the old city of Kokand, which was only defended by a hastily raised and ill-armed Muslim militia, and easily captured it. The sack of the city was followed by a massacre in which at least 5,000 people were killed, local estimates being more than double this figure. Only a handful of fugitives lived to tell the tale, and among them was Mustafa Chokayev, the leader of the government, who eventually found his way to Europe. Muslim resistance to the Revolution was henceforwards to be hardened into the Basmachi movement which will be described later.

The creation and extinction of the Kokand government, both within a period of three months, are among the most significant events of the whole Russian Revolution, which claimed to have granted self-determination to hitherto subject peoples. The resolution taken at the Fourth Extraordinary Regional Muslim Congress to set up an autonomous Turkestan was the first sign of a corporate national consciousness shown by the people of Turkestan, and the first (and the last) attempt to attain their ends by constitutional means. The resolution of the Congress expressed 'the will of the peoples of Turkestan to self-determination in accordance with the principles proclaimed by the Great Russian Revolution and proclaims Turkestan territorially autonomous in union with the Federal Democratic Republic of Russia. The elaboration of the form of autonomy is entrusted to the Constituent Assembly of Turkestan, which must be convened as soon as possible. The Congress solemnly declares herewith that the rights of national minorities settled in Turkestan will be fully safeguarded.'[38] The failure of the Kokand government to achieve any of its aims was due not to the inevitable defects of inexperience, bad organization and incomplete representation (the people of the two khanates, including the non-Turkic Tadzhiks, were for obvious reasons excluded), but to the simple fact that the Muslims were unarmed and were opposed by a large armed foreign element brought there as a result of conquest and colonization. That Lenin and the other Soviet leaders realized this, and also that the high-handed attitude of the Tashkent Soviet was the very negation of all declared Communist principles, is abundantly clear from contemporary Soviet literature, and particularly from the book by Georgiy Safarov mentioned earlier. From 1919 onwards, serious and by no means entirely unsuccessful efforts were made to cover up and push into the background this early Communist flouting of the most elementary principles of self-determination and to arrange for Muslim participation in republican and local government. At no time, however, did the Soviet authorities ever contemplate taking either of the two steps which are the inevitable prelude to the acquisition of real independence by former colonial territories, namely, the withdrawal of foreign armed forces and the removal of all barriers to international intercourse. It is noteworthy that the standard Soviet description of the Kokand government of 1918 is as follows: '*Kokand Autonomy*. A counter-revolutionary bourgeois nationalist organization in Kokand which at an "all-Muslim" Congress held in Kokand on the 26th November 1917 declared itself as "the government" and called upon the Turkestan Council of Peoples' Commissars at Tashkent to hand over its power. Under the flag of "Kokand" the Turkestan counter-revolution tried to establish the old order and *to wrest Turkestan from Soviet Russia*. (The italics are mine.) On the 20th February 1918, Red Army forces with the help of the poor people of Uzbekistan occupied the old city of Kokand and liquidated "Kokand". The leaders of "Kokand" with a small force fled from the city and continued their struggle against Soviet power in the ranks of the Basmachi.'[39]

It has been said that the reason why the Russians, of all the nineteenth-century imperialist powers, never lost their empire was because they never lost their nerve. However true this may be, the years 1918 to 1924 were a testing time which would have given pause to all but the very strongest nerves, and however much the Soviet Government may have been disturbed by the uncompromising attitude of the Tashkent Soviet, any other kind of attitude would almost certainly have resulted in the loss of Turkestan to the Russian or Soviet empire, although probably not of the Steppe Region. After the collapse of the provisional government in Petrograd in October 1917, Turkestan was virtually cut off from metropolitan Russia and there was no hope of obtaining military reinforcements from there. If the Muslims had been allowed to participate in the Tashkent Soviet and eventually in the Turkestan Republican Government, or had been allowed to set up a parallel government in Kokand or elsewhere, they might perhaps have consolidated their position and acquired a prescriptive right to the government of their own country of which it would have been difficult to deprive them. As it was, the summary and brutal liquidation of the Kokand government merely sparked off a series of unco-ordinated guerrilla risings which, although highly embarrassing to the Soviet regime, were not calculated to promote any coherent nationalist movement. But although bad organization, lack of arms and internal rivalry prevented the so-called Basmachi* movement from succeeding, it was a clear indication of the disillusionment of the Muslims with the new regime and of the desperation resulting from mal-administration and the famine and misery which came in its train.

* 'Basmachi' was a word in general use throughout Turkestan with the meaning of raider or marauder.

A detailed account of the activities of the Basmachi rising would be out of place in the present narrative.* Briefly, it can be said to have included four phases, the first of which was the revolt in Fergana (January 1918 to November 1919) in which the rebels were joined for a time by Osipov, the defecting Commissar for War in the Tashkent government, and by the so-called Russian 'peasant army' made up of Russian settlers from around Dzhalal-Abad. The Fergana rebels under their leader Madamin (Muhammad Amin) captured a number of towns in the *oblast* and eventually set up a provisional government and established contact with Admiral Kolchak's Siberian forces. Madamin also received an Afghan delegation who offered him arms and financial help. In September 1919, however, the Red Army defeated Ataman Dutov, whose forces had for two years prevented contact between European Russia and Turkestan, and Red reinforcements were now able to reach the Soviet Government in Tashkent. By the end of the month Osh and Dzhalal-Abad had been recaptured and the new provisional government came to an end. The second phase opened with the arrival in Tashkent of the Turkestan Commission under General Frunze. This had been appointed by Lenin to curb what was understood to be the excessive power exercised by the Turkestan government and to ensure the participation in it of the Muslims. Attempts were made to stop the Muslim population from supporting the Basmachis by stepping up military operations, and also by the distribution of food and seed and by encouraging Muslims to become members of the Communist Party. These measures had the effect of bringing about the defection from the Basmachis of the Russian 'peasant army' and later of Madamin himself. But these successes were largely superficial; Soviet requisitions of labour and property continued and an even more redoubtable leader of the revolt in Fergana appeared in the person of Kurshirmat (Kurbashi Shir Muhammad).

The third phase began in September 1920 with the extension of the movement to Bukhara. In September 1920 the Red Army launched a successful attack on Bukhara and the Emir fled to eastern Bukhara, or what is now Tadzhikistan. A so-called Young Bukharan government was set up which, however, being closely

* A full account of the movement can be found in *Central Asian Review*, 1959, No. 3, pages 236–250.

associated with the Jadid movement, soon found itself at logger-heads with the Soviet authorities. A very confused situation now ensued. Bukhara became a rallying point for Muslim intellectuals from many parts of Russia; among them was the Bashkir leader Zeki Validov Togan, who arrived in Bukhara in 1921 and set about organizing the secret Turkestan National Union which aimed at a genuinely national government for Turkestan free from Russian domination. In eastern Bukhara the Emir had joined Ibrahim Bek who, although violently anti-Russian and anti-Soviet, was a conservative Muslim and therefore strongly opposed to the Jadid movement. During the summer of 1921 he was being attacked by the Red Army forces and was at the same time being approached by negotiators from the Young Bukharan government acting to some extent under the instructions of the Soviet authorities. At one time the Russian Red Army commander appeared to be ready to intrigue with Ibrahim Bek against the Young Bukharan government. Meanwhile in Fergana the Basmachi movement gained new vitality. Well armed, well mounted, and with considerable popular support, the rebels gained control of all the countryside and of the towns of Margelan, Namangan and Andizhan as well. Under Kurshirmat's command they destroyed cotton mills and railway lines; and they made contact with Togan's National Union and with various Russian anti-Bolshevik groups. In September, however, the Red Army was reinforced by two divisions and after furious fighting near Margelan, Kurshirmat was defeated and fled to east Bukhara, where the rising had not yet reached its zenith.

The fourth and final phase of the Basmachi movement began in October 1921 with the arrival in Bukhara of Enver Pasha, Turkey's Minister for War until her defeat in the First World War in October 1918, and one of the original leaders of the Young Turk movement. After his disgrace in Turkey, Enver escaped to Germany and in 1920 arrived in Moscow, where he offered his services to the Bolshevik Government. The latter, thinking that a person of his prestige would be able to placate the Central Asian Muslims and win them over to their side, allowed him to go to Bukhara where he quickly abandoned any idea of throwing in his lot with the Bolsheviks. Togan, who was still in Bukhara, tried to dissaude Enver from joining the Basmachis, declaring that he could be of greater use in Afghanistan;

but Enver ignored this advice and, after leaving Bukhara, ostensibly on a shooting expedition, made his way to eastern Bukhara, to make contact with Ibrahim Bek. Ibrahim regarded him with suspicion as an unorthodox Muslim innovator and at first held him prisoner. Later, his suspicion was partly allayed by a letter from the Emir, then in Afghanistan, and in January 1922 Enver was released and began to rally the Basmachi forces in eastern Bukhara.

It is probable that in taking up the cudgels for Islam and the Central Asian Muslims, Enver was actuated more by personal ambition than by religious zeal; but a man of his personality, courage and experience could not but have a tonic effect on the ragged forces of the Basmachis. He soon collected a considerable following and inflicted a number of defeats on the Red Army. By May 1922 he had established contact with the Basmachis in Fergana and also with the Turkmen leader, Dzhunayd (Junayd) Khan, who was offering strong resistance to the Bolsheviks in the Karakum desert. By July, however, the tide had turned against Enver: contrary to advice given to him by Togan, he had peremptorily refused a Soviet peace offer and the Red Army now returned to the attack with renewed vigour. Enver might have resisted this had it not been for dissension and treachery on the part of the other Basmachi leaders, and particularly of Ibrahim Bek who continued to distrust him. Eventually, on August 4, 1922, he was surprised near Bol'dzhuan, and was killed after desperate fighting. Deprived of Enver's able leadership, the Basmachi resistance movement was doomed. By the autumn, resistance had virtually ceased in Fergana; joined now by Togan, they continued to fight on in eastern Bukhara until the end of 1922. By the end of 1923 the backbone of the movement was broken, although sporadic activity by splinter groups continued until the late 1920s. Ibrahim Bek withdrew to Afghanistan in 1926, whence he continued to conduct raids into Soviet territory. He was captured by Soviet troops in 1931 and executed.

The immediate causes of the Basmachi movement were the excesses of the early unrepresentative Soviet Government of Turkestan and the sacking of Kokand. Whether it can be fairly described as it has been by some writers as a great pan-Turk national movement is, however, doubtful. The Basmachi leaders who achieved the greatest renown were not the intellectuals or the reformists, but conservative reactionaries, some of them little more than swashbuckling brigands, who were as much opposed to the Jadids and Young Bukharans as they were to the Russians. While the relatively lenient policies introduced by the Turkestan Commission certainly reduced the popularity of the Basmachi rebels among the Muslim population, there is little doubt that dissension in the ranks of the rebels and the sheer weight of Russian arms were the overriding factors.

Before proceeding to describe the formation of the Central Asian Republics and the consolidation of Soviet rule, some brief digression must be made in order to recount developments in the two semi-independent khanates of Khiva and Bukhara. In both of these the situation differed markedly from that in the Steppe Region and Turkestan. In the first place, there were no considerable bodies of Russian officials and settlers who could set themselves up as representatives of the Revolution and take charge of the administration. Nor did the Tashkent Soviet in the early stages of the Revolution dispose of sufficient military forces to undertake the forcible subjugation of the khanates. Secondly, in both khanates there were more or less clear-cut internal problems, which had nothing to do with the Revolution or with the Russians. In Khiva there was the age-long rivalry between the town-dwelling Uzbeks and the nomad Turkmens; while in Bukhara the reactionary government of the Emir was opposed by the Young Bukharans and Jadids.

Up to the Revolution, the Uzbek sedentary population of Khiva had been protected from Turkmen depredations by the presence of a small Russian garrison. When this garrison was evacuated early in 1918 the Uzbeks were left at the mercy of the Turkmen raiders, whose leader, Junayd Khan, now instituted a campaign of terror and wholesale plunder. Among the Uzbeks there was a small party known as the Young Khivans which, like the Young Bukharans, was modernist in outlook and constituted the sole force capable of rallying the Uzbek population of Khiva against the Turkmens. In their desperation, this party appealed to the Soviet Government, and in January 1920 a small Red Army force of some 800 crossed the Amu-dar'ya into Khiva and quickly drove Junayd Khan and his forces into the Karakum desert. The Red Army now took charge and in June created the Khorezmian People's Soviet Republic under the nominal control of the

Young Khivan Party. For the present, this Republic was to preserve much the same degree of independence as the khanate had had in Tsarist times.

In Bukhara, the modernist party, the Young Bukharans, decided to ally themselves with the Bolsheviks even earlier than in Khiva: but Soviet penetration was to be postponed until later. In March 1918, the Tashkent Soviet dispatched a detachment of 80 Red Guards in the company of 200 Young Bukharans to deliver an ultimatum to the Emir, coupled with a threat of force. This attempt was repulsed by a fanatical mob stirred up by the mullahs and the Turkestan government was obliged to sign a treaty with the Emir by which it not only recognized the independence of Bukhara and undertook to restore the territory which Russia had taken from it since 1855, but even to provide the khanate with arms. The Emir, who in April 1917 had issued a manifesto promising limited reforms, now treated the Young Bukharans to a reign of terror. At the same time, he declared a Holy War on the Russians and tore up large stretches of the railway track in order to prevent a second Soviet invasion; and he concluded agreements with Persia and Afghanistan for the supply of arms and made contact with other counter-Revolutionary organizations including the Basmachis, and also with the British forces in Persia.

In the absence of sufficient military forces to bring the Emir of Bukhara to heel, the Turkestan government busied itself with conducting propaganda inside the khanate and with trying to reconcile the two factions among the remnants of the Young Bukharan party which had settled in Tashkent and Samarkand after the failure of the first attempt to establish the Revolution in Bukhara. Of these two factions one was nationalist in its outlook and opposed to the idea of class war, while the other was essentially left wing and adhered to the principles of the Revolution. During 1919 a compromise was reached by the creation of a new 'Revolutionary Young Bukharan Party'. This, however, soon failed to satisfy the extreme left wing. The ensuing conflict alarmed the Turkestan government, and more particularly the Turkestan Commission which had arrived at the end of 1919, since the Young Bukharan exiles were relied upon to bring about the final overthrow of the Emir's government. In the summer of 1920, the moderate faction was disciplined and brought into line by a resolution passed at a conference between the two factions. This resolution flattered the Young Bukharan moderates by describing them as 'richer culturally than the Bukharan Communists', but actually foreshadowed their eventual disappearance, and by implication that of the Jadids, as a political force. Nevertheless, the government of the People's Republic of Bukhara which was set up after the final defeat and collapse of the Emir's regime in September 1920 was in no sense Communist or even socialist: although the programme included promises to reduce the power of the clergy, to improve the administration and confiscate the Emir's property, there was no mention of the dictatorship of the proletariat or the liquidation of private ownership.

Another area where the establishment of Soviet authority had been vigorously contested was Transcaspia. Even before the 'October' Revolution, there had been the beginnings of a nationalist movement among the Turkmens. A group of Turkmen intellectuals formed a regional Turkmen Congress which seemed at first to challenge the authority of the local Soviet established in Ashkhabad at the end of 1917. The decision taken by the Executive Committee of this Congress in February 1918 to create a Turkmen army on the basis of the old Tsarist Turkmen cavalry squadron billeted near Ashkhabad, excited the alarm of the Tashkent Soviet, which dispatched a Red Army force under Kolesov to deal with the matter. This small national rising was suppressed before it could get under way, but by July 1918, as the result of the excesses of the drunken Commissar Frolov, to whom the crushing of the counter-revolutionaries had been entrusted, the Russian Social Revolutionaries rose against the Ashkhabad Soviet and Bolshevik rule in Transcaspia came to an abrupt end. The provisional government which succeeded it was scarcely any better or stronger and soon appealed for assistance to the British Military Mission in Mashhad in north-east Persia, which had been sent there to take all possible steps to ward off an expected German advance through the Caucasus into the Middle East. The small force at the Mission's disposal did what it could to stiffen the resistance of the provisional Transcaspian government to Red Army attacks and also to give economic and financial assistance to what seemed to be the only stable authority likely to offer any resistance to the Germans. In June, the British force which, contrary to Soviet statements, had never exceeded 1,000 men, was withdrawn to Persia. Without their support the Transcaspian forces were easily defeated and by February 1920 the whole of Transcaspia was in Bolshevik hands.

By the end of 1920 the greater part of the Steppe Region and Turkestan had passed under direct Soviet control, although sporadic resistance continued in Fergana, eastern Bukhara and in parts of Kazakhstan. Direct Soviet administration, such as it was, consisted of the Kirgiz (Kazakh) Autonomous Soviet Socialist Republic, and the Turkestan Soviet Republic, while the two People's Republics of Khiva and Bukhara, although still nominally independent, were subject to close Soviet supervision. Many Western historians have stigmatized the early Soviet Government of Central Asia not only as tyrannical but as grossly inefficient and lacking in any co-ordinated plan. When, however, it is recalled that for two years after the 'October' Revolution the whole region was almost completely cut off from Europe and that during this period the Bolsheviks had at their disposal only troops which were largely undisciplined and poorly armed, the progress made by the end of 1920 in establishing the new regime and in stamping out resistance must be seen as no mean achievement. Indeed, first-hand observers of the developments in the first two years of the Revolution in Central Asia are amazed that order and progress should ever have been created out of the chaos which reigned between 1917 and 1920. One of the most important of these observers was Colonel F. M. Bailey who, as an officer of the Indian Political Service was perfectly familiar with the problems of colonial administration, including that of Asian nationalism. His account,[40] at times almost bald in its unpretentiousness, of his experiences in Turkestan in 1918 and 1919 shows clearly that the reins of government in those years were in the hands of men most of whom were lacking not only in political and administrative experience but in any but the most elementary education. A large proportion of them were adventurers and opportunists belonging to minorities who were mistrusted by both Russians and Muslims alike, and who had little to lose and no sense of loyalty either to the Tsarist regime or to the Revolution. The violent and unprincipled conduct of these people was a byword among the Muslims as well as among the large Russian population of Tashkent, the great majority of whom were opposed to the

Revolution. Some of them met a violent end and most of the others disappeared completely after the arrival in 1919 of the Turkestan Commission. Nevertheless, the part which they played in what is now known as 'the triumph of the Revolution' in Central Asia was decisive in the sense that it intimidated and oppressed the local population to such an extent that they eventually welcomed the relatively orderly and moderate regime ushered in by the Turkestan Commission.

It has been argued that if the principles of the Revolution in respect of self-determination had been faithfully applied to the Steppe Region and Turkestan, the spirit of nationalism which the Revolution undoubtedly evoked would eventually have resulted in the formation of one or more Muslim states. These might have preferred association with the rest of the Muslim world rather than with a Communist or any other kind of Russia wishing to control their political, cultural and economic destinies. This undoubtedly was the idea which from 1917 onwards began to germinate in the minds of the very small number of Muslim intellectuals with enough political comprehension to understand what the Revolution meant. Whether such an idea could have been translated into reality, even supposing that the Soviet Government had been disposed to favour it, is quite another matter. The history of the first six decades of the twentieth century has shown that the relinquishment of paramount power over backward peoples, even where it can be effected gradually and with due preparation by a stable metropolitan government, is likely to be attended by grave and sometimes insoluble problems. In 1917 the possibility of an orderly transfer of power to the former colonial territories of the Tsarist empire was so remote as to be almost inconceivable. The Tsarist Government had never contemplated the eventual grant of independence or self-government and had consequently made no preparation for it; neither an indigenous civil service nor indigenous security forces existed even in embryo. Moreover, the total collapse of the metropolitan government was almost immediately followed by the disintegration of the colonial administration. An orderly and gradual transfer of power was therefore quite out of the question and, even if Lenin had decided to abdicate all responsibility for the administration of the former empire and to leave the people of Central Asia to their own devices, it is improbable that the immediate result would have been any different from what happened during the first two years of the Revolution, namely, the seizure of power by the European settler population. The gradual restoration of central authority and control, which was made possible after the defeat of Admiral Kolchak's forces and the arrival in Central Asia of better equipped and disciplined Red Army troops, seemed to the Soviet Government the only practicable course open to it. Once order had been re-established, they could proceed to the consolidation of Soviet power, that is, to the reconstitution on different lines of the Russian empire.

CHAPTER VII

THE CONSOLIDATION OF SOVIET POWER

'By the end of 1920,' writes Alexander Park,[41] 'the Soviet Government had repudiated, in fact if not in principle, its early promise to the nations of Russia of the right of self-determination up to and including secession. In Central Asia as in numerous other parts of the Tsarist empire, Stalin's 1918 formula of "self-determination for the toilers" had furnished the practical basis on which the Soviet Government supported or opposed the claims of national groups for self rule, and the Red Army had become the real instrument of "self-determination". But doctrine had also evolved towards a new concept of self-determination as a demand not for separation from Russian but for national equality in the socialist order. And this in turn had given rise to a further notion of the socialist state in Russia as a hierarchically organized union of autonomous and federated national Soviet Republics. In the course of the Revolution and Civil War, Bolshevism thus adopted the idea of a federal socialist commonwealth both as a counterpoise to non-Russian tendencies towards separation and as a device for guaranteeing those national rights which the Soviet regime had pledged itself to honour.'

The history of the consolidation of Soviet power in Central Asia really begins with the arrival in Tashkent of the Turkestan Commission whose first task was to draft a constitution for the Republic of Turkestan to replace the draft Constitution submitted to Moscow by the Turkestan government in the summer of 1918. This first draft had stipulated a degree of genuine autonomy which Moscow was not prepared to concede, and although the draft was never formally rejected, Moscow refused to grant the Republic a charter of autonomy within the Russian Soviet Federated Socialist Republic (RSFSR). In September 1920, under the guidance of the Turkestan Commission, a new constitution was adopted which conformed to Moscow's requirements and stipulated that the control of foreign affairs, foreign trade and defence should be the exclusive responsibility of the Federal Government. The special Soviet interpretation of the term autonomy thus adopted was later to apply to all the Union Republics of Central Asia and to Kazakhstan, all of which up to 1964 were still officially described as 'fully sovereign states'.

At this point the non-Soviet historian must again find himself at cross purposes with Soviet historians. Impartial examination of the available evidence leads inevitably to the conclusion that the form of government under which the Muslim peoples of Central Asia were destined henceforward to live was not of their own choosing but imposed on them from Moscow, which in future was to exercise an even greater degree of control over their lives than St Petersburg had previously. From the old imperialist 'white man's burden' standpoint it would be possible to admit this state of affairs while insisting that it was either inevitable or made necessary by the stubbornness and ignorance of the people, who did not know where their own interests lay. This, however, is not the argument advanced by the Soviet authorities. Starting from the premise that the Tsarist conquests saved the Muslims of Central Asia from the predatory designs of the Western imperialists, they claim that the Russian people have always been the Muslims' best friends, that the Civil War was exacerbated by capitalist intervention and that collectivization, cultural reform, colonization and the control of economy, defence and foreign policy from Moscow were brought about by the will of the Muslim peoples themselves and opposed only by reactionaries working in the name of Islam or in the pay of foreign powers. History written from this angle tends to be selective and to be concerned with material aims and results rather than with actual events and spiritual reactions. If there ever existed any day-to-day chronicle of events which frankly recorded the impression which they made on the actual Muslim participants, it has never been made available for examination, and when it is recalled that in the early 1920s when the new form of government was taking shape at least 96 per cent of the population was still illiterate, it would hardly be surprising if no very clear recollection of the events of those years still remains, particularly in view of

the efforts made by the authorities to gloss over any mass expression of opposition to the Revolution. This is not to say,
however, that a very fair idea of what actually happened cannot
be gained by filling in the gaps in Soviet official history from the
local press and other literature published in Tashkent during the
1920s. Although very little of the latter was written by Muslims
and therefore hardly represents the Muslim point of view, the
Russian authors were often professional men who had received
little or no training in the Marxist presentation of facts and were
apt to report events exactly as they had occurred. An illuminating
example of this kind of writing is a small book of Ye. Kozlovskiy[42]
which describes the part played by the Red Army between 1917
and 1927. The author was clearly a professional soldier who was
perfectly familiar with local conditions and knew and cared next
to nothing about politics and ideology. He does not mince words,
as do later historians, about the gross inefficiency of the early
Soviet regime and the obvious hostility to it of the local
population.

Under the new Constitution adopted in September 1920, the
Turkestan ASSR comprised exactly the same territory as the
former Turkestan Governorate-General, that is to say, the five
oblasts of Syr-dar'ya, Semirech'ye, Fergana, Samarkand and
Transcaspia, and the Amu-dar'ya Military Division. As before,
the khanates of Khiva and Bukhara, now transformed into
People's Republics, were sandwiched between Transcaspia and
the remaining *oblasts*, and although the treaties which now allied
them to Moscow described them as politically independent, they
were in fact no more free from Russian control than they had
been during the Tsarist regime. By the introduction of specially
selected instructors and advisers, many of them Tatars, and by
the conclusion of economic and military agreements this control
was extended to cover practically the whole life of the new
republics; but the illusion that some degree of freedom had been
granted was achieved by the annulment of all previous agreements
between Russian governments and the khanates and of all concessions formerly held by Russian individuals and firms. The
Soviet Government was aware by this time that it could not
bulldoze the people of Central Asia into complete submission
immediately and that particular caution was necessary in the
khanates, where some degree of economic independence had

existed in Tsarist times. By the end of 1922, however, they decided to declare openly that the whole of Turkestan, including the Khorezm and Bukharan republics, was to become a single economic unit. In November a Central Asiatic Economic Council was formed consisting of representatives of the three Central Asian republics, its function being to integrate the whole economy including agriculture, irrigation, communications and monetary systems. In December, in his report to the 10th All-Russian Congress of Soviets on the formation of the Soviet Union, Stalin announced, 'Two independent Soviet republics, Khorezm and Bukhara, being People's Soviet, but not Socialist Republics – remain for the present outside the framework of this Union solely and exclusively because they are not yet socialist. I have no doubt – and I hope you too have no doubt – that, in proportion to their internal development towards socialism, they likewise will enter the structure of the Union state now being formed.' After this, complete absorption became a foregone conclusion.

Lenin believed, and probably continued to believe until the end of his life, that when backward countries were 'liberated' either with or without Soviet assistance, they would naturally and quickly gravitate towards a Marxist form of socialism. This belief is axiomatic to the whole Communist creed and its failure to materialize is always attributed to some outside agency such as imperialist intrigue or pan-Islam. In Khiva and Bukhara the new-fledged nationalist governments, although they had only been able to come to power with Soviet assistance, had no liking for Marxist socialism and did their best to prevent its introduction. With the presence of Red Army garrisons in their countries, however, they were powerless to resist for long. In both republics a situation developed between 1920 and 1922 which bore some resemblance to that prevailing in the mandated territories of the Middle East at the same period. There the mandatory power maintained its own armed forces, superintended the training of local armed forces and police, and virtually took charge of the administration by means of a cadre of advisers who set up political, judicial and economic institutions on Western democratic lines. As long as the mandate lasted, the control exercised by the mandatory power was paramount in respect of foreign relations and internal security. In Khiva and Bukhara the Soviet

Government exercised the same kind of control, and they also regulated the republics' economy. There were, however, two important differences: in the first place, the Western institutions set up in the mandates, although unfamiliar, were not entirely unintelligible or repugnant to the people; secondly, the Western mandatory powers were intent on reducing rather than increasing their control, for they were precluded from perpetuating it partly by their obligations to the League of Nations, and partly, perhaps principally, for geographical reasons. Neither of these circumstances hampered the Soviet leaders, who had realized from the start that the future of the kind of Soviet Union which they had in mind would depend on the exercise of uniform central control over all the nationalities. Their temporary toleration of the Young Khivan and Young Bukharan governments, therefore, was only a prelude to the complete absorption of the khanates into the Soviet system.

As already noted the main problem of the Khorezmian Republic was the age-long friction between the settled Uzbek and the nomad Turkmen population. Had these elements been able to compose their differences, the task of the Soviet Government would have been made much more difficult. Safonov, the Soviet equivalent in Khiva of a High Commissioner, was well aware of this problem and proceeded to take its solution into his own hands. He began by convening an all-Turkmen Congress in the town of Porsa, and by various promises to the Turkmen leaders secured their support in his opposition to the Young Khivan government. Serious disturbances in the town of Khiva in March 1921 were followed by the capture of government offices by Red Army troops and the overthrow of the government. A revolutionary committee consisting of two Uzbeks, one Turkmen, one Kazakh and a member of the Komsomol was set up in its place and although the existing constitution remained nominally in force and the remnants of the Young Khivan party continued to resist, the stage was now set for a complete Soviet takeover. In October 1921 several members of the government were executed or imprisoned on a charge of counter-revolution, a systematic purge of hostile elements was instituted during 1922, and in October 1923 the Constitution was changed so as to disenfranchise 'all non-toiling elements' and the Khorezmian People's Republic was declared the Khorezmian Soviet Socialist Republic.

In Bukhara, the process of absorbing the People's Republic into the Soviet socialist system followed much the same pattern as in Khiva, and here too the presence of the Red Army was the deciding factor. There were, however, some important differences. It was seen in the last chapter that the Government which took control of Bukhara on the overthrow of the Emir's government in September 1920 was that of the 'revolutionary Young Bukharan Party', which was an uneasy coalition of Young Bukharan, or Jadid, and Bolshevik elements, the leader of the party being Faizullah Khoja (Fayzulla Khodzhayev), who managed to retain his position until 1937 when he was tried and eventually executed on a number of charges including that of nationalism. Although this government was superficially more socialist and 'progressive' than the Young Khivan government, reactionary elements were more firmly entrenched in Bukhara, especially in the outlying districts. The conflict between urban and nomad elements was not so acute as in Khiva; on the other hand, the Basmachi resistance movement was in full swing and not only had the open or tacit support of some of the Young Bukharans and of officials of the previous regime, but was stiffened by such experienced and sophisticated personalities as Zeki Velidi Togan and Enver Pasha. The constitution of the Bukharan People's Republic was a genuinely progressive document which in other circumstances could have been the foundation of a genuinely democratic regime. While it marked a radical change from the former despotic system and was interlarded with Soviet terminology, it was in many respects quite un-Soviet in character: for example, it specifically safeguarded the possession and disposal of private property and declared that 'no published laws of the Republic may contradict the foundations of Islam'. Clearly such a constitution could not satisfy the Soviet leaders for long. As in Khiva, a purge of government and party officials was carried out during 1922. But even this was not completely effective, and in June 1923, Stalin pointedly referred to the fact that the Bukharan Council of Ministers contained eight merchants, two members of the intelligentsia and one mulla, but no peasants. A new and much more far-reaching purge ensued: the Council of Ministers was dissolved and reconstituted to include workers and peasants; more and more officials were arrested; and the Constitution was amended to disenfranchise anyone likely to oppose a Soviet Socialist regime. Finally, in September 1924 Bukhara was proclaimed a Soviet Socialist Republic.

The stage was now set for the next step towards the political unification of Central Asia. This was the so-called national delimitation on the basis of Lenin's Nationalities Policy. This delimitation, which was to involve the setting up of five National Republics covering the entire territory of the former Governorates-General of the Steppe Region and Turkestan and the khanates of Bukhara and Khiva, was destined to last, with some minor modifications, for at least forty years, and was generally expected to be permanent until the 1960s when signs of an impending change began to appear.

The Nationalities Policy has been strongly criticized on the grounds that the labelling of nationalities which it involved was arbitrary and artificial, and that it was merely a device to enable Moscow to 'divide and rule' while ostensibly adhering to the Communist principle of self-determination. In retrospect this criticism seems to be well grounded; even so, it would be a mistake to dismiss the Nationalities Policy as entirely cynical and lacking in any kind of justification. Viewed dispassionately and without regard to the high-sounding moral and ethical claims for and denunciations of it made by supporters and opponents of the Soviet regime, it can also be seen as a practical expedient for maintaining the integrity of the Russian state and for restoring and preserving law and order. If the Soviet leaders sought moral justification for a policy prompted by material considerations, they were by no means the first imperial rulers to do so.

Quite apart from real or imaginary internal threats and the menace of bourgeois nationalism, the Soviet leaders were confronted with another possibility which seemed to make the political unification of Muslim Central Asia an urgent necessity. As early as 1918, Sultan Galiyev (or Mir Sayyid Sultan Ali oghlu, to give him his proper name), a Tatar Muslim Communist holding a high position in the Commissariat of Nationality Affairs, began to develop a movement which in Soviet eyes amounted to counter-revolution. This movement centred round a conviction that the exclusively German or Russian interpretation of Marxism was unsuited to the Muslim world, and that it would eventually become obscured by Great Russian chauvinism. Sultan Galiyev aimed at modifying Marxism as conceived by the industrial West in order to render it applicable to the fundamentally agrarian society of Asia. Although a Communist, his ideas were bound up with Islamic tradition. His plan had several stages and was to begin with the creation of a Muslim state on the middle Volga, which he insisted on calling by its original Tatar name of Idel. To this state were to be joined, first the Turkic Muslims of Russia, and later all the other Russian Muslims. This Muslim state or federation was to organize the propagation of Communism in the non-Soviet East, and finally to help 'colonial and semi-colonial' territories in establishing political domination over their imperial rulers. The considerable response accorded to Sultan Galiyev's movement in Central Asia and the Caucasus drew attention to its potential danger. In 1923, he was denounced, arrested and dismissed from the Party. He ultimately disappeared and was believed to have been executed in 1930. Whatever the strength of Sultan Galiyev's following, his was the last expression of the all-Union Muslim point of view to appear in the USSR. Some people and among them Mustafa Chokayev, President of the ill-fated Kokand government of 1918, maintained that the 'plan of dividing Turkestan into tribal states', that is, the national delimitation of 1924, was the direct result of Sultan Galiyev's attempted 'counter-revolution'.

A detailed description of the national delimitation is outside the scope of the present study. Indeed, the factual information on which such a description ought to be based is not, and probably never will be, available. This is to be regretted: for a complete account of the mechanics of an administrative operation which, in spite of enormous difficulties, was virtually carried out in little over a year might be of value in other areas where similar problems are being encountered. As it is, the difference between Soviet and other accounts of the operation is so great as to make both versions barely credible. The Soviet contention is that agreement was reached as between the existing Republics, that is to say, the Kazakh and Turkestan ASSRs and the Khorezmian and Bukharan Soviet Socialist Republics; there were naturally many claims and counter-claims, but these were all settled in a spirit of give and take and true Bolshevik co-operation. The six peoples or groups of peoples, among whom the territory of the former Governorates-General of Turkestan and the Steppe Region and the khanates of Bukhara and Khiva was now to be apportioned, were the Kazakhs, Kirgiz, Karakalpaks, Turkmens, Uzbeks and Tadzhiks. All these were classified as 'nations', although only the Kazakhs, and possibly the Turkmens, had ever thought of themselves as such. As conceived in Moscow, the Nationalities Policy consisted in dividing the country into national formations coinciding as far as possible with the linguistic limits of each group, and later in developing national languages on the basis of living dialects. That such a division could have been achieved simply by the representatives of the peoples concerned was clearly impossible. Quite apart from the difficulty of reaching agreement among peoples who were to a large extent intermingled, the 2 or 3 per cent of literates throughout the region could hardly be expected to provide the necessary technical experts for such an operation. There was no doubt some deference to local opinion, and this resulted in some advantage for the Kazakhs who were politically the most advanced; but by and large the decision was imposed from above and enforced by the presence of the Red Army.

It is, of course, easy to visualize other solutions of the Central Asian nationalites problem which, although politically less convenient for the Soviet regime, would have accorded more closely with the natural nation-forming processes already in operation. Bennigsen and Quelquejay consider that a more natural and more practicable arrangement would have been the creation of three nations composed of the Kazakh-Kirgiz group, the Uzbek-Tadzhik group and the Turkmen group.[43] On the other hand, the wholesale condemnation of the Soviet Nationalities Policy and the national delimitation of 1924 is, perhaps, unjustified. As the self-appointed heirs to the Tsarist empire, the Soviet leaders undoubtedly felt some responsibility for Central Asia, or at least for the 2 million Russians living there. Rightly or wrongly they thought that to leave the region to its own devices would entail deplorable consequences for all concerned, and they adopted what seemed to them the best way of restoring law and order within the framework of the Russian state.

The nearest correspondence to the old administrative divisions was in the Kazakh ASSR which comprised all four *oblasts* of the Steppe Region, as well as some additional territory in the north, a considerable part of the Transcaspian *oblast* and almost all the Syr-dar'ya and Semirech'ye *oblasts*. The Turkmen SSR comprised the rest of the Transcaspian *oblast*, most of Khiva and a small part of Bukhara. The Uzbek SSR, together with the Tadzhik ASSR which was associated with it until 1929, consisted of the rest of Khiva and Bukhara, a small part of the Syr-dar'ya *oblast*, and the greater part of the Fergana and Samarkand *oblasts*. The Kirgiz SSR comprised parts of the Samarkand, Syr-dar'ya and Fergana *oblasts*, and the southern part of the Semirech'ye *oblast*. In 1929 the Tadzhik ASSR was raised to the status of SSR and the possibility of a fusion of the Uzbek and Tadzhik peoples was thus removed. Other changes in status since 1924 were the raising of the Kazakh ASSR to SSR status in 1936 and of the Kirgiz Autonomous Oblast to ASSR in 1926 and SSR in 1936. The Karakalpak Autonomous Oblast formed in 1925 within the Kazakh ASSR was raised to ASSR in 1932 and transferred to the Uzbek SSR in 1936. Except for the Tadzhik ASSR, which was associated with the Uzbek SSR, all the ASSRs were regarded as part of the RSFSR until the constitution of 1936. Apart from these changes in status, there have been only minor adjustments in the republican frontiers but frequent changes in the internal administrative divisions of the republics.

Anyone familiar with the problems of colonial administration in areas like the Steppe Region and Turkestan will recognize in the National Delimitation of 1924 an administrative measure, which, from the Soviet-Russian imperial point of view, was eminently sound and indeed inevitable if the empire was to be kept in being. Here was an area which, with the exception of the two khanates, had been regarded as an integral part of Russia for half a century. Consequent on the breakdown of the Tsarist colonial administration it had fallen a prey to disorder and was exposed to attempts by reactionary internal forces as well as by foreign powers to 'wrest it from Soviet Russia' – a highly significant expression which is still used in the most modern official histories. The Tsarist administrative division of the region had proved unsatisfactory owing mainly to the ill-fated decision not to extend direct Russian rule to the khanates. Any inhibitions which the Tsarist Government may have had about removing these medieval excrescences were not felt by the Soviet Government, which quickly realized that their liquidation was an essential preliminary to the consolidation of Soviet power. There can be little doubt that in the circumstances any imperial government – and no impartial person can regard the Soviet Government as anything else – would have acted in much the same way, or that the new administrative division, although not ideal, was in some respects better than the old one. Moreover, if the Soviet Government had ever entertained any idea of granting the peoples of Central Asia *genuine* independence based on ethnic and linguistic grouping, the National Delimitation would have proved a useful interim measure. As it was, it provided the basis for a new and much more efficient system of colonialism.

The grounds on which non-Soviet historians have criticized the National Delimitation are not uniform. Most of them are agreed that the principle of 'divide and rule' weighed heavily with the Soviet authorities, and some of them argue that the tortuousness of the inter-republican frontiers resulted from a desire that no republic should have economic predominance over the others. Other historians, and particularly Alexander Park, maintain that the economic superiority of Uzbekistan in both agriculture and industry was inevitable since the Uzbeks with their long tradition as oasis-dwellers were the most skilled in agriculture and had the best lands, while their urban development and fuel resources favoured the exploitation of industry. It can also be argued that since there was to be a socialist redistribution of wealth in all the republics, and since the whole economy was to be regulated from the centre, the Soviet authorities did not regard economic equality as between the republics as being either possible or necessary. On balance, it seems probable that the principle uppermost in the Soviet mind was that of language, primarily because they wished for political reasons to separate as far as possible the main tribal units. A clear-cut linguistic or ethnic division would have been impossible without recourse to an arbitrary exchange of populations, and this, curiously enough, the Soviet Government never seems to have contemplated. A new administrative division based *approximately* on language appealed to the Soviet authorities as the best way of breaking with Tsarist tradition and of contributing to their new nation-forming plans. It is, indeed, even conceivable that the linguistic frontiers were based on some pigeon-holed Tsarist scheme worked out by some Central Asian expert such as Nalivkin. The linguistic frontiers were not necessarily designed for the socialist system; they would have suited any form of administration equally well, and in effect they resulted in the creation and perpetuation of a new kind of national consciousness which was later to prove highly embarrassing to the Soviet regime.

The new republican governments, even underpinned as they were by Russian officials and experts and enjoying the support of the Red Army, were faced with a formidable task. The people had quickly realized that the Soviet yoke was not likely to be any lighter than the Tsarist: from a material point of view their condition was at first much worse than before the Revolution owing to the disruption in economy and communications; the promised redistribution of wealth and land could not be put into immediate effect; and declared Soviet views on religion, family life and private property were alarming in the extreme. Intensive Soviet campaigns against all kinds of 'feudal survivals', such as the veiling of women and the Ramazan fast, which the people regarded as an essential part of their lives, resulted in widespread arrests and denunciations. Most puzzling of all, nationalism, which, the people were told, had existed among the various new nations for countless generations but had only now been given expression in the new Republics, was soon declared to be a crime against the state for which officials could be executed or at least dismissed from their posts. The new Republics were to be 'national in form, but socialist in essence': the Uzbeks, for example, might have their national flag, their national language and some (but not all) of their national cultural traditions; but there was no question of their being Uzbek citizens or Uzbek patriots; their patriotism, their military service, their work and their productivity were due to the Soviet state as a whole and not to the Uzbek SSR.

On the other hand, although the Soviet authorities in pursuit of their material goal were prepared to ride roughshod over many susceptibilities and traditions, their methods also included certain innovations which had a strong appeal for the people and which had, for various reasons, been withheld by the Tsarist regime just as they had elsewhere by other imperial governments, and by the governments of independent Asian countries. I have dealt with the question of education in greater detail in another chapter but it may be appropriate to mention here the often expressed view that in introducing universal compulsory education the Soviet regime laid up trouble for itself. In most colonial empires, it is pointed out, nationalist movements have been started by highly educated people, many of them having received their education in the metropolitan country. But the nuisance value and frequent success of these movements stemmed not so much from the enlightenment of their leaders as from their ability to incite, and in many instances delude, their fellow countrymen, the vast majority of whom had remained ignorant and illiterate. Whether or not the Soviet authorities knew or thought they were taking a calculated risk in extending popular education on a scale hitherto unknown in any other Asian country except Japan, there can be no doubt whatever that the rapid spread of literacy, and later of higher education, did more than anything else to distract the attention of the people from the rigours and repressions which accompanied the new regime and to reduce their susceptibility to the infiltration of nationalist ideas. That universal education is calculated to promote rather than endanger orderly government is a principle still apparently not grasped by many Asian regimes which continue to devote the major part of their efforts and treasure to the building up of armed forces rather than to education, and are in consequence frequently shaken by revolt and subversion, as often as not originating in the armed forces themselves.

Although the most violent physical and most determined cultural opposition offered to the Soviet regime occurred in the settled districts of the Central Asian Republics, it was in Kazakhstan that the Soviet authorities encountered the greatest difficulty in consolidating their power. This was due partly to the greater homogeneity and thus more developed national consciousness of the Kazakhs, and partly because the elusive nature of Kazakh nomad society rendered it largely impervious to Soviet indoctrination and to the attractions of the Soviet educational policy. In spite of the early disappearance of the Alash Orda, the so-called socialist government of the Kazakh ASSR remained distinctly nationalist until 1927. The thought uppermost in the minds of the Kazakhs was how to get rid of the Russian settlers. This they attempted to do by declaring that the Kazakhs must have priority in matters of land distribution and by relegating the Russian and Ukrainian settlers to the most unproductive tracts. Such anti-European discrimination was, however, put an end to during the Party Secretaryship of Goloshchekin, who not only vigorously defended the position of the one and a half million European settlers in Kazakhstan, but encouraged further colonization, particularly in connexion with the building of the Turksib (Turkestan-Siberia) railway which was opened in 1930.

It soon became clear to the Soviet Central Government that the only way in which the nomad society of Kazakhstan, and to a lesser extent of Turkmenistan and Kirgizia, could be brought into the Soviet fold was by compulsory stabilization. The settlement of nomads and the combination of animal husbandry with land cultivation was a process which had begun even before the coming of the Russians, notably in the south of the Steppe Region and in Semirech'ye. In theory, it had been encouraged by the Tsarist Government, but any well-meant efforts on the part of the local administrators had been largely stultified by the centrally controlled settlement policy which resulted in most of the best lands being given to Russian and Ukrainian settlers. Early Soviet attempts at stabilization were hesitant and proved largely unsuccessful. Forcible stabilization was not resorted to until the beginning of the first Five Year Plan in 1928, which included the introduction of collectivization of agriculture throughout the Soviet Union. The first action taken in Kazakhstan was the expropriation of herds and land belonging to rich peasants locally known as *bays* and in Russian as *kulaks*. Farm implements, buildings and transport were confiscated and distributed among poor peasants who were organized into collective and state farms. By 1932 up to 60 per cent of the population had been herded into these farms, most of which were either under Russian management or under the control of Russian collective farms. By this time discontent among the Kazakhs was widespread and they resorted to the wholesale slaughter of cattle. Many of the collective farms collapsed and the whole process of stabilization came under fierce official criticism. It was admitted that not only had the collectivization and stabilization of the nomads been far too high-handed, but that the whole approach to the matter was wrong, based as it was on the premise that stable agriculture was necessarily superior to pastoral nomadism. A new policy was evolved which included the establishment of what was called 'a roving cattle economy' (*otgonnoye zhivotnovodstvo*, or *otgon*) which allowed for the use of both summer and winter pastures and therefore some degree of seasonal nomadism. A slow recovery began in 1934; but the whole Kazakh economy, based as it was on animal husbandry, had been struck a crippling blow from which it never completely recovered. There was also a heavy loss of human life: the 1939 census showed a drop in the total number of Kazakhs of nearly a million for which no official explanation has ever been forthcoming. An unspecified number are said to have emigrated to China and the fate of the remainder is unknown. In general, Kazakh nationalists were made responsible for the failure of early attempts at sovietization and in March 1935 a number of them, including Kulumbetov, the Kazakh Vice-Premier, were executed.

The essence of the Soviet Nationalities Policy was economic and its declared object was 'the liquidation of existing inequality' among the nations making up the former Russian empire. It was believed that once inequality had been eliminated all bourgeois nationalist and separatist tendencies would disappear. If, as Alexander Park maintains, the policy was 'conceived in honesty' it quickly encountered realities which showed that it could not be made to correspond to the will of the people, however much it might contribute to their ultimate material good. In the first place the minute native intelligentsia, which alone had the necessary education and political consciousness to qualify for administrative and political activity, was stigmatized as the 'exploiting' class, and therefore excluded from politics. Secondly, the Soviet tendency to prefer the 'proletariat' to the peasantry, although it had little national significance for the more homogeneous population of western Russia, had unfortunate results in the Muslim borderlands, where the politically conscious industrial proletarian minority was mainly Russian and Ukrainian, that is European, and the peasant majority Asian. This tended to perpetuate and even to extend the colonialist concept of enlightened European tutelage over backward native peoples.

The Soviet leaders were no doubt well aware of the contradictions which were developing between Soviet ideals and hard reality. Lenin in particular frequently inveighed against the danger of Great Russian chauvinism. He may have believed that education and administrative training would eventually result in complete *korenizatsiya*, a new word whose literal rendering is 'nativization', but although the training of native personnel was begun in the 1920s, it proceeded very slowly; for instance, in Kazakhstan by 1930 only 26·5 per cent of all clerical posts were held by Kazakhs. In the meanwhile, Soviet Russian standards and procedures had been adopted and the whole administration so Russianized that it could not be 'nativized' merely by introducing more and more Russian-trained indigenous personnel.

There were other all-Union institutions which inevitably made for centralization and russianization. Muslims, most of whom had previously been exempt from conscription, were now drafted into the preponderantly Russian Red Army; various planning, construction and youth organizations were conceived on an all-Union basis, and their membership cut across national boundaries. Finally, the greatest instrument of centralization, the Party, was, after the first outburst of national fervour, to become more and more susceptible to the mystique of Russian traditionalism and nationalism, which had never really disappeared from Russian life. The final discrediting in 1937 of Pokrovskiy's theory of history which condemned the Tsarist conquests and annexations as 'an absolute evil' was the beginning of a long process tending towards the rehabilitation of the Tsarist regime and of Russia's historic mission as a mentor of backward peoples. It was the Party which developed and is still propagating this idea.

From the early days of the Revolution it had been clear to the Soviet leaders that the only way in which central control over the outlying parts of the empire could be combined with the nominal grant of self-government would be through the agency of the Communist Party. The difficulty in Central Asia was to strike the balance between the chauvinism of the Russian colonists who in the beginning had seized power to the complete exclusion of the Muslims, and the developing nationalism of the numerically superior Muslims, which as education gained ground, might become what was later known as national Communism. Owing to the high-handed attitude of the Tashkent Soviet from 1918 onwards, practically nothing was done to recruit Muslim Communists until the summer of 1920. The membership of the Turkestan Communist Party had by 1921 risen to 65,000, but Moscow quickly realized that this was spurious and that the Party's ranks were being largely filled not only by Russian colonizers but by Muslims with an eye to the main chance. A purge ensued and by 1923 the total had dropped to about a quarter of the 1921 figure. Spirited efforts were now made to train and educate Muslim Party members and candidates for membership, but in 1926 it was recorded that 70 per cent of the Party members in the Turkmen SSR were 'technically illiterate'. By 1927 the party membership in the Uzbek, Turkmen and Kirgiz SSRs had risen to about 16,000, of whom at least half, and probably much more, were Russians. In spite of numerous setbacks, which included frequent nationalist 'deviations', the Party persisted in its efforts to build up a Muslim Communist *élite* which would contain enough reliable members to forestall the development of any dangerous nationalism. At what stage and to what extent they can be said to have achieved this aim are matters which will be discussed in greater detail in a later chapter. Up to 1963, however, the proportion of active non-Muslim Party officials in the various Republics was considerably greater than the non-Asiatic proportion of the population, this in the case of Kazakhstan being considerably over 50 per cent.

Other institutions which the Soviet authorities set up to aid in the consolidation of their power were the Komsomol, or Young Communist League, the Trade Unions and the Koschi, which Park has described as 'a mixture of rural trade union and co-operative with a predominantly political character'. The Komsomol performed the dual role of a training ground for future Party members and an active instrument in the Party's campaign for increased productivity, abolition of nationalist survivals and the like. The Tsarist Government had never attempted anything in the way of youth organization, and recruitment to the Komsomol hung fire until the late 1920s. The proportion of Muslims to non-Muslims in its membership is difficult to determine, but it seems probable that the proportion of non-Muslims had always been lower than in the Party itself. At the outbreak of the Revolution, the Trade Union movement was only in an embryo stage in Central Asia and its membership was almost entirely confined to Russians who made up over 90 per cent of the industrial workers. By 1927 the Trade Union membership had risen to 238,029 of whom 78,906 were Muslims. In the Agricultural and Forestry Workers Union, however, the Muslims outnumbered Europeans by nearly two to one. As elsewhere in the Soviet Union, trade union officials were not necessarily representative of the workers in the sense of having been workers themselves; the trade union apparatus was rather an official body designed to exercise control primarily over the native workers.

The *Koshchi* (the word simply means 'ploughman', or 'hired labourer'), although a kind of trade union, was distinct from the Agricultural or Forestry Workers Union (*rabzemles*) which restricted its membership to hired workers. The Koschi on the other hand, included landless and small peasants, tenant farmers, share croppers and village home-craftsmen. It was a Soviet creation and was designed to incorporate and control the small peasant organizations which had grown up during the Civil War but had been ignored by the Tashkent Soviet. It was used by the Soviet authorities to aid in the promotion of class war as opposed to nationalism and also in the creation of local government bodies on Soviet lines. It was given official status in March 1922 and a charter specified its various tasks which included political indoctrination of the rural population and encouragement of friendly relations between the Muslim and European workers. Anyone who had supervised or hired labour, private traders, middlemen, and active members of religious organizations were debarred from membership. There is no doubt that the Koshchi union quickly caught the popular imagination and the people flocked to become members. It performed a useful role in explaining the aims of the Party and in preparing for the great agrarian reforms which were applied between 1925 and 1927 and will presently be described. During this period, however, the authorities decided, probably with good reason, that the Koschi was becoming infiltrated with elements hostile to the Soviet regime. It was accordingly announced that it no longer 'represented the interests of the agricultural proletariat' and was deprived of its official status. In 1927 it was transformed into 'a voluntary social organization', and although it still remained nominally in existence until 1931, it had long ceased to have any effect on political life.

The first stage in the consolidation of Soviet power in Central Asia had been the National Delimitation. This was not only an important administrative expedient for the restoration of law and order out of chaos, but it served as a spectacular renunciation of the whole imperial principle and by creating a whole set of new administrative terms strove to give the impression that colonialism had disappeared for ever. For some time, however, the change was only dimly apprehended by the Muslim peoples as a whole and its effect was virtually confined to the urban population, itself quite unrepresentative of a country the vast majority of whose population gained its living by agriculture. To reach this population the Soviet authorities had to undermine the whole traditional system of agricultural and agrarian relationships. The only way in which this could be done was by the creation of an artificial revolution; for the Russian Revolution in the sense of a peasant war against the landowners had never spread to Central Asia. Here there were no class distinctions and few if any cultural barriers; the patriarchal system was so firmly established that the idea of seizing a landlord's property simply did not occur to the peasants. Moreover, in many parts of the country, and particularly in Turkmenistan, the land was already communally owned by tribes or family unions and the notion of confiscating this land and distributing it to individuals seemed to the tribal leaders the very negation of socialism. The first task of the authorities was consequently to implant a sense of grievance in the countryside and by a widespread propaganda campaign to produce among the 'have-nots' a feeling of hatred for the 'haves'. Before this could be done, however, steps had to be taken to remove the only genuine existing hatred, that of the Muslim population for the Russians who had seized their lands and had gone on seizing them during the first two years of Russian colonist domination of Turkestan. A decree of March 4, 1920, ordered the return to the Muslim peasants of all land seized from them by Russian settlers and by May 1921 687,841 acres of such land were said to have been redistributed to 13,000 native households, mainly in Semirech'ye.

There is no doubt that by confining the first stage of agrarian reform to the main areas of Russian colonization in Turkestan, namely, the former Semirech'ye and Syr-dar'ya *oblasts*, the new regime succeeded in giving the impression, which it had failed to do earlier, that it was in fact intent on the abolition of national inequality. But although the Marxist socialist system as applied to Central Asia might involve, and has indeed involved, a greater degree of national equality than exists in some other colonial empires, this was not the primary purpose of the agrarian reforms. 'In turning the peasant against the landlord,' writes Alexander Park, 'the Bolsheviks were not aiming merely to put an end to historically derived inequalities in the countryside; they sought rather to destroy the landlord as a political, economic and social force in the village . . . the land reform was to be an instrument for cutting the peasant loose from every tie with the past. By destroying every competing authority it sought to make the Soviet system the only source of guidance in the village.'

The second stage of the agrarian reforms, their extension to the uncolonized areas, began in 1925 and by the end of the year it was claimed that in Uzbekistan all land holdings exceeding 135 acres had been expropriated and redistributed. By 1927, it was declared that the average holding per household was only 8 acres. Expropriation and redistribution were not completed throughout the whole region until 1929. In spite of the good impression created by the action taken against Russian colonists, of the vast propaganda campaign and of the care taken to avoid antagonizing religious elements, there was considerable resistance to the reforms, on the part not only of the landowners, but also of the peasants themselves, who often sided with their previous masters in order to preserve the *status quo*. In Turkmenistan, where much of the land was communally or tribally owned, resistance was offered by whole communities. Had the people realized that land distribution was only a prelude to collectivization, which had begun in other parts of the Union in 1928, that is, at least a year before redistribution of land was complete in Central Asia, there is no doubt that resistance would have been much stronger, although faced with the ever-present Red Army it would have had no hope of success.

With the completion of the agrarian reforms in 1929 the consolidation of Soviet power in Central Asia and the Steppe Region was accomplished. By destroying the traditional system of land tenure and water rights the Soviet regime had struck at the very roots of Muslim society. Education was soon to produce a sufficient nucleus of supporters of the regime to ensure penetration into the most remote rural districts of the conviction that the new regime had come to stay and that active opposition to it was hopeless. Passive resistance, however, particularly in cultural matters, was destined to continue even into the next generation, and even in the 1960s it had by no means died out.

CHAPTER VIII

CENTRAL ASIA UNDER SOVIET RULE

By 1927 Soviet physical control over the five republics now comprising the entire territory of the Steppe Region, Turkestan and the khanates of Bukhara and Khiva was complete. Henceforward the Muslim peoples of the region were to play no decisive part in shaping their destinies. With the ever-present Red Army, the increasing number of Russian settlers and the absence of any hope of assistance or intervention from outside they became resigned to their lot and were not disposed to offer any other than passive resistance. During the ensuing 35 years there were in fact few events and no positive developments which could be said to have taken place on the initiative of the local inhabitants. Soviet history of these years, in so far as it has been written at all, consists almost entirely of a catalogue of achievements in the fields of industry, agriculture, irrigation, communications and culture, all of which are attributed to the 'triumph of the Revolution' and few if any of which bear the stamp of native genius. This kind of history, if indeed it can be called history, is in striking contrast to the published accounts of what has happened during the same period in the Muslim countries of the Middle East and South Asia. Here the story is of frequent changes of governments and even of regimes, of conflict now with neighbours, now with the West, of tribal revolt and internal disturbance, of the rise and fall of public figures, and in general of increased stature and significance in the modern world. In the Central Asian republics the standard of living, education, communications, public health and productivity rose much higher than in all but one or two of the Muslim countries of non-Soviet Asia; but this was the result of determined and relentless planning from the centre rather than of national development brought about by the will of the various peoples concerned. This is not to minimize the part actually played by the Muslim peoples in providing the necessary labour and in acquiring new skills which could be used in developing the economy. After physical opposition as expressed in the Basmachi revolt had been forcibly overcome, active resentment gradually gave way to resignation, and this under the influence of more efficient administration, skilful propaganda and better organized education and recreation, in turn produced a considerable degree of co-operation with the new regime. From the point of view of the masses, efficient colonialism provides solid material advantages which may make up for the absence of the spiritual satisfaction which may or may not accompany national independence. It is of course idle to speculate on the eventual outcome of an experiment which has not yet outlasted two generations, but it is necessary to draw attention to the fact that the peoples of Central Asia, in the circumstances which have prevailed during the past 35 years, can hardly be expected to have had a history in the accepted sense of the word.

Much of the foregoing could be said to apply to any colonial territory where national consciousness either does not exist or where its expression by means of nationalist movements is proscribed. Thus the recorded history of Turkestan from 1865 until 1917 is simply the history of Tsarist administration there, as well as, to some extent, of that of the rulers of Kokand, Khiva and Bukhara. It is the story of what happened in these regions irrespective of the wishes and actions of the people. It was much the same for British and French colonial territories so long either as national consciousness did not exist or as nationalist movements were suppressed. In neither case, however, was it found possible or thought desirable to take measures which would result in the permanent suppression of any form of nationalist activity even though this was likely to prejudice the security or economy of the metropolitan power. The reasons for such restraint were various; they included the growth of liberal ideas at home, the vastness of and the density of population in the territories concerned, preoccupation resulting from two World Wars, and pressure exercised by foreign powers. Some of these circumstances might be said to have existed in Tsarist times and to have had some effect in restraining the Tsarist Government from completely annexing Bukhara and Khiva; but as has been shown earlier, there were no nationalist movements to suppress since national consciousness only began to appear in Central Asia after the Revolution of 1905 and was even then moderate in its aspirations and restricted to certain peoples. National consciousness of a more definite kind appeared after the 1917 Revolution and resulted in sporadic nationalist movements; but after the end of the Civil War and the final suppression of the Basmachi revolt, a situation was created in which the new regime was able to harness national consciousness to its own requirements and in which most of the restraining factors just mentioned were simply inoperative: there were no liberal ideas at home; the territory though vast was sparsely populated; and pressure and intervention by foreign powers had come to an end by 1920. The Soviet Government proceeded to take advantage of this situation with a ruthless determination the ultimate effects of which were seriously underestimated by the West as well as by adjacent Middle Eastern and South Asian governments.

In order to bring about the conditioning of the peoples of Central Asia to the new regime the Soviet Government adopted three principles from which it has never deviated: the maintenance in the area of large and predominantly non-Asian security forces; the segregation of the Central Asian peoples from all contact with the outside world by the establishment of an efficient system of non-Asian frontier guards; and the institution of a widespread system of education and propaganda designed to condition the people to the new regime and insulate them from all outside influences. Although the third measure would not have been possible without the existence of the first two, it was incomparably the most important of the three in dealing with the Muslim masses of Central Asia, where it was not a question of re-education, as it was in western Russia, but of the introduction of education and political indoctrination where virtually none had existed before. There can be no doubt that the effect of education on a previously illiterate population was profound: it occupied their minds in a way that they had never been occupied before; and if it did not succeed in implanting, as the Soviet Government had hoped, a love for the Russian people, it at least fostered a hatred for the Muslims' previous pastors and masters, and gradually induced what Stalin called 'a taste of the material good of the Revolution'.

In the material as well as in the cultural sense much more 'happened' to the peoples of Central Asia during the first 35 years of consolidated Soviet rule than in approximately the same period of consolidated Tsarist rule, that is to say, from 1881 until the Revolution. During the earlier period the Muslim peoples enjoyed a much higher degree of security than previously, but they hardly changed their way of life at all. The Tsarist regime evidently wished them to do so and held very much the same views about the deadening influence of Islam as their Soviet successors; but they lacked the necessary urge and dynamism and were moreover beset with many internal and external embarrassments. A very fair idea of *what* has happened to the Muslim peoples during the Soviet regime can be gained by examining the innumerable Government decrees relating to the economy, education and the like and seeing the extent – the very considerable extent – to which they have been translated into reality. In the present chapter an attempt will be made to review conditions existing up to the early 1960s in various material fields about which accurate information is now readily available. *How* these things have happened is much less easily determined since all extant Soviet accounts written after the late 1920s are merely studies in black and white – descriptions of a struggle between the forces of reaction and progress, the former being always actuated by the worst and the latter by the best and purest motives. None of these accounts devotes any space to a fair exposition of views which ran counter to Soviet plans on conservative or other grounds. Large-scale opposition to such sweeping measures as collectivization and the expansion of cotton cultivation at the expense of cereals was attributed to the lowest motives and then swept aside. Another factor which makes the study of Soviet histories of the Muslim republics a sterile process is their remarkable sameness: apart from the difference in economic resources, the tales of achievements and shortcomings are all strikingly similar. This is not to say that the accounts were necessarily untrue; the results were the same because the plans and the degree of official disregard of local opposition were the same. This, however, was only true of Central Asia; elsewhere in Asia, for example, in Georgia and Armenia, the Soviet approach was different.

By far the fullest and best documented account of what went

on in Central Asia during the Soviet regime is to be found in Baymirza Hayit's *Turkestan in the Twentieth Century*.[44] Himself an Uzbek, Dr Hayit grew up in Soviet Uzbekistan, defecting to the West during the Second World War. He describes in great detail the strong spiritual resistance offered by Muslim intellectuals to the Soviet assault on their cherished traditions and way of life, and the manner in which this resistance was steadily worn down by the Soviet authorities. He writes, nevertheless, that 'it was not until 1937 that the social life of Turkestan was determined by communism. Up to then, the Turkestan Communist leaders had tried to let the people live in their own way, and at the same time to fulfil Soviet state plans. Therefore the people were able to live either secretly, or frequently quite openly, according to their own customs.' He goes on to state that all this changed after the purge of the Party and state machine which took place in 1937. This purge was part of the so-called Great Purge (known in Russian as *yezhovshchina*, from the name of the then head of the NKVD, Yezhov) which convulsed the whole of the USSR between 1936 and 1938; but it had a particular effect on the Central Asian Muslims, coinciding as it did with the abolition of national military formations and the introduction of universal conscription in the Soviet armed forces. Dr Hayit incidentally asserts that of the 1,500,000 Turkestanis called up for military service in the Second World War, 800,000 deserted to the Germans.

The fact that social life remained in many ways unchanged until 1937 can hardly be attributed to a Soviet belief that the old way of life was compatible with the new productivity plans. Indeed, the whole trend of Soviet propaganda between 1927 and 1937 suggests the exact opposite. But the rumblings of discontent among the intellectuals and the suspected existence of nationalist aspirations among the Muslim Communist *élite* may have indicated the advisability of postponing further pressure until a suitable opportunity presented itself. The Union-wide purge of 1936 with its object of harrying out 'enemies of the people' from wherever they might be lurking offered just such an opportunity. In Central Asia justification for the purge was found in a so-called nationalist plot in Uzbekistan. Whether or not a real plot existed and, if it did, whether it constituted a real threat to the Soviet regime are questions to which it is impossible to provide an answer. But the trial of the alleged participants and the arrests and executions which followed it were events of great significance and therefore deserve special mention here.

The affair began with the secretary of the Komsomol of Uzbekistan accusing Fayzulla Khodzhayev, the Prime Minister, of having buried his brother according to Islamic rites. In June 1937 at the 7th Congress of the Uzbek Communist Party Khodzhayev was dismissed from office and ordered to report to Moscow where he was at once arrested. In September, Akmal Ikramov, Secretary of the Uzbek Communist Party, was accused in a newspaper article of being a nationalist. He too was ordered to report to Moscow, but was soon sent back and was arraigned before the Central Committee of the Uzbek Communist Party in Tashkent. He was then arrested and in March 1938 he and Khodzhayev with twenty-one other accused, among them Bukharin and Rykov, were publicly tried in Moscow. Both men were found guilty on a number of charges and executed.

It is improbable that the truth about this affair will ever now be known, and the authorities are evidently determined that it shall pass out of history. Although a full account was published in the verbatim Report of Court Proceedings in the *Case of the anti-Soviet 'bloc of Rights and Trotskyites'* (Moscow, 1938), no mention of it is made in the Soviet Encyclopaedia. The second volume of the history of the Uzbek SSR has not yet appeared, but the matter is not referred to at all in a work called *Materials for the History of Soviet Uzbekistan* (published in Tashkent in 1957). Nor does it figure in the list of outstanding events in Uzbekistan since the Revolution which adorns the walls of the Historical Museum in Bukhara. There remains a strong suspicion that these two men, like many others in different parts of the Soviet Union, were victimized *'pour encourager les autres'*. Both men had long revolutionary records; both had been associated with the Jadid movement, although Khodzhayev had to some extent broken with it when he joined the Revolutionary Young Bukharans who constituted the first government of the Bukharan Peoples Republic. Ikramov, the son of a well-known Tashkent cleric, had joined the Communist Party in 1918, was elected First Secretary of the Uzbek Communist Party in 1924 and remained in this post until his arrest. Both seem to have been sincere supporters of the Revolution, but both had openly expressed doubts about the genuineness of Soviet claims to have abolished colonialism.

Ikramov in particular had actually challenged Stalin on this point at a Conference of the Central Committee of the Russian Communist Party which he had attended in 1923. At the trial both men admitted having worked for national independence. What exactly they meant by this was not explained, but it seems probable that they had never visualized the separation of any part of Central Asia from the Soviet Union. In any event, they vigorously denied having any association with anti-Bolshevik elements either inside or outside the USSR. Until 1956 both Khodzhayev and Ikramov were treated as 'unpersons', but in that year Ikramov was suddenly rehabilitated and in 1959 was accorded a brief entry in the Small Encyclopaedia. His trial and execution were not, however, mentioned.

In Central Asia the Purge was not accompanied by any disturbance or resistance. According to Dr Hayit, there was hardly a family which was unaffected by the Purge and the people as a whole were stunned. Since then many persons have been accused of harbouring nationalist sentiments, but there has never been any further suggestion of a nationalist plot or movement. Even during the War there were no serious outbreaks or disturbances although Dr Hayit mentions one or two isolated attacks on police stations.

Quite apart from the provision of manpower, Central Asia played an important part in the War from the Soviet point of view. A large number of factories were transferred from the western part of the Union and this naturally contributed towards the rapid industrialization of the region. After the War, and particularly after 1950, economic and living conditions began steadily to improve and visitors to the Republic testified to the general appearance of well-being. Foreigners, it is true, were not allowed into the rural districts, but there was no reason to suppose that these failed to benefit by the general improvement in conditions. The people were resigned to their lot and seemed to be materially, if not spiritually, contented with it. But, as someone said of social life in Bulgaria in the days of Turkish rule, 'Bondage has this one advantage: it makes a nation merry. Where far-reaching ambition has no scope for its development the community squanders its energy on the trivial and personal cares of its daily life, and seeks relief and recreation in simple and easily obtained material enjoyment.'[45]

Political Organization and Administration

The system of political organization and administration was confirmed by the Constitution of 1936, and until November 1962 there was no fundamental change. Nominally, each republic was administered by a Presidium and a cabinet of about 23 Ministries, the great majority of which were concerned with various branches of industry and agriculture. Executive government was in the hands of a Supreme Soviet while local government devolved upon *oblast* (province), *rayon* (county), town, settlement and village soviets, all of which were elected bodies. Most of the Ministries were held by members of local nationalities, but the authority of some of them, for example the Ministry of Foreign Affairs, was purely fictitious. Ministries with an All-Union significance, such as those of Communications and the Committee for State Security, were usually held by non-Asians. In theory, representation of the republics at the centre was secured by the Soviet of Nationalities, but in fact the connecting link between the centre and the republics, and indeed the government of the republics themselves, was in the hands of the Communist Party. On the whole, the administration worked smoothly, but it was subject to periodical exposures and purges, most of them connected with shortcomings in production of various kinds. There was a tendency on the part of Western students of Soviet affairs to attribute these exposures and the dismissals which usually followed them to political causes, and there is no doubt that the central authorities sometimes read political or even nationalist motives into routine cases of nepotism and misappropriation of public funds. It was seldom possible to follow the fortunes of officials dismissed for inefficiency or dishonesty, but in many cases their punishment seems to have stopped at dismissal from the Party. Many of the cases of misconduct and abuse of authority were characteristic of colonial regimes where locally appointed officials do only lip service to Western methods of administration and develop a remarkable skill in adapting Western bureaucracy to their own private ends. When eventually local malpractices were discovered, their treatment was often reminiscent of what sometimes happened in the less efficient Indian states during the period of British rule. For example, in 1961 after having been found guilty of gross inefficiency, corruption and nepotism, the

Kirgiz First Secretary of an *oblast* Party committee in Kirgizia was promoted to the post of Minister of the Interior. Four months later, after a letter had been received from Khrushchev, he was removed from this higher post and dismissed from the Party. His 'promotion' to cabinet rank was perhaps too *naïve* an admission of the fact that his new post would be much less influential, and probably less lucrative, than that of *oblast* Party Secretary. In an Indian state, gross abuses and maladministration of this kind would have been brought to the attention of the Political Resident; an official would have been found responsible, but the abuses hushed up, and the official appointed to a higher post; later, when the affair had been made public and the official named, the British Government representative would write to the ruling prince and demand the official's instant dismissal and punishment.

In 1957 it was announced that henceforward the republics would have greater responsibility in certain matters which had hitherto been controlled by the centre. But no amendment was made to the Constitution in which the limits of republican responsibility are clearly defined, and it does not seem that any change did in fact take place. In 1962, on the other hand, certain measures were introduced which seemed likely to have the effect of increasing rather than lessening central control. To begin with, it was decided to set up a Central Asian Bureau to work under the direct guidance of the All-Union Communist Party's Central Committee Presidium. It was stated that this Bureau would not take over the functions of republican Central Committees but would 'extend help to the Party Agencies of the Central Asian republics in improving the guidance of industry, construction and agriculture, co-ordinating the work of the Party, Soviet and economic agencies of these republics'. The Bureau, whose Chairman was a Russian, was to consist of the Party First Secretaries of the republics of Uzbekistan, Tadzhikistan, Kirgizia and Turkmenistan, the First Secretary of the Chimkent Oblast Committee of the Kazakh SSR, and also the heads of four new Central Asian economic organizations to be set up at the same time, namely, the Central Asian Council of National Economy, the Central Asian Construction Agency, the Central Asian Directorate for Cotton Growing, and the Chief Directorate for Irrigation and the Construction of Sovkhozes. At the same plenum of the Central Committee of the Communist Party Khrushchev announced a major reorganization of the Party to make it more efficient in guiding industry and agriculture. He declared that, under the existing territorial division, Party Committees were concerned with industry and agriculture alike, but in practice they tended to neglect industry and construction in favour of agriculture, or vice-versa, depending on the problems currently stressed by the All-Union Central Committee. Reorganization of the Party on a production basis, said Khrushchev, with separate bureaux and committees for industry and agriculture, would overcome these difficulties. Decrees ordering wholesale changes in the system of administration then followed. The general pattern was that in each republic the Central Committee was now to have two new bureaux – one for industry and one for agriculture. Lower down the scale, most *obkoms* (Oblast Party Committees) were to be split into industrial and agricultural commit-tees, subordinate respectively to the Industrial and Agricultural Bureaux of the Central Committee, but in *oblasts* where either industry or agriculture was negligible there was still to be only one *obkom*. Under the industrial *obkoms* would come the *gorkoms* (Town Party Committees) and the Party organizations of industrial undertakings situated outside urban areas, while the agricultural *obkoms* would control rural Party organizations. The rural *raykoms* (Rayon Party Committees) were abolished and replaced by Party committees of new *kolkhoz-sovkhoz* Production Directorates. All this resulted in drastic changes in the territorial administrative divisions of some of the republics. For example, the three *oblasts* into which Turkmenistan was previously divided were abolished. The Agricultural Bureau of the Central Committee assumed direct control of the Party Committees of 21 Rural Production Directorates which replaced the previous 39 rural *raykoms*. The Industrial Bureau of the Central Committee took charge of the 7 existing *gorkoms* of Krasnovodsk, Nebit-Dag, Cheleken, Mary, Chardzhou, Tashauz and Ashkhabad, as well as of two Zonal Industrial Production Party Committees.

The same principle was extended to such other republican organizations as the Komsomol, Trade Unions, and to the Ministries of Education, Culture, Health and Social Insurance, all of which were divided into Agricultural and Industrial sectors. Local government was also reorganized: where there were two

Oblast Party Committees there were now to be two soviets, one for the urban and industrial population, and the other for the rural, agricultural population. Rural *rayons* were amalgamated so that in nearly all cases they coincided with the areas covered by the Kolkhoz-Sovkhoz Production Directorates. This entirely novel system of administration seemed to imply that production was henceforward to be regarded as the sole basis and purpose of life and that government would be replaced by economic management.

Although the system and machinery of government are uncharacteristic of the local population and unrepresentative of their wishes, it cannot be described as inefficient. With some evasions and delays government decrees are put into operation without demur and although government in the past was harsh and oppressive it is probably not felt to be so at present.

Nationalism

Before proceeding to describe material developments under the Soviet regime, some mention must be made of the extent to which nationalism can be said to have persisted among the Muslim peoples of Central Asia. The matter is so complicated, and impartial investigation so clearly impossible, that no precise conclusion can be expected; it may, however, at least be possible to clear away a certain amount of misconception.

Like many other 'isms' nationalism is a word with no accepted semantic 'referent', that is to say, it does not immediately suggest the same thing to everyone. Elie Kedourie in his admirable and provocative essay on the subject[46] defines it as follows: 'Nationalism is a doctrine invented in Europe at the beginning of the nineteenth century. It pretends to supply a criterion for the determination of the unit of population proper to enjoy a government exclusively its own, for the legitimate exercise of power in the state, and for the right organization of a society of states. Roughly, the doctrine holds that humanity is naturally divided into nations, that nations are known by certain characteristics which can be ascertained, and that the only legitimate type of government is national self-government.' A by-product of imperialism, nationalism is normally in direct conflict with imperial authority and first showed its head in the nineteenth-century European empires of Austria, Turkey and Russia. As all these empires were in conflict with each other, the standard imperial attitude towards nationalism quickly came to be that it was a bad thing in one's own empire but a good thing in other empires. A natural outcome of this was that while nationalist movements occasioned much genuine self-sacrifice among the actual participants and some sincere sympathy and practical support among liberal opinion abroad, they were also actively aided and in some instances initiated by foreign powers from motives which were not purely altruistic or ideological. Thus, British intervention in Greece in the 1830s was aimed as much at checking Russia as at championing the Greeks, while Russia's support of Bulgarian and Serbian independence was actuated as much by her designs on Turkey as by her desire to support her co-religionists.

The same equivocal attitude towards nationalism persisted into the twentieth century, when its theory and practice were extended to Asia and later to Africa. It had already become clear that no subject nationality could gain or sustain political freedom un-aided. A new phenomenon was that in the great majority of cases hitherto subject nationalities now gained their freedom without fighting and without self-sacrifice, as the result of the liquidation of empires. That of the Turkish empire resulted from military defeat; that of the British and French empires was voluntary although partly induced by circumstances outside British and French control. By 1960 all the peoples of the Asian mainland who had come under European or Turkish imperial domination in the nineteenth century or earlier had become politically independent, with the exception of the Aden and Persian Gulf Protectorates and Soviet Asia, the latter accounting for about one-third of the total area of Asia, with an indigenous population of over 25 millions. This has meant that while old-fashioned British and French imperialists may deplore the fact that nationalism has helped to deprive them of the greater part of their empires, the British and French peoples as a whole no longer regard nationalism as an ever-present internal menace of which their enemies continually seek to take advantage. Since, however, all the countries of the Western *bloc* regard the Soviet Union as a potential enemy, they are interested in the possibility of nationalism inside the Soviet Union partly because they genuinely believe that the peoples concerned would be better off

The Country and the People

1 The Darkh Gorge in the Zeravshan Valley

3 Ploughing virgin soil in the Kazakh Steppe

2 A mountain torrent in the Tien Shan Mountains

4 Turkmen women

5 Tadzhik women greeting a veterinary
surgeon on a Soviet collective farm

6 A scene from *Abay*, a Kazakh play

7 Old men chatting in a tea-house
attached to an Uzbek collective farm

Before the Russians

9 The tomb of Timur (Tamerlane the Great) in Samarkand

10 (*opposite*)
The Shah-i-Zindah
Mausoleum in
Samarkand

11 The Mausoleum of
Shah Ismail of the
Samanid dynasty
(tenth century) in
Bukhara

12 Muzaffar-uddin,
Emir of Bukhara
(1860–85)

Central Asia under the Tsars

13 General Kaufman,
Governor-General
of Turkestan (1867–82)

14 General Kolpakovskiy,
Governor-General
of the Steppe Region (1881)

The Soviet Period

18 The Polytechnic Institute at Dushanbe

17 A section of the great Fergana Canal

19 Building the Kayrak-Kum
Hydro-electric Station

20 At a teachers' training
college in Tadzhikistan

outside Soviet control, and partly, perhaps principally, because they think that widespread nationalist outbreaks would bring strategic and economic embarrassment to the USSR. It is considerations of this kind which impel some people to look eagerly for signs of nationalism among the nationalities of Central Asia as well as in other parts of the Soviet Union.

The Russian attitude to nationalism on the other hand, has not undergone the same change. As the paramount power in the largest centrally controlled multi-national empire still in existence the Russians continue to have a morbid dread of nationalism both in its active form as affording possibilities for foreign exploitation, and in its more passive aspect of stubborn adherence to tradition and failure to conform to modern techniques. It is this very real dread which causes the Soviet Government to wage constant war on nationalist survivals inside the USSR and to announce its determination to uproot the slightest traces of them which remain. At the same time the Russians retain their belief in the active or notional support of nationalist movements abroad as a means of embarrassing their enemies. Up to 1956, by which time a large number of Asian countries had already obtained their independence, they continued to support all national movements whether directed against imperial rulers or against the 'bourgeois nationalist' governments which had succeeded them and which they continued to regard as 'lackeys of imperialism'. At the 20th Party Congress of February 1956, however, a new policy was inaugurated: it was admitted that many countries had now become politically independent; but they still needed what was called 'national liberation' in order to free them from Western economic, and in some instances, military tutelage. This could be seen as a kind of compromise between the practical needs of the Soviet state and the ideological requirements of the Communist Party. The Soviet people, and particularly those of non-Russian nationality, were expected to believe, and probably to some extent did believe, that as they had already been 'liberated' by the Revolution, they had no need of nationalism. By continually referring to British imperialism and to British imperialist designs on Russia's Muslim borderlands as if they still existed even after the transfer of power in India, the Soviet Government hoped to distract attention from the fact that the only white empire left in Asia was the Soviet empire itself.

In spite of constant Soviet harping on the subject of nationalism in Central Asia it is unlikely that the Russians ever thought of it in the same terms as of nationalism elsewhere in the Union. They were perfectly familiar with the implications of nationalism among the other Slav peoples, among those of the Baltic states, of the Georgians, and even to some extent of the Tatars. These were all peoples with clearly defined cultures and more or less clearly defined territories, and during the Revolution the Soviet Government was faced with their actual or attempted secession. As has been pointed out earlier no coherent desire for separation was ever expressed by the Muslims of Central Asia; but this does not mean that the Russians did not genuinely fear that the Central Asians, not to speak of the Azerbaydzhanis, might follow the example of the Poles, Finns and the other Baltic peoples. They also believed that Britain knew of this desire and was anxious and able to exploit it.

In Central Asia the situation with regard to nationalism, nationality, national consciousness and nation-forming has always been difficult to determine. It has been said that nationalism is that something in virtue of which a nation continues to exist even when it has lost its autonomy. This certainly was and is true of the Poles, Esthonians, Latvians, Lithuanians and Georgians. But what of peoples who had never known autonomy because they had never been formed into nations? In Central Asia natural nation-forming processes had begun with the breaking up of the old Muslim *Umma* at the end of the nineteenth century, when the three literary languages of Arabic, Persian and Chagatay began to be replaced by literary Kazakh, Uzbek and Turkmen. At this period it looked as if three national groups were emerging from the welter of Central Asian peoples, namely, the nomad Kazakh-Kirgiz, the Uzbek-Tadzhik and the Turkmen groups. Had the Tsarist regime persisted, it is highly probable that these three groups would have continued to form and would eventually have developed nationalisms to plague the Tsarist imperial government in the traditional manner. With the Revolution the natural process became an artificial one, and the new regime favoured the creation and development not of three but of six national groups, each of which was provided with a national language and national territory. These were classed as 'nations', two other groups – the Uygurs and Dungans being classed as '*narodnost*', that is to say, nationalities with a national language but no national territory. This arrangement had the effect of applying a kind of homeopathic treatment to the incipient disease of nationalism; it appeared to recognize the existence of nationalism and to stimulate its growth artificially while keeping it under close control.

Some students of Central Asian affairs argue that in spite of its artificiality the National Delimitation of 1924 resulted in the creation of fully-fledged nations. To such persons the expression 'Central Asian nationalism' would presumably convey the existence of national consciousness, if not of nationalist movements, within the confines of each republic. There are some indications that the Soviet authorities themselves may incline towards this view, and in so far as the peoples now regard themselves as grouped by nations rather than by tribes or clans they may well be right. A different view was taken by most of the Muslim refugees from Central Asia now living in exile. These maintained that the National Delimitation was an attempt to disrupt the natural unity of the Muslims of Central Asia, whom they prefer to describe as Turkestanians. When they speak of Central Asian nationalism they mean a corporate feeling among all the Muslims of the area formerly made up of Turkestan, the khanates and the Steppe Region who could and would form a nation-state if they were given the opportunity. This kind of nationalism, if indeed it can be called nationalism, derives in Kedourie's words, 'the greater part of its strength from the existence of ancient communal and religious ties which have nothing to do with nationalist theory, and which may even be opposed to it'. In theory ties of the same kind should unite in one nation-state the Arab states of Asia all of which have been almost completely independent for nearly twenty years, but among whom inter-state rivalry shows no sign of abating.

In speaking of nationalism in Central Asia there is a tendency to confuse nationalism with national consciousness. National consciousness may and does exist strongly among national communities in many countries, including Great Britain and the United States, without there being any question of its developing into nationalism aiming at separation and independence. There is no direct evidence available of the existence of Uzbek or other particularist national consciousness in Central Asia apart from vague charges preferred in the Soviet press; but it may well exist. There is equally no direct evidence either of an active corporate or communal feeling among the Muslim peoples or of any inter-republican hostility; but the first unquestionably does exist, while the second most probably does not. Of the existence even in embryo of nationalist movements of the kind experienced in other empires there are few if any characteristic indications. Elsewhere, and before the Revolution in the Russian empire, such indications have included the existence of easily identifiable, nationalist leaders either at large or in exile, internal disturbances and acts of sabotage, the existence abroad of dedicated nationalist committees receiving active support from foreign governments, and a more or less steady stream of refugees into adjoining countries. In empires other than the Russian and Soviet there have been added the phenomena of the nationalist press and literature and the presence of active, or at any rate vocal, opposition groups in parliament. Of all these hitherto characteristic indications of nationalism the only one which can be discerned today in relation to Central Asia is the existence abroad of a few nationalist organizations most of them formed and all of them financed from foreign, usually private, resources. These organizations engage in radio and other propaganda directed to the peoples both of the Soviet Union and of the free world. There is no reliable information about the extent to which the peoples of Central Asia are affected by this propaganda. It is reasonable to suppose that it plays some part in keeping alive their national consciousness, but hardly that it encourages them to take active steps to achieve liberation.

The absence of characteristic indications of nationalism or nationalist movements does not, of course, rule out all possibility of the existence of deep-rooted, clandestine organizations which, although at present rendered impotent by Soviet security measures and lack of outside support, are only biding their time until more favourable circumstances should present themselves. If such organizations ever existed, it is probable that they are becoming progressively weaker; but even without such organizations national consciousness could persist almost indefinitely. Indeed, the very absence of ability, or even perhaps inclination, to take any positive action is inclined to make men think and brood all the more. There is ample evidence of continuing and even increasing adherence to Islamic culture and of harking back to the past in various cultural and traditional matters; but this is not the stuff of which nationalist movements are made. There is also some first-hand evidence among the titular nationalities of the Central Asian Republics of a kind of divided loyalty and patriotism. For example, it seems perfectly possible for a Turkmen Party member holding an important and lucrative post to be a sincere admirer and supporter of the Soviet regime, while at the same time being genuinely proud of the qualities and achievements of the Turkmen people as the mainstay of the Turkmen SSR. It would be much more difficult even to hazard a guess about the loyalties harboured among the 125,000 Uzbeks living in the Turkmen SSR. Many of these may well be convinced Party members and as such convinced Soviet patriots; but it seems unlikely that they would take any pride in the achievements of the Turkmen SSR or even of the Uzbek SSR, in which they are, for reasons not of their own making, prevented from living. Leaving aside the extreme case of the Kazakh SSR, where the Kazakhs make up only 29 per cent of the total population, the state of national sentiment in a republic like the Tadzhik SSR is even more uncertain. Here 1,051,000 Tadzhiks make up only 55 per cent of the population, while there are over half a million Tadzhiks living in the neighbouring Uzbek and Kirgiz SSR and something over two millions in Afghanistan.

As stated earlier, the existence of nationalism in Central Asia cannot be finally proved or disproved. It is highly probable that the great majority of Central Asian Muslims strongly resent the presence in their midst of the Russians and other non-Asians and dislike almost equally the Tsarist and Soviet regimes which have interfered with their cherished beliefs and way of life. This could have accounted for the mass defection of Muslim soldiers of various nationalities to the Germans during the last war; but neither the cause nor the fact of this defection could be said to constitute nationalism in itself, nor is it easy to see in what sort of nationalism it would have resulted in the event of Germany's having won the war. It is not on record that the defection was the result of German propaganda; but the Soviet authorities probably thought that it was and this would account for the mass deportation of Muslims and others from the Crimea, the Volga Region and North Caucasus on the grounds of collaboration with the Germans when the latter's forces approached these regions. The full facts about the extent of this collaboration are not known, but even if it was as widespread and concerted as the Russians made out at the time, there is nothing to show that it was directed towards or could have resulted in the formation of new nation states. What is often called nationalism – Kurdish nationalism, Pathan nationalism, Druse nationalism among others – may be not so much a desire for self-government and civic freedom as simply an age-long addiction to lawlessness and a chronic dislike of any kind of regular government. Even in Europe the frontier and the strictly limited jurisdiction of state authority are concepts which were only dimly grasped as late as the middle of the eighteenth century and they are still barely understood by many Asian and African peoples. The fact is that in the great majority of cases it is imperialism which has brought nationalism, and eventually nations, into being by demonstrating not only the advantages of orderly government, but also the power and influence which lies within the grasp of anyone who has both mastered Western democratic techniques and has the ability to influence the masses of his own countrymen. In the Russian and Soviet empires things did not develop in this way. There was ample demonstration of the advantages of security and orderly administration on Western lines, perhaps even more of it than in some other empires; but nationalist movements were never allowed to gather momentum and there is no single instance of a national figure like Gandhi, Nkrumah or Makarios who after long struggles against his colonialist masters was able to lead his people after independence had been granted. The Russians simply do not see any sense in this kind of thing and its occurrence in other empires has merely aroused their contempt or suspicion.

Up to 1960, it looked as though the so-called federal system inaugurated in 1922 had come to stay and that the Soviet Communist leaders were satisfied that under it national consciousness which they continued to describe as 'nationalist survivals', would either be harmless or would gradually fade away. In 1960, however, it became clear that the authorities had decided to revert to what was said to be Lenin's original plan, that of a unitary multinational state. By this was meant a state in which there would be no separate nations and in which separate nationalities would only be recognized in a broad cultural sense; that is to say, the cultural entity of 'great historical ethnographic regions', of which Central Asia would be one, would be recognized, but such barriers to unity as frontiers and linguistic differences would be made to disappear. The reasons for this change of policy were both economic and political, the latter including what Soviet leaders evidently felt to be the growing need to face the world, and perhaps in particular China, not with a so-called federation or a commonwealth of nations – *sodruzhestvo natsii*, an expression sometimes used of the Soviet Union – but with a unitary state, which is perhaps another way of saying Greater Russia. There is at present no means of telling how far the significance of this change has been apprehended in the Central Asian Republics – it has been explained that the stages preliminary to final separation, *sblizheniye*, or coming closer and *sliyaniye*, or merging – would take a very long time. It is probable that even if those who harbour some sentiments of republican patriotism realize that their republics are doomed to eventual extinction, they will accept the inevitable with resignation.

The Economy

At the end of 1957 the Research and Planning Division of the Economic Commission for Europe published its report entitled *Regional Economic Policy in the Soviet Union: The Case of Central Asia*.[47] This was the first authoritative, objective and clear statement of facts and potentialities of the Soviet economy in Central Asia which had been made readily available to the countries of the West. The report was 'based partly on published statistics, partly on information supplied directly to the Secretariat by the All-Union or Central Asian authorities and partly on information obtained by members of the Secretariat during a visit to two of the Central Asian republics – Uzbekistan and Tadzhikistan – in March '57'. It was thus issued with the collaboration of the Soviet authorities. A Russian version of it was prepared but so far as is known it was not given any wide circulation in the Soviet Union. It was strongly criticized by the Soviet delegation at a plenary session of the ECE in April–May 1958, and also in the Soviet press. The report dealt only with the four southern republics, and not with Kazakhstan.

Before the publication of the ECE report, a general picture of the economy of Central Asia had been extremely difficult to obtain. A fairly full and accurate description of the economy during the first ten years of the Soviet regime could be derived from early contemporary Soviet literature. This literature, though difficult of access, is still extant and has been admirably analysed by Alexander Park.[48] Soviet reporting during the first and second Five-Year Plans (1928 to 1937) was characterized by a great deal of exaggeration and by statistics which, if not deliberately misleading, were at least difficult to follow. Appreciations of the economic situation made by Western economists during this time were considerably affected by their political opinions: those of the Left were inclined to take Soviet assessments at their face value and to voice their unstinted approval of Soviet motives, methods and achievements; those of the Right dismissed Soviet statements as propaganda, questioned the motives and soundness of Soviet economic policy, and prophesied imminent collapse. During the war, Western estimates of Central Asian economy, in so far as they were made at all, were less critical of Soviet aims and achievements; but after 1945 the expression of extreme views again became usual. Objective assessments were, of course, made from time to time by more cautious students of Central Asian affairs who doubted the wisdom of stigmatizing Soviet Central Asian economy as 'unbalanced' and therefore doomed to eventual failure, and who found in Soviet methods and achievements matter both for criticism and for approval. But such assessments were usually attacked by the Left as attempts to damn Soviet achievements with faint praise, and by the Right as 'fellow-travelling'.

Alexander Park has pointed out that the early Bolshevik leaders were confronted with two possible alternatives. Either they 'could extend and consolidate the system of Great Russian political administration in the border region under the guise of proletarian political tutelage and so establish an enlightened colonial system . . . or they could undertake a programme of accelerated industrialization which would transform the overwhelmingly rural national republics and regions into centres of native proletarian strenght'. The Marxist-Leninist theory of Revolution naturally impelled them towards the latter course; but before they could actually embark on it, they were confronted with an economic reality resulting from the complete collapse of the Russian economy brought by seven years of war and revolution.

Any survey of economic development in Soviet Central Asia naturally falls into two periods separated by the Second World War. The first period was one in which Soviet policy had perforce to aim primarily at the expansion and intensification of agricultural production. This meant delay in the creation of a native industrial proletariat, for not only was the maximum available manpower required for agriculture, but it lacked the necessary technical knowledge for employment in industry. As a result, the new industries set up in the first period were manned overwhelmingly by non-Asian settlers and new immigrants from the western parts of the Soviet Union. In the second period, however, with the growth of industry, stimulated as it was by the transfer of industrial plant during the War, increasing numbers of Asians were receiving vocational and technical training and more and more began to enter industry.

Before the Revolution the integration of the Central Asian economy with that of Russia as a whole had already begun, and the effect was apparent not only in agriculture but in the cottage industries. The demands of Russian industry were leading to the abandonment of the production of foodstuffs in favour of cotton. In 1912, the Tsarist Minister of Agriculture had already decided that 'every additional ton of Turkestan wheat is a competitor with Russian and Siberian wheat, every additional ton of Turkestan cotton is a competitor with American cotton. It is therefore better to supply this region with imported cereals even if they are more expensive, and make its irrigated land available for cotton cultivation'. At the same time, Russian-manufactured goods were rapidly displacing locally produced textiles, and other consumer goods. With the Revolution the process of integration came to an abrupt halt, and as a result of the precipitate policy of nationalization engaged in by the Turkestan Council of Peoples Commissars the very important cotton industry and the less important extracting industries (coal, oil and other minerals) nearly did likewise. In addition, insecurity and the breakdown of communications had seriously affected the local production and distribution of foodstuffs and famine conditions were soon widespread. By 1921 the Soviet leaders had learnt two severe lessons. The first was that the primary products of the borderlands –

cotton in the case of Central Asia – were essential for the preservation of the Russian state, and the second that there could be no question of creating a socialist economy and native industrial proletariat in Central Asia until the pre-Revolutionary level of economy had been restored. The extent to which the first lesson had been taken to heart can be seen, in Park's words, 'in Zatonskiy's rejoinder to Stalin at the 10th Party Congress in 1921: if the strengthening of the centre required it, a policy of plunder in the borderlands would be proper and correct'.[49]

The Soviet Government now concentrated on what it conceived to be its primary task of bringing back Central Asia to its pre-War function as a source of technical crops and raw materials for the industries of Great Russia. As a result of the New Economic Policy introduced at the 10th Party Congress, the Turkestan government denationalized half the enterprises which it had seized during the Civil War. During the period of the New Economic Policy, the Moscow government did not lose sight of its socialist ideals. While it was intent on restoring as rapidly as possible the pre-Revolutionary level of economy and to this end allowed a certain amount of freedom to private enterprise, it concentrated its energies on developing the state sector of economy and proposed to control private enterprise and cottage industries by a system of producer co-operatives. It also did what it could towards the creation of a native industrial proletariat by constantly enjoining local Party authorities to recruit more Asian workers into industry. In spite of this, however, employment in industry remained predominantly European, partly because of lack of training and inclination among the Asian masses and partly owing to discrimination by the still mainly European controlling element. Thus, according to the 1926 census, in Turkmenistan only 306 of the 2,861 factory workers and only 836 of the 8,489 railway workers were Turkmens. In Uzbekistan the situation was slightly better: of 14,321 factory and 11,582 railway workers, 4,246 and 994 respectively were Uzbeks.

By 1927 there were unmistakable signs of recovery in certain fields. Gross production in the cotton ginning industry had risen from 4 per cent of the 1913 level in 1920 to 70·6 per cent. In the same year, the value of Central Asian petroleum production was only 22·4 per cent of the 1913 figure; but by contrast coal production had exceeded the 1913 level by 42 per cent in 1924–5, and by

1927 it had reached 259 per cent. At the beginning of the Five Year Plan period (1928 to 1937) the output of Central Asian industry as a whole was still about half the 1913 level. It was said to have increased more than twelve-fold between 1926 and 1940, but it must be remembered, as pointed out in the ECE report, 'that Central Asian industry was extremely small in 1926 and a percentage increase over a period of years of the order of magnitude just mentioned is no unique performance for a country in a reconstruction period, or at the very first stages of industrial development. To mention only one other example; in Pakistan the index of industrial production rose more than four-fold in the six years from 1950 to 1956, but the average annual increase of *per capita* national income was no more than 2 per cent owing to the smallness of the industrial sector and to an unfavourable evolution of the terms of trade.' In 1940, 225,000 persons were employed in industry in the four southern republics, by which time most of the cottage industries had disappeared. In 1914 less than 21,000 had been employed in factories and mills. It is not known what proportion of either of these figures consisted of local nationalities, but the latter did not include the considerable number of Asians employed in cottage industries throughout the territory, including the khanates. It is reasonable to suppose that a considerable part of the handicraft workers had been drawn into industry, but probably only in the lower grades of employment. In 1934, for example, all the workers in the huge Tashkent textile combine were Russians.

It was in the post-war period after 1950 that the main expansion of the Central Asian economy took place. A considerable proportion of the natural increase of the labour force in the rural areas now began to take up employment in the towns, but whereas before the Revolution the proportion of urban and rural populations had been much the same in Central Asia as in the rest of Russia, the share of the urban population in Central Asia now fell considerably behind that of the rest of the Soviet Union. In 1957 it was only 32 per cent in Central Asia as against 43 per cent in the Soviet Union as a whole, and in 1959 these figures had risen to 38 per cent and 48 per cent respectively. As was to be expected, industrialization did not proceed at the same rate in Central Asia as in the USSR as a whole. According to the ECE report, 'the share of population in industry is no more than half that of the Soviet Union as a whole: Central Asia has about 2 per cent of Soviet gross industrial output but more than 6 per cent of the population . . . nevertheless . . . the region is by now much more industrialized than neighbouring Asian countries, India not excepted.' It must, however, be remembered that by 1959 over 30 per cent of the total population of the five Central Asian republics was made up of immigrant non-Asians. The proportion of nationalities employed in the various industrial enterprises was always difficult to determine, but in certain known cases the proportion of non-Asians remained very high, for example, in 1957 only 11 per cent of the workers in the Tashkent textile combine mentioned earlier were Uzbeks. In India, on the other hand, both during the British period and after, the number of non-Asians employed in industry, or indeed in any other capacity, was negligible.

It is not possible here to do more than glance at the development during the Soviet period of some of the main branches of Central Asian economy. This economy remained in the main agricultural, although in Soviet reporting prominence was always given to industry. For example, in the *Great Soviet Encyclopaedia*, in the description of the economy of *oblasts* where 98 per cent of the population is engaged in agriculture and where industry is confined to a few small factories and repair workshops, priority is always given to the latter. Progress in both heavy and light industry has, of course, been remarkable; but the fact remains that the most important economic asset of the whole region is cotton, which has both agricultural and industrial characteristics, since cotton ginning and the production of cottonseed oil, fertilizers and cotton-picking machines, are among the principal industries. According to the ECE report[50] 'Central Asia can be characterized as a region equipped with a fairly broad range of consumer goods industries, producing for the local market but dependent on imports for nearly all capital goods, and with scarcely any export industries save crude processing such as cotton ginning, oil pressing and silk spinning. Apart from some exports of ores and mineral oil, the region is therefore completely dependent on its agriculture, and above all on its cotton, to pay for necessary imports of cereals, timber and industrial goods.'

Cotton, cultivated almost entirely by artificial irrigation on collective farms that amount to huge plantations, remained the major crop. Over five times as much cotton was being grown by 1957 as on the corresponding territory before the Revolution, when the share of cotton was about one-fifth of the sown irrigated area. Even before the Revolution, Central Asia accounted for 88 per cent of the cotton produced in the Russian empire, whose comparatively low internal requirements had to be supplied to a great extent by imports from abroad. By 1957, Central Asia was providing 85 per cent of a greatly increased internal consumption, leaving some over for export. This result had been obtained by trebling the area under cotton, and raising yields per acre by two-thirds, mainly through the increase in irrigation and the introduction of improved methods of cultivation. But in spite of the size of the Central Asian cotton crop, up to 1957 only about 4 per cent of the spinning and 5 per cent of the weaving of cotton was done there. This meant that more than 90 per cent of the Central Asian cotton was exported as raw fibre to other parts of the Union, and this situation is not likely to have changed much since.

The agriculture of the four southern Central Asian republics differed considerably from that of the rest of the Soviet Union. Except for shipments of tinned and fresh fruit and a small amount of packed meat and fish, food was produced primarily for local consumption. But quite apart from cotton which constitutes the main agricultural crop, these republics are important as suppliers of raw silk and wool, at least 90 per cent of which is spun and woven elsewhere in the Union. Before the Revolution about two-thirds of the total sown irrigated area was given up to grain, but this share has now been reduced to no more than 10 per cent.

Although livestock breeding has never been practised to the same extent in the southern republics as in Kazakhstan, it was none the less considerable. The Civil War and collectivization resulted in a serious reduction of herds which were only brought back to pre-Revolution level in 1940. Even in 1957, when the population was 75 per cent larger than before the Revolution, the numbers of cattle were only 17 per cent higher. The numbers of sheep, on the other hand, greatly increased. Numbers of livestock per inhabitant, although smaller than before the Revolution, continue to be larger than in such neighbouring countries as Afghanistan and Persia.

The character of agriculture in Kazakhstan differs considerably from that of the southern republics. Only in the south does it follow the typical Central Asian pattern of cotton, rice and fruit, grown on irrigated land. In the north it is more of the West Siberian type, that is to say, livestock breeding, and the dry-farming of cereals. Before the Revolution the population of the north was still mainly nomadic and therefore occupied primarily with livestock breeding. During the collectivization period (1928–32) the production of livestock dropped catastrophically, and it was only in the late 1950s that the position began to improve substantially. In 1954, Khrushchev told the Central Committee of the Communist Party that at the end of 1953 Kazakhstan had only 17,000,000 sheep and goats as against a figure of 19,000,000 for the year 1928; but by 1960 the figure had reached 28,000,000. In 1953 the Virgin Lands campaign was inaugurated. This resulted in the ploughing up of considerable areas of potential pasture land, but by 1961 it was still difficult to say to what extent the campaign had been successful. In that year the sown area was over 28 million hectares as against 9 million in 1953 but the yield of wheat, although much larger for Kazakhstan than previously, seems to have been less than was expected, and the operation was subjected to severe official criticism. It was also unpopular among the Kazakhs, partly because it seemed, perhaps wrongly, to threaten their traditional industry of stockbreeding, and partly because it resulted in the introduction of a further 600,000 or more non-Asian immigrants.

As already indicated, great strides were made in the development of both heavy and light industries. Geological prospecting disclosed large deposits of ores and other minerals, apart from oil, gas, uranium and hydro-electric power capable of supporting types of industry which consume large quantities of energy. Heavy industry was mainly limited to the extraction of coal and oil, and some ores, mainly lead and copper, most of the latter being exported in crude form to metallurgical centres in Siberia. After 1950, however, a start was made in processing metals locally. Steel and an increasing range of engineering products were produced, but according to the ECE report, local production accounted 'for only around 1 per cent of the Union total, while more than 6 per cent of the population of the Soviet Union live in Central Asia'. In the few industries which existed before the

Revolution the increase in output was spectacular, while in the many newly created industries there was a steep rise in output, especially after 1950. For example, the output of coal increased from 200,000 tons in 1913, to nearly 6 million tons in 1955, and 8½ million tons in 1961, this in the four southern republics alone. In Kazakhstan, where coal was not exploited at all before the Revolution, the output in 1961 was 34½ million tons. The manufacture of cotton cloth, which was either non-existent or minimal before the Revolution, had risen to 117 million metres by 1940 and to 278 million metres by 1955.

The economic achievements in Central Asia and Kazakhstan during the Soviet period must mainly be attributed to Russian dynamism, planning and administration. Industrial development depended to a very large extent on the non-Asian element in the population. After 1945 there was a considerable increase in the number of people belonging to the local nationalities employed in industry; but there was also a very large increase in the immigrant non-Asian population. Left to themselves as an independent nation or nations, the people of this region would hardly have developed their economy to the same extent, nor in all probability would they have wished to do so. It is sometimes argued that they would have grown rich from selling their cotton and other valuable commodities in whatever markets they pleased. However this may be, the 'full sovereignty' which was claimed for them never included freedom to conduct trade relations with any other country outside the USSR. It was, of course, true that the native population was too sparse to exploit to the full the natural resources of the region, and it has always been officially claimed that the assistance provided by the Russians in manpower and 'know-how' was merely that of an 'elder brother' anxious to help the Asians to place the resources of underdeveloped areas at the disposal of the whole Soviet community.

Living and Labour Conditions

In order to see in proper perspective the development of living and labour conditions under the Soviet regime some notice must be taken of the analogies and differences between Soviet Central Asia and adjoining Asian countries. Most of these countries have been affected by Westernization in respect of their administrative systems, agricultural methods, communications and consumer goods, but none of them to the same extent as Soviet Central Asia. The main factors which have affected living and labour conditions in the Soviet Muslim republics are first, state control of economy, finance and labour legislation exercised from the centre; secondly, the very high rate of white colonization; thirdly, collectivization; and fourthly, the emphasis placed on industrialization, which has resulted in the steady drift of population from rural to urban areas. These factors, except for the first and third, could have been put into operation without the introduction of a socialist system under the overriding control of the Communist Party, and while there is no doubt that the latter played an important part in forcing the pace of Westernization and industrialization, it would have been able to achieve very little without white colonization. Colonization is a phenomenon which is entirely absent from the adjoining countries and has, indeed, never been practised on the same scale anywhere else either in Asia or Africa. Whatever ethical objections there may be to it, there is no doubt that the presence in Central Asia of large numbers of Russian, Ukrainian and other non-Asian Soviet settlers, who are hardworking and to a large extent free from colour prejudice, has contributed considerably to the development of industry and agriculture and thus to the material well-being of the local population.

Although by Western standards the economy of the five republics would be thought of as predominantly rural, and therefore employment to be mainly in agriculture, prominence in all Soviet economic surveys is always given to industry. There is, of course, no doubt whatever that the number of people employed in industry has increased out of all knowledge. For example, it is claimed that before the Revolution the numbers of people employed in industry in what are now the Turkmen and Kazakh SSR were approximately 2,000 and 8,200 respectively. By 1955 these figures had already risen to 150,000 and 700,000 and are now without doubt very much higher. Money wages in industry in Central Asia are the same as elsewhere in the Soviet Union for comparable work, but a greater proportion of the industrial workers in Central Asia are unskilled or belong to light industries which normally pay less than heavy industry, of which there is relatively little in Central Asia. In addition, families are larger in

Central Asia and therefore there are greater differences in consumption standards per head in earnings per worker. In general, it can be said that in the larger towns and settlements the standard of living has risen in correspondence with the rise of industry, and by Asian standards it is now high. For example, an objectively written account of living conditions in the oil installations at Nebit-Dag in Turkmenistan stated that 'at the present moment in Nebit-Dag there are no Turkmen workers' families without radio loudspeakers or radio sets, gramophones, sewing machines, and electric or flat irons'.[51] Such conditions were probably of very recent standing, but they are typical of a large number of industrial undertakings.

There is a widespread tendency among all, and particularly among Soviet, sociologists to regard as beneficial and 'progressive' the adoption by Asian peoples of many of the features of the Western way of life simply because they are new and Western. Thus taps and flush systems from which no water comes and which have to be helped out by the homely, slighted bucket – a frequent occurrence in Central Asian towns – may still be regarded as symbols of modernization and therefore as superior to the older and more reliable methods. Such Western appliances as bedsteads, chairs and cutlery may give the illusion of Western civilization, but they are not necessarily conducive to health and happiness, or even to productivity. But if much of the Westernization of traditional life in Central Asia may seem to be superficial and meretricious, there are many solid improvements introduced by the Soviet Government during the past quarter of a century, effects of which can be seen in the substantial increase and decrease in the birth and death rates and in the general air of well-being in the appearance of the population as a whole.

In the report of the U.N. Economic Commission for Europe referred to earlier it was commented that average living standards for Soviet Central Asia as a whole 'were probably one-fifth to one-fourth lower than the Soviet average' but that 'this regional disparity in living standards cannot be regarded as large compared with those found in other countries. There is hardly any European country without regions where *per capita* income or consumption is one-fifth or more below the national average.' The report continued: 'The conclusion that average living standards in

Central Asia are only one-fifth to one-fourth below those of the Soviet Union as a whole is tantamount to saying that they are on much higher levels than those in the neighbouring Asian countries, and that they have improved very considerably in the three decades since the end of the Civil War. This statement remains true even though there are certain fields, such as dwelling space per head in towns and *per capita* consumption of animal food, where there has been very little change in quantity, although some improvement in quality, during the period of Soviet rule.' Although the information available to the compilers of this report, both from published sources and at first hand, was evidently far less complete than it would have been in other analogous areas, there is no doubt that it accurately sums up the situation not only in the four Central Asian republics with which it specifically deals, but also in Kazakhstan. But the conclusion just quoted falls very far short of Soviet claims as contained in propaganda directed both to the Soviet public and to foreign countries. It would, for example, be impossible to find in Soviet writing any support for the statement made elsewhere in the report that 'there can be no doubt that on average the non-Asians living in the region are better off than local nationalities', and that although 'it would seem that a minority of the Asian population . . . enjoy higher standards than the average European, either in Central Asia or in the Soviet Union as a whole . . . the living standards of the majority of the Asian population falls significantly short of the average for the Europeans.'*

Most of the measures which have resulted in improved living conditions are standard throughout the Union and have been subjected to only slight modifications to suit local conditions. In the early years of the regime there was great resentment at official interference in the traditional way of life, particularly after 1938. Later, however, and particularly after 1950, most of the enforced changes relating to public health, availability of commodities, housing and the supervision of public conduct were accepted as a matter of course, although ways were constantly sought – and found – of evading the regulations in these respects. Judging from the newspapers, cases of private trading were still common in

---

* The Soviet point of view in this matter is set forth in *Equality of Rights between races and nationalities in the USSR*, by Tsamerian and Ronin. Paris: The United Nations Educational, Scientific and Cultural Organization, 1962.

the 1960s and seemed likely to continue. As in other colonial territories the local Asian population displays great resource and ingenuity in circumventing controls devised by Europeans primarily for Europeans. On the other hand, some All-Union institutions such as the body of voluntary guardians of public order and morals known as the *druzhinniki* are reminiscent of similar Muslim institutions which operated in the khanates until their abolition in 1921.

The distribution and availability of food and commodities of all kinds greatly improved during the Soviet regime. Before and during the Tsarist regime, and probably up to the 1930s, the supply of food and the other necessities of life had alternated between plenty and extreme scarcity amounting to famine. Famine conditions due to harvest failures coupled with inadequate means of moving supplies to distressed areas were still a recurrent possibility in many parts of Asia in the 1960s. By 1950, however, the spectre of famine had virtually disappeared from Soviet Central Asia and the sales of meat, sugar and dairy products had begun to rise steeply. In 1955 sales in state and co-operative shops were still some 25 per cent lower than in the Soviet Union as a whole, but they did not represent the total consumption of food, partly because farmers producing part of their own food account for a larger share of the population in Central Asia than elsewhere. Sales of such commodities as confectionery, tobacco, radio sets and toys were 30 per cent less in Central Asia, but of textiles only 13 per cent less.

Although there was considerable improvement in the housing situation in rural areas, that in the towns remained unsatisfactory in the 1960s owing to the rapid increase in urban population. In 1963 the allotted dwelling space per inhabitant was still 6 sq. metres, thus showing no advance over the 1940 figure. It is also interesting to note that the same living space per person over 12 was stipulated by government regulations for the living quarters at the 'Spassky Zavod' copper works operated under a British concession up to 1919 at Uspenskiy near Karaganda. Building programmes, and particularly the quality of building, was subjected to a running fire of criticism in the Soviet press during the 1950s and 60s; but there is no doubt that a great deal was achieved particularly in the building of entirely new settlements and new self-contained districts known as *mikrorayons* with shops, schools, kindergartens, cinemas, etc., added to existing towns, such as Frunze.

The collectivization of agriculture which was completed in the early 1930s resulted in the collective farm or *kolkhoz* becoming a more or less typical unit in the rural areas. Living conditions in these farms, which would sometimes contain many thousand workers, varied very much according to the type of farming engaged in. For example, the incomes in money and kind earned by members of cotton farms in Uzbekistan were far higher than those earned in ordinary cereal- and livestock-producing farms. On the other hand, opportunities for owning private property seemed to be greater in the latter. For example, in 1961 the press quoted a case of a *kolkhoz* in Turkmenistan which owned only 560 sheep and goats while 10,470 were privately owned by the *kolkhoz* workers. In the same year, new decrees were enacted in Kirgizia, Kazakhstan and Turkmenistan limiting the number of livestock in personal ownership outside the collective and state farms. Since, however, it did not seem possible to limit the numbers privately owned inside the farms, the probability of these decrees having been enforced did not seem to be strong. Although the farms were under the supervision of local Party committees, they enjoyed a considerable degree of autonomy. There was also a marked tendency for clans and extended families to congregate in a single *kolkhoz*, a phenomenon subjected to continual criticism. A *kolkhoz* was frequently based on an existing village which remained its headquarters while additional buildings were erected to accommodate the workers. Thus, in 1953, the Voroshilov *kolkhoz* in the Pokrovka *rayon* of the Issykkul' *oblast* of Kirgizia had its administrative headquarters in the village of Darkhan, while its 2,588 workers, almost entirely Kirgiz, were housed in 627 homesteads in Darkhan itself and the neighbouring village of Chichkan. This *kolkhoz*, said to be typical of its kind, was self-contained in both material and cultural respects, possessing among other things an electric flour mill, seven-year and secondary schools, a club and a library.

In the field of public health and medical services, comments the Economic Commission for Europe's report, the standard in Central Asia 'has improved so strikingly in the period of Soviet rule that the relevant comparison is no longer with neighbouring Asian countries, but with the countries of Western Europe . . .

the number of physicians per thousand, which before the Revolution had been much lower than it is in the neighbouring Asian countries today, now equals that of the Western European countries, and the number of hospital beds per thousand inhabitants is five to fifty times higher than in Asian countries, and more than half that of the advanced Western European countries.' Judging from the Central Asian press of the 1960s there was still much room for improvement in such matters as rural medical services, the building programmes for hospitals and dispensaries, and sanitation in the hospitals. Nevertheless, progress in all the health services was little short of remarkable, and appeared to be continuing. Thus, in Tadzhikistan, the republic with the fewest number of non-Asian inhabitants, there were 15,605 hospital beds in 1962 compared with only 6,816 in 1950.

In the early years of the Soviet regime, many of the innovations which resulted in improvements in the material standard of living met with strong local resistance. Soviet writers are wont to claim that this resistance sprang entirely from ignorance and prejudice fostered by religious and other reactionary elements. This was no doubt partly true, but there was also a feeling, which has by no means disappeared, that the innovations were objectionable not so much in themselves as because they were imposed by foreigners. Be that as it may, active resistance to the process of Westernization gradually disappeared. Although one would hardly expect any extensive labour or social disturbances to be reported in the Soviet press, it is significant that the only disturbances even rumoured have been among the non-Asian inhabitants of Central Asia. For example, the serious riots reported to have taken place in Temir-Tau near Karaganda in October 1959 seem to have involved only the Russian and Ukrainian workers, which may perhaps account for the subsequent appointment of a Kazakh, Arstanbekov, for the first time, to the important post of Chairman of the Committee of State Security of Kazakhstan.

Under Soviet rule living conditions in Central Asia and Kazakhstan gradually became far less precarious, and brigandage and other forms of violence which had continued even during the Tsarist regime, particularly in the nomad areas, became almost unknown. But if life became less dangerous it also became more dull, and this probably accounted for the serious increase in drunkenness among the Muslim population. On the other hand, hooliganism, of which there were frequent official complaints, seemed to be confined mainly to the non-Asian element, particularly in the New Lands area of Kazakhstan. Reported cases of criminality among the Muslim population seemed to consist mainly of 'speculation', that is to say private trading, embezzlement of public funds, idling or 'parasitism', with an occasional case of abduction.

Public Works

Soviet achievement in public works during the first 40 years of the Soviet regime was considerable and in some fields remarkable. There is no doubt that the Soviet Government attached greater importance to and made more capital investment in public works than did the Tsarist Government during a period of comparable length. Whether the Tsarist regime could have done more in the then existing circumstances or whether the Soviet achievement would have been possible without the Communist Revolution are questions which can never be answered. In their natural desire to acquire the maximum credit for the Soviet regime, Soviet propagandists tend to obscure certain facts which if borne constantly in mind show the Soviet achievement to be rather less miraculous than is often supposed.

During the nineteenth century the Russians had acquired control over a vast region with a sparse but resentful population, no railways or even roads, where building, agriculture and irrigation were carried on with techniques over a thousand years old, and where industry was confined to silk, cotton and carpet weaving, and a few domestic handicrafts. Fierce armed resistance continued in Fergana until 1876 and in Transcaspia until 1881, in which year the first railway of some 145 miles was built. Many roads and towns had, of course, been built before this, but the Russians could hardly be expected to have embarked on a programme of public works until local resistance had been overcome and the security of communications assured. They thus had at their disposal a period of barely 35 years before the outbreak of the Revolution, a period which included the strikes and disturbances incident on the Revolution of 1905, not to speak of the Russo-Japanese war. All things considered, what was achieved in this period was creditable, although undoubtedly marred by much inefficiency, muddle and corruption, phenomena which were not to disappear during the Soviet regime. This regime, too, began its life with a period of disorders and economic stagnation, and it was not until 1927 that large-scale construction could begin. Up to 1962 the Soviet regime also had had at its disposal a period of 35 years, and this too had been to some extent disrupted by the Second World War. Although its achievements were far more spectacular, the Soviet regime had a number of initial advantages over its Tsarist predecessor: a good road and railway system already existed; there were good port facilities on the Caspian and Aral Seas; the anomaly of the Bukharan and Khivan vassal states had been removed; there were many well-built towns all over the region; and there were some two million Russian and Ukrainian settlers to eke out and stiffen the backward and still resentful local population.

By far the greatest Soviet achievement was in the building of irrigation works, many of which served the double purpose of irrigation and electrification. In Chapter I a brief account was given of the old irrigation system and also of the larger irrigation works built in the khanates either before or independently of the Russian administration. In Chapter V it was stated that the only major projects completed by the Russians during the Tsarist regime were those of the Golodnaya Step' (the Hungry Steppe) and the Murgab River. Neither of these works was completed before 1895 and then only after numerous organizational and engineering failures and mistakes. Moser in his history, *L'Irrigation en Asie Centrale*,[52] wrote that most of the work done between 1884 and 1894 was in the planning of vast and in some cases unrealizable projects and in the repair of existing canals that formed part of the ancient system. Part of the Tsarist failure to develop irrigation in Central Asia can be attributed to the reluctance to contemplate the wholesale removal of the traditional methods of irrigation, based as these were on the system of small holdings. In addition, the khanates of Bukhara and Khiva were outside the scope of Russian planning. But the main cause was the absence of any co-ordination of state and private resources and planning coupled with the fact that Russian engineering was a good deal behind that of Western Europe. There is, however, no reason to suppose that these defects would not have been removed in the normal course of events.

Under the Soviet regime the traditional system of irrigation was doomed from the beginning of collectivization. Large-scale projects were quickly envisaged, but lack of resources, skilled personnel and equipment prevented any such projects from being undertaken until the middle 1930s. Nevertheless, Soviet historians claim that the irrigated area of Turkmenistan was almost doubled between 1924 and 1938, one of the works completed being the considerable Bosaga-Kerki Canal, while in Tadzhikistan the first stage of the Vakhsh Valley project was completed by 1935, and a new system of canals constructed with a total length of 13,000 km. Soviet sources also state that by 1938 the irrigated area in Uzbekistan had risen to 1,480,000 hectares compared with only 80,000 hectares during the Tsarist regime. (It should be noted here, however, that more than half the territory of Uzbekistan had previously formed part of the khanate of Bukhara.) The first major engineering project was the great Fergana Valley Canal built by mass manual labour in 1939. The Fergana Valley irrigation system was later extended in the 1940s to include the North and South Fergana Canals. Construction was necessarily slowed down during the War but by 1947 large new projects were on the way. By 1957 it was claimed that the total area of 3·6 million hectares irrigated before the Revolution had risen to 7 million hectares, for all five republics. After 1951, a number of large-scale projects were embarked upon all over the region, and the greatest of these, the Kara-Kum Canal, was completed in 1962. This project was first envisaged in 1946 and work upon it was begun in 1954. The canal extends from Bosaga on the Amu Dar'ya River to Ashkhabad and is approximately 500 miles in length. It was primarily designed for irrigation of land, but will also carry a certain amount of navigation. A far larger project than this – the main Turkmen Canal – was announced in 1950 by the Council of Ministers of the USSR. This canal was to run from Takhiya-Tash on the Amu-Dar'ya to Krasnovodsk on the Caspian, with a branch running south-westwards to join the Sumbar River. The whole of northern and western Turkmenistan would thus be supplied with water and a large part of the Kara-Kum desert be made fertile. The project – larger than any other canal project in the world – was to have been completed between 1951 and 1957. Preparatory work was begun immediately and continued until March 1953, when the feeder canal at Takhiya-Tash was opened amid a blaze of publicity. Progress reports continued during March, but after the beginning of April 1953 all mention of the canal disappeared completely from the Soviet press. The project had clearly been abandoned after three years' intensive work and publicity. No reason was ever given for the dropping of this gigantic undertaking, and the incident is only mentioned here as an example of the difficulty of accurate reporting on the affairs of Central Asia.

There was without doubt much faulty planning, miscalculation, unjustified delay and waste in connexion with Soviet irrigation projects in Central Asia. Nevertheless, in spite of the gloomy prognostications of Western students of Central Asian affairs, achievement was on a remarkable scale. Moreover, the earlier tendency to boast and exaggerate was much less evident by the early 1960s when a number of further projects were either planned or actually under way. Of these the principal are the continued development of the Golodnaya Step' which is now under the control of the new Central Asian Bureau; the Charvak Hydraulic Complex on the Chirchik River, begun in January 1963 and due for completion in 1969, and the Toktogul Hydraulic Complex at the upper reaches of the Naryn River in Kirgizia.

In railway and road construction the Soviet achievement has been far less spectacular than in irrigation. This may be partly because full details of new roads and narrow gauge railway lines are not published, no doubt for security reasons. By comparison the Tsarist achievement appears much more impressive, especially when consideration is given to the difficulties which had to be faced. Before the building of railways could be begun a system of post roads was established throughout the conquered region and by 1868 a regular post-route had been established between Tashkent and Orenburg. The major and most important part of the Central Asian railway system had already been completed before the Revolution, and the Turksib railway, the purpose of which was to make Siberian grain available so that cereals could be subordinated to cotton in Central Asia, had already been planned and surveyed. Its completion in 1930 was hailed as a triumph of revolutionary energy and Soviet achievement, but in normal circumstances it would probably have been completed long before then. Other major works of railway construction completed during the Soviet period included the Mointy-Chu stretch west of Lake Balkhash, the Amu-Dar'ya Valley line from Chardzhou to Kungrad, and most recently the so-called Friendship Railway from Aktogay on the Turksib to the Sinkiang Frontier, where it was designed to connect with a Chinese railway from Lanchow. By 1963, however, the Chinese section was still far from completion and the rate of progress was unknown. In 1957, an elaborate programme of road and railway construction in northern Kazakhstan was published, this being designed to meet the growing needs of this rapidly developing area.* This programme, which included the building of over 1,000 miles of broad and narrow gauge railway, and a large number of roads, was due for completion by 1965.

In town building and planning the Soviet regime worthily carried on the tradition established by its Tsarist predecessors. Apart from the capital cities of Dushanbe and Frunze, which were little more than villages 40 years ago and now have populations of over 220,000, a large number of entirely new smaller towns have been built, and industrial settlements are constantly being developed into cities.

Foreign Relations

At no time since the establishment of recognized frontiers can the peoples of what are now Central Asia and Kazakhstan be said to have had any effective relations with the peoples of the adjoining countries. As originally aligned during the Tsarist regime, the frontiers took no account of nationality or language, with the result that hundreds of thousands of Turkmens, Uzbeks, Tadzhiks and Kazakhs, and a much smaller number of Kirgiz, remained within Persian, Afghan and Chinese territory. At the time of the Russian conquest, the Russian Government was only just becoming dimly aware of the implications of nationality and nationalism in Europe and certainly took no account of them whatsoever in Asia. They recognized the existence of what Gorchakov, the Minister for Foreign Affairs, called in 1864 'properly constituted states', but they were not interested in the national composition of those states, nor, in a political sense, in the national composition of the territory which they had just conquered. The vague contacts maintained by the vassal states of

* For a complete description of this programme see *Central Asian Review*, 1958, No. 3.

Bukhara and Khiva with other Muslim states such as Turkey and Persia had no juridical significance.

One of the essential features of a Soviet Union republic is that it must border on a foreign state, and since each Union republic is officially described as 'fully sovereign' its government naturally includes a Ministry of Foreign Affairs, if only for form's sake. In fact, all relations with adjoining states have always been the exclusive concern of the Central Government in Moscow, and none of the fifteen republics has ever maintained any representation abroad, with the sole exception of the Ukrainian and Belorussian delegates to the United Nations.

Unlike its Tsarist predecessor, the Soviet Government at first displayed great interest in the fact that the existing frontiers of the Russian empire partitioned, as it were, what it regarded as the national territories of the newly identified nations of Central Asia. During the decade following the Revolution several attempts were made to persuade the Turkmen, Uzbek, Tadzhik and Kazakh elements in Persia, Afghanistan and China to regard themselves as belonging to the newly formed national republics which adjoined their territories. These attempts were uncoordinated and they conflicted with the Soviet Government's other aim of competing with the West for the favours of the Persian, Afghan and Chinese governments. In the first few years of the Revolution it was by no means certain what form the governments of these countries would eventually take; but when it became clear that they would be strongly nationalist and that any attempt to create trouble among their populations or to bring about secession of part of their territories would be strongly resented, the earlier policy was abandoned. Some interesting information on the subject of Soviet attempts at subversion and intervention in Persia and Afghanistan is contained in the memoirs of G. S. Agabekov, a Soviet Armenian secret agent who defected to the West in 1930. The lurid title of *OGPU, the Secret Red Terror* given to the English translation of these memoirs prevented them from being taken seriously; in fact, however, they constituted an authentic and ungarbled account of the early Soviet intelligence and subversive operations in the borderlands of Central Asia. Agabekov recounts, for example, how the Soviet Consul General in Meshed failed to exploit the mutiny which broke out in the Persian garrison stationed in the Turkmen country round Bojnurd in 1926, and also the ill-fated military intervention in support of King Amanullah of Afghanistan which was mounted from Uzbekistan in 1929. None of these or of any other similar Soviet gambits had any connection with the national sentiments of the people living on either side of the Soviet frontier, but it is possible, and even probable, that the Soviet authorities genuinely thought that the minorities in Persia and Afghanistan were anxious and ready to be liberated from Persian and Afghan rule. Had they in fact been so ready, there would have been little to stop them from throwing in their lot with the newly formed national republics that adjoined their territory.

During the 1930s both Persia and Afghanistan were under strong nationalist governments which established their authority throughout their countries and there was no further talk of Soviet liberation of minorities until 1945, when Persia was again weak and disturbed. Once again, however, the Persian Government, with the active moral support of the West, was able to reassert its authority and the Soviet 'forces of liberation' were compelled to withdraw.

The character of relations between Soviet Central Asia and China, or more specifically, with what is now known as the Sinkiang-Uygur Autonomous Region, was different. Russian influence in Sinkiang was first established in the 1870s when Russian troops occupied for ten years part of the Ili Valley round Kuldja. After the Revolution, Russian influence increased rather than slackened, and continued up to and beyond the Chinese Communist Revolution of 1949. The frontiers of the Kazakh, Kirgiz and Tadzhik SSR march with those of Sinkiang for nearly 1500 miles, and although the Kazakhs, Kirgiz and Tadzhiks played no part in initiating or maintaining Russian or Soviet influence in Sinkiang, which was largely commercial and technical, there have been important movements of population back and forth across the frontier. During the second half of the nineteenth century about 100,000 Uygurs and Dungans (Chinese Muslims) moved into Russian territory where they are still settled, and after the 1916 Revolt in Turkestan and the Steppe Region, some hundreds of thousands of Kazakhs and Kirgiz emigrated into Sinkiang. Some further emigration of Kazakhs into Chinese territory took place in the early years of the Revolution, but many of the emigrants are said to have returned since to Soviet territory, others having made their way into Gilgit and thence to Turkey, where they are now settled. More recently, in 1962 some 6,000 Kazakh families from the Ili Valley took refuge in Soviet territory.

The long frontier with Sinkiang constitutes one of the Soviet Union's most delicate border problems, particularly since the Chinese Communist Revolution of 1949. Until that year, the situation of the 4,000,000 Muslims in Sinkiang in respect of foreign interference with their settled way of life was much better than that of the Muslims of the Soviet Union, and the number of Chinese colonists and officials in the area had not exceeded 300,000. Before the coming of the Russians the Muslims of both eastern and western Turkestan probably accorded greater respect to China than they did to the rulers of Persia or Afghanistan. It may be true that later, according to Owen Lattimore, 'the Central Asian peoples have always tended to accord prestige and admiration more readily to Russia than to China'[53] but the Russians themselves have not always been certain of this. After 1949, and particularly after the constitution of the Sinkiang-Uygur Autonomous Region in 1955, they seemed to have been nervous lest the resurgence of China as a great power intent upon re-establishing her old imperial frontiers might prove an attraction for the Asian peoples of the Soviet Union. From this time onwards there was a marked absence of any detailed reference to China in the press of the Soviet republics adjoining Chinese territory and particularly of any mention of the considerable economic development of Sinkiang. In 1962, on the other hand, a volume published in Alma-Ata entitled *Studies in the History of Kazakhstan and Eastern Turkestan* – the latter an expression which is highly distasteful to the Chinese – contained two historical articles which were quite clearly anti-Chinese in tone. The first extolled the resistance offered to the Chinese by the Muslims during the national uprising of 1864, while the second endeavoured to show that a prime factor in the revolt of 1964 in Sinkiang was the realization by the Muslims that greatly superior living conditions prevailed in Kazakhstan and Soviet Central Asia.

During the 40 years which followed the frontier delimitation of 1924 the peoples of Soviet Central Asia were subjected to a steady stream of propaganda designed to show how favourably their situation compared with that of those peoples of Asia who continued in one way or another to be the victims of Western imperialism. This propaganda was probably not successful in removing the feeling that they themselves were still under the domination of the Russians, but it did convince them not only that their material condition was better than that of the Persians, Afghans and others, which indeed it was, but also that they enjoyed a much higher degree of physical and spiritual freedom, which they did not. In Central Asian universities and Academies of Sciences students were taught to think of the cultures of other Asian peoples as continuing to be 'oriental' while their own had become 'Soviet', and it was significant that when the name of the Institute of Oriental Studies in the Moscow Academy of Sciences was changed in 1960 to the Institute of Asian Peoples, no corresponding change was made in the Institute in the Uzbek Academy of Sciences, which is still known as *Institut Vostoko-vedeniya*, or Institute of Oriental Studies, because it is concerned only with oriental, that is, non-Soviet countries and peoples.

It is hardly possible to form any notion of how the attitude of the peoples of Central Asia towards their neighbours would have developed if the natural nation-forming tendencies had been allowed to proceed. They might, and most probably would, have wished to join forces with their co-nationals in the adjoining countries, and the resistance which they would inevitably have encountered from the governments of those countries would probably have resulted in hostilities. Up to 1963 there was no indication that the Soviet Government would permit any direct trade relations between the Asian republics and their non-Soviet neighbours. There was, however, a distinct prospect of the extension of centrally controlled commercial contacts with adjacent countries. For example, in Afghanistan, north-south roads, the building of which was never attempted during British rule in India, were by 1961 being constructed under Soviet supervision, and north-south railways may soon follow. Similarly, the linking of the Central Asian railway system with the Persian Gulf and Indian Ocean through Persia, and through Afghanistan and Pakistan respectively, presents no great engineering obstacles.

CHAPTER IX

THE CULTURE OF THE PEOPLES OF CENTRAL ASIA AND KAZAKHSTAN

SINCE UNDERSTANDING of the term 'culture' is by no means uniform, any description of the culture of a people should necessarily begin by stating what particular meaning is to be attached to the word in the given context. In his book *Sociology*, Ginsberg gives a useful summary of some of the best-known concepts of culture.[54] Anthropologists, he says, understand by culture 'that complex whole which includes knowledge, belief, art, morals, law, custom and other capabilities and habits acquired by man as a member of a society'. This definition is considered by others to include not only culture but civilization. Professor MacIver, for example, distinguishes between culture and civilization: 'our culture is what we are, our civilization is what we use'.[55] Culture he considers to be 'the expression of our nature in our modes of living and of thinking, in our everyday intercourse, in art, in literature, in religion, in creation and enjoyment'. Civilization, on the other hand, includes the whole mechanism or apparatus which man uses in his endeavour to control the conditions of his life including the whole machinery of social organization.

The Soviet understanding of culture is somewhat different. It is broadly defined as 'the combination of the material and spiritual values created and developed by humanity in the course of its history'.* This again seems to embrace both civilization and culture, but Communist writers tend to avoid the word civilization and break down culture into two parts – material and spiritual culture. To the first belongs primarily 'the state of productive forces and the labour habits of people'. To the realm

* The adjective *kul'turnyy* is currently used in the USSR in the sense of 'well-mannered' rather than 'cultured'.

of spiritual culture belongs 'the state of education, knowledge, art and other forms of social consciousness, the development of which is conditioned by the material conditions of social life'. With this general definition few people will disagree; but Marxist-Leninist ideology adopts the special view that the highest form of culture is socialist-spiritual culture which 'having developed in different national forms and being profoundly international in character, ensures rapid adherence to a progressive culture, which allows nations to preserve the best features of national culture to the fullest extent, and contributes to their mutual enrichment'. The standard Soviet description of the ideal culture for the national republics of the Soviet Union is that it should be 'national in form and socialist in essence'.

The most notable work dealing with any aspect of the culture of Turkestan which has so far been published is V. V. Barthold's *Istoriya Kul'turnoy Zhizni Turkestana*. The literal translation of this title is *The History of the Cultural Life of Turkestan*, but a more accurate description of the book would be 'A History of Civilization in Turkestan'. Of the book's twelve chapters, five are devoted to the progress of civilization before the coming of the Russians, six to Turkestan and southern Kazakhstan under Russian rule, and the last and longest chapter to Russia's relations with the three Uzbek khanates. The book is mainly historical and the principal subjects dealt with are urban development, agriculture, commerce, law, religious organization and education. Languages are only dealt with very briefly and there is scarcely any mention of literature or the fine arts. The practice of religion or its spiritual effects is not dealt with at all, although there is some mention of outbreaks of religious fanaticism. The book was published in 1927, ten years after the Revolution, yet there is only the barest reference to the new regime and none at all to its actual or possible effects.

Apart from the difficulty of deciding on what interpretation and on what aspects of culture to concentrate, there is also the problem of the marked difference between the cultural life of the nomads and of the settled peoples. While information on the urban and agricultural civilization and culture of Turkestan is fairly plentiful, thanks to the industry of Barthold, that on the early culture of the Kazakhs is extremely scarce. Writing in 1941, M. Vyatkin, one of the best and most objective authorities, said that 'research on the former culture of the Kazakh people is one of the most backward sections of the historical study of Kazakhstan; comparatively little has been done even on the first stage of scientific investigation – the collection of material'.[56] A final difficulty lies in the fact that whereas in the earlier part of the Soviet period the emphasis was on the distinctiveness of the cultures of the newly emerging nationalities, the more recent tendency is to point to their interresemblance.

With these variations in mind it seems best to concentrate on providing as much information as space will allow about the spiritual characteristics of the peoples of Central Asia as they were irrespective of the Western impact and as they have been affected by or have resisted that impact. The subjects selected for examination are 1. social grouping; 2. religion; 3. language; 4. literature; 5. education; 6. the fine arts, drama, etc. These matters have been referred to earlier but only fleetingly; it is now proposed to examine them in greater detail.

The present survey is primarily concerned with cultural developments since the Western impact but it is necessary to glance at the cultural influences to which the peoples of Central Asia had been subjected before the coming of the Russians. Although there is evidence of a fairly advanced state of culture in Central Asia from the Greco-Bactrian period onwards, and particularly during the dominion over most of the region by the Persian Sasanian dynasty (third to seventh century), very little is known of its nature. Long before the Russian people had accepted Christianity, that is to say, before the end of the ninth century, Islamic culture had reached a high degree of development in Turkestan, although it had barely begun to have any effect on the Steppe Region. Iranian influence, which had begun during the Sasanian period, continued with hardly a break up to the end of the Samanid dynasty in 999, for the impact of pure Arab culture, as distinct from the Persianized Islamic culture which spread rapidly over Turkestan during the ninth and tenth centuries, was comparatively slight. The overthrow of the Samanid dynasty by the Karakhanids ushered in what is sometimes called the Turkish period, although Barthold is of the opinion that the culture of such Turkic peoples as the Karakhanids, Karluks and Tokuz-Oguz was largely derived from their contact with the Chinese. The Mongolian period contributed little or nothing which was essentially Mongolian to the culture of the peoples of the region, but the *pax Mongolica*, which came to an end with the Timurid dynasty, gave an important fillip to urban culture and the flourishing of the arts. After the overthrow of the Turkicized Mongol Timurid dynasty by the Uzbeks, the peoples of Central Asia were not subjected to any further foreign cultural influences until the coming of the Russians. Although from the end of the Timurid dynasty up to the Russian conquest all the various rulers in Turkestan and the Steppe Region were of Turkic origin, Islamic and Iranian culture retained an important hold over the minds of the people; and this in the absence of anything which could be called cultural regimentation.

Social Grouping

Long before the coming of the Russians the tribe or clan had ceased to have any significance as an economic or political unit in Central Asia. Up to the fifth or sixth centuries AD, the economic unit was the patriarchal joint family whose members possessed their lands and herds in common. Thereafter, these family communities, according to the Soviet ethnographer Abramzon, began to break up into 'conjugal families', that is, consisting of two generations only. Such families were, however, often united by economic and ideological bonds and formed in consequence 'family unions'. This double process of the break-up of the joint families and the reunion of conjugal families into family unions was still in progress at the time of the Revolution of 1917; but since the beginning of the twentieth century the small conjugal family predominated everywhere. The large joint families which persisted among the nomads and the unions of conjugal families had lost their economic significance, but they retained most of their customs and traditions, as well as their moral codes.

In 1917 the unit of Muslim society in Turkestan was the conjugal family consisting of the parents, the married sons (who remained in the family until the death of the father), unmarried daughters and the grandchildren. Although the primitive clan had ceased to exist as a unit, groups of families frequently considered themselves as descended from common ancestors and therefore related by blood. It was these real or, more often, imaginary blood ties which regulated the rules of exogamy (marriage outside the tribe) and endogamy (marriage within the tribe or clan). Among the Kazakhs and most other nomads except the Turkmens, exogamy was obligatory. Among the Turkmens, sedentary Uzbeks and Tadzhiks, endogamy was the general rule. Where exogamy was practised, a Muslim man could marry a non-Muslim woman provided she belonged to one of the revealed religions (*Ahl al-Kitab*, that is, Christians or Jews), but a Muslim girl could only marry a Muslim. Parental control in all matters relating to the family, including marriage, was complete. This was characteristic of Islamic society, but many such practices as *kalym* or bride-price, *kaytarma* or retention of the bride until the bride-price had been paid, and *amengerstvo* or marriage of a man to his brother's widow, had nothing to do with Islam, although Soviet writers often claim the contrary. These customs, which were much more prevalent among the nomads than among the settled people, had already begun to die out before the Revolution under the influence of the new capitalist economy introduced by the Russian conquest, but without much pressure being exercised by the Tsarist authorities. The Soviet regime, on the other hand, considered that the very nature of Islamic society militated against the building of socialism, and they therefore proceeded to take active steps for its destruction. These included the stabilization of the nomads, socialization of land and water rights, and finally, collectivization. Polygamy, marriage of girls under eighteen, and a number of other practices such as *kalym* and *kaytarma* were forbidden by law. Endogamy and the veiling of women were not actually made illegal but were made the subject of vigorous propaganda campaigns. These measures have certainly accelerated Westernization, although in some respects the effect produced has been much less than was estimated, while in others it has been the contrary of what was intended by the authorities. For example, a Soviet ethnographical survey carried out in the Khorezm *oblast* of Uzbekistan in 1954–6 revealed that a number of traditional social customs were still very much alive and had even imposed themselves on such exclusively Soviet organizations as the collective and state farms, where *brigades* or working parties were formed on clan or family lines. Attempts to achieve the equality of the sexes and the abolition of arranged marriages, particularly of minors, were less successful than was expected. In the 1960s there were no statistics to show the actual number of child marriages which still took place, but figures showing the attendance of girls at school indicated that the rate of truancy was very high between the ages of 13 and 17, and this was more than once attributed by the press to the fact that girls left school in order to get married. The vast majority of such marriages, and indeed of all marriages among the Muslim population, were arranged by the parents, another 'survival' strongly disapproved of by the authorities.

From the number of exposures and criticisms of social survivals which continued to appear in the Soviet Central Asian press throughout the 1950s it might be assumed that little progress had been made in the modernization of social conditions among the Muslims of Central Asia and Kazakhstan, and that there was even some kind of organized opposition to such modernization. Such an assumption would be far from correct. The abandonment of the old ties of tribe, clan and joint family and the adoption of the Western form of family life are phenomena which were occurring all over the Middle East, usually without any coercion or even encouragement on the part of governments. In Soviet Central Asia there had been both coercion and encouragement as well as steady propagation of the modern as distinct from the traditional way of life by means of formal education, literature, films and radio, all of which were far better organized and penetrated much more deeply into rural areas than in the non-Soviet Muslim world. It seems that given the necessary facilities, knowledge and know-how, the Muslim East is perfectly ready to accept the material and external appurtenances of Western civilization. In an interesting study of this subject published in 1959,[57] Alexandre Bennigsen wrote as follows: 'The masses do not engage in any conscious or organized opposition, but, since it takes them some time to understand, they retain "innocently" the traces of their past. For the intelligentsia, the problem is somewhat different: here it is a question of the resurgence of "capitalist" consciousness, which probably exists in the heart of every man; . . . but here too in the matter of certain external survivals, there is no question of opposition to the system; indeed, it seems that the Muslims of the USSR, peasants, workers and intellectuals alike, are really trying to adapt themselves to the way of life of the "model man" advocated by the authorities. It is for this reason that there is no fundamental contradiction in the mind of the Party member who secludes his wife and at the same time undertakes to explain to his compatriots why women ought to be emancipated. This divergence between the conscience of the individual and that of the citizen – a perennial problem confronting every regime – would not constitute a danger to the regime, even if it partly contravenes some Marxist principles.' Why, asks Bennigsen, were the authorities still so dissatisfied when 'the great Russian dream' – the ethnic fusion of the Russians with the other races of the Union – now seemed to be theoretically possible? The fact seems to be that in the case of the Muslim nationalities, this symbiosis was as far away as ever, perhaps even farther. The tribe, the clan and the joint family having all virtually disappeared as political, economic and, latterly, even as social units and the idea of nationality and of the nation having been impressed upon the people for forty years, the originally synthetically formed nations now seemed to those who belonged to them to have acquired a self-contained individuality which had nothing to gain by fusion with the Russians. Intermarriage between Muslims and Russians, without which fusion would be impossible, was still extremely rare, and in the case of Muslim girls virtually non-existent. The present social grouping, therefore, of the nation composed of small families on the Western model seems no more likely to lead to fusion than the older system which it has replaced.

Religion

Apart from a few vestiges of Shamanism among the nomads, religious belief and practice among the indigenous people of Central Asia have, since the Arab conquests of the seventh and eighth centuries, been confined to Islam. Up to the establishment of the Soviet regime with its policy of cultural regimentation, Islam was unquestionably the strongest and most durable cultural influence to have taken root in Central Asia. Before the coming of the Russians, Islamic culture not only survived but was actually embraced by all non-Muslim invaders such as the Karakhanids and Mongols. Only a small proportion of the upper classes was affected by Russian culture during the Tsarist regime, which, although it hated and feared Islam, adopted a fairly tolerant attitude towards it. Even the openly hostile Soviet attitude towards the Islamic creed and way of life by no means eradicated Islamic influence; and its effect would probably have been very much smaller if the beginning of the Soviet regime had not coincided with the collapse of the Ottoman empire and the abolition of the Caliphate.

From a theological point of view, Islam probably had its apogee in Central Asia during the Samanid dynasty, which was overthrown by the Karakhanids at the end of the tenth century. Under the Samanid dynasty, Bukhara became an important centre of Islamic learning, and it was here that the *madrasah*, or Muslim higher educational establishment, had its origin. The heyday of Islamic culture in Central Asia was during the fourteenth and fifteenth centuries, when Samarkand might have been considered as its centre. At this period, learning and the arts were inseparably associated with Islam and derived great benefit from the close contacts which Central Asia was able to maintain with the whole of the Muslim world. The state of learning, and even of popular education, was probably on a par with that of Western Europe, and far above that of Russia, which was then under the domination of the Mongols who, although converted to Islam, communicated nothing of their spiritual culture to the Russian people.

After the end of the Timurid dynasty at the beginning of the sixteenth century, the creative power of Islamic culture declined; but the influence of Islam, and particularly of the clergy, on the lives of the people increased. This process continued even during the Tsarist regime when, as has been noticed in an earlier chapter, the authorities were slow to recognize the strongly entrenched position of Islam. In 1900, it was estimated that in Turkestan alone, without counting the khanates of Bukhara and Khiva, there were 1,503 congregational mosques and 11,230 parish mosques with a total of 12,499 imams to minister to 6,000,000 persons, that is, one mosque for every 471 believers.

The policy of the Tsarist regime towards Islam was inconsistent and confused. During the early stages of the Russian advance into the Steppe Region in the second half of the eighteenth century, the Russian Government regarded Islam as a stabilizing and pacifying influence, and, as noticed earlier, actually ordered the building of mosques in the Kazakh Steppe. Later, however, when the authorities realized to what extent justice and the agrarian system were tied up with Islamic law, they began to regard the clergy, and particularly the Kazis, or administrators of the *shariat* or canon law, with strong disfavour. Kaufman, while looking on Islam as a baneful and dangerous influence, considered that it could best be countered by a policy of indifference. He did not advocate any interference with religious observance, or in the educational or legal systems except where the latter was concerned with taxation. But he did all he could to minimize the authority of such Muslim dignitaries as the Kazi Kalan, or Supreme Judge, whose office he eventually caused to be abolished. He thought that in this way Islam would eventually wither away. Kaufman's successors, none of whom approached his administrative ability and personality, pursued a somewhat different and more indulgent policy. Attempts were made to find out more about Islam, and particularly about the customary law (*'adat*) operating among the nomads. Every now and then, however, there arose foreboding about the increased power of Islam. For instance, in a report compiled in 1886 on the Syr-dar'ya *oblast*, it was noted that 'the propagation of Islam among the nomads by *ishans* (religious leaders) from Bukhara, Samarkand, Kokand and Tashkent has increased since our pacification of Central Asia'. After the Andizhan rising in 1898, the Russian authorities became seriously alarmed. An attempt was made to penetrate the secrets of Sufi mysticism and to find out what was being taught in the Muslim schools. The services of both Russian and local scholars were enlisted and a large amount of material was collected. According to Barthold, however, much of this was of a superficial character.

Among the tasks undertaken by the Pahlen commission of 1908–9 was the codification of the *shariat*. Barthold's strong criticism of the way in which this matter was handled may have been prejudiced, but almost certainly reflected local opinion. According to him, the codification was based, not as it should have been on a Russian translation of the *Hidayah*, a famous work on Muslim jurisprudence by Burhaneddin Marghinani, himself a native of Turkestan, but on an English summary of the work which had been compiled for use in the Indian courts. It was thought that since the Muslims of both India and Turkestan belonged in general to the Hanafite sect, this summary would do very well for Turkestan. In the event, only extracts from the summary were included in the proposed codification, and these without reference or notes. The result was quite unworkable and was never brought into use.

It is tempting to compare the Russian attitude towards Islam in Central Asia with the British attitude towards it in India. The relations between the British authorities and the Muslim clergy were relatively good, in spite of considerable interference with the operation of Muslim law. The British had a far greater respect and understanding of Islam than the Russians. There were, however, several factors which made the situations in the two countries quite different. Having themselves been conquerors of the country in a previous era, the Muslims of India regarded the British with feelings of respect and sympathy amounting at times to confederacy; the British were one of the 'Peoples of the Book', whereas the Hindus were not; finally, in the communal conflict which racked India during the latter part of the British period, the Muslims were in the minority and regarded the British as their natural protectors. None of these circumstances prevailed in Turkestan and the Steppe Region, where an additional reason for hostility and tension between conquerors and conquered lay in the fact that the Russians themselves had lived for 250 years under Muslim domination and harboured a hereditary, although partly subconscious, feeling of resentment against Islam. It is also true that in Central Asian Muslim society, particularly in the cities, obscurantism, hypocrisy and corruption of various kinds had sunk to depths which were unknown in Muslim India.

The Russian Revolution was immediately preceded by the Revolt of 1916, which, although not in any way attributable to the Russian attitude towards Islam, undoubtedly aroused Muslim religious fanaticism directed against the Russians. Accordingly, one of the first acts of the Bolshevik leaders was to address in December 1917 the following conciliatory appeal:

Muslims of Russia, Tatars of the Volga and the Crimea, Kirgiz and Sarts of Siberia and Turkestan, Chechens and mountain Cossacks! All you, whose mosques and shrines have been destroyed, whose faith and customs have been violated by the Tsars and oppressors of Russia! Henceforward your beliefs and customs, your national and cultural institutions, are declared free and inviolable! Build your national life freely and without hindrance. It is your right. Know that your rights, like those of all the peoples of Russia, will be protected by the might of the Revolution, by the councils of workers, soldiers, peasants, deputies!

The way in which Muslim political organizations were at first encouraged and created and then finally destroyed has been described elsewhere. Events quickly showed that Islam with its distinctive social, educational and judicial systems was much less likely to reach a workable compromise with the new regime than the Orthodox Church of Russia. The fact is that Islam has never experienced a Reformation or Renaissance which could loosen the bonds of medievalism and allow it to come to terms with modern life. The chances of a new, vigorous, ruthless and atheistic force such as Bolshevism being able to gain the co-operation of the Muslim clergy were in any event remote, but it is probable that the latter by their intransigence made things worse than they need have been. Even before the Revolution they had vigorously opposed the reformist Jadid movement, and continued to do so even when it eventually found itself in opposition to the Soviet authorities. But the Soviet view that the strong reactionary conservatism of the clergy resulted solely from a desire to retain their own vested interests was almost certainly an oversimplification of the facts. Dr Baymirza Hayit[58] considers that this conservatism stemmed rather from the age-long need to defend Islam from the attacks of infidel invaders – the Mongols, the Kalmyks and finally the Russians. Be that as it may, their unreasoned and unyielding resistance to reforms of any kind only accelerated the downfall of the clergy and increased Soviet hostility to the very existence of Islam both as a creed and as a way of life.

As a religion, Islam came under the general fire directed against supernatural beliefs and was not subjected to any special treatment, except that since Islam, like Communism, had claims to universality, it was regarded as potentially more dangerous than, for instance, the Orthodox Church. As a way of life Communism regarded Islam as infinitely more pernicious and objectionable than any branch of Christianity. It saw it as backward, as militating against material progess and as having been promoted and per-petuated, first by feudal Eastern potentates and later by Western imperialists, for their own anti-social ends. It was against the less fundamental aspects of Islam that the Soviet attack was mainly directed: the veiling of women, pilgrimages to holy places and tombs, festivals which interrupted work, and such practices as circumcision. This attack was still actively maintained in the

1960s. Foreign reports of the actual persecution and suppression of Islam have, however, been greatly exaggerated. The practice of Islam in accordance with Koranic precepts was never formally forbidden and in its campaign against what it regarded as harmful customs the Soviet Government never went to such lengths as the nationalist governments of some non-Soviet Muslim countries. After the early crude violence of the League of the Godless, atheist propaganda was of a more calculating and 'scientific' description. On occasions, anti-Islamic propaganda was deliberately played down, and when Germany attacked the USSR in 1941 the support of Islam, as of other religions, was actually enlisted: Mufti Abdurrahman Rasul, so-called leader of the Soviet Muslims, issued a manifesto which urged Muslims to 'rise in defence of the Fatherland against the enemy threatening destruction and misfortune to all Muslims, children, brothers and sisters in our religion', and to 'organize religious services in houses of prayer and mosques and consecrate them to victory of our army'. After the Second World War, the Soviet authorities either became undecided in their attitude towards Islam, or changed their views to accord with contemporary political considerations. In a decree of November 11, 1954, just before the beginning of a new Soviet drive in the Middle East, reference was made to 'certain mistakes in the conduct of scientific and atheistic propaganda' and to Lenin's warning issued in 1921 about the need to avoid the more offensive type of anti-religious utterance. During the next two years there was a marked decline in anti-Islamic literature published in Central Asia; but from 1957 onwards there was an increased official demand for more atheistic literature and lectures, as well as strong criticism of the quality of the existing material. Judging from the works of such writers as Klimovich, Prokof'yev and others this latter criticism was well founded: according to Bennigsen and Carrère d'Encausse[59] these writers were bureaucrats without any imagination who for years were content to repeat *ad nauseam* a few elementary propositions. 'The result of their efforts is at once pedantic, laborious, jejune and intolerably boring.' At times, too, the Soviet Government seemed to incline towards the view held by Kaufman, that the best attitude to adopt toward Islam was one of indifference, since it would inevitably die out when confronted by a more dynamic and progressive civilization. It is incidentally interesting to note that this great administrator to whom the rapid consolidation of Russian rule in Central Asia is largely due, is now regarded as an 'unperson': his name does not appear in the 2nd Edition of the Soviet Encyclopaedia.

To follow the fortunes of Islam in Central Asia and Kazakhstan during forty-five years of Soviet rule and to assess its status and influence at the end of that period are matters of extreme difficulty. From the point of view of status, Islam was probably at its lowest ebb at the time of the German invasion in 1941. In that year, no doubt with the object of raising Muslim morale, four 'spiritual directorates' were created throughout the USSR, that with jurisdiction over Central Asia and Kazakhstan having its headquarters at Tashkent. Between 1917 and 1941, all religious schools and theological colleges had been closed and all religious instruction came to an end except for the small amount that could be given privately by mullas, a large number of whom are said to have disappeared, mainly during the purges of 1932–8. The Mir-i-Arab *madrasah* in Bukhara, which was originally founded in 1535, was closed after the Revolution but reopened in 1952. A second *madrasah*, that of Barak Khan, was opened in Tashkent in 1958, these being the only two Muslim theological colleges in the whole of the USSR. Details about the closing of mosques and about the number in use at any given period as well as of the number of officiating clergy, are impossible to obtain since there are wide discrepancies both within and between official and private sources of information. It can, however, be said with a tolerable degree of certainty that whereas in 1917 there were not less than 20,000 mosques in Turkestan (including the khanates) and the Steppe Region, the number in use throughout the region in 1953 was between 200 and 300, according to an estimate made in that year by the Mufti of Tashkent – and even this was almost certainly an exaggeration. The number of officially recognized mullas was unknown but there was believed to be a very large number of unofficially recognized clergy who officiated at marriages, funerals and the like. As elsewhere in Islam, the entire religious establishment was supported by contributions from the faithful; but control over the spiritual directorate was exercised by the Council for the Affairs of Religious Cults established in 1944 and attached to the Council of Ministers of the USSR. This Council dealt with all matters affecting religious sects apart from the Orthodox

Church. It was represented in each SSR or ASSR by a similar Council attached to the republican Council of Ministers. At *oblast* level there was a representative attached to the executive committee of the local Soviet.

Although the foregoing facts and figures give some idea of how the actual fabric of Islam fared during the Soviet period, they do not reflect the extent to which Islam remained a living force among the people or how far they responded to the very strong pressure brought upon them by the present regime to abandon the practice of Islam and all that it stood for. The Soviet assault on Islam within the confines of Russia began at a moment when, as already mentioned, Islam had just suffered two severe shocks to its temporal and spiritual prestige: the collapse of the Ottoman empire after the end of the First World War, and the abolition of the Caliphate which occurred a few years later. The psychological effect of these events was strongly felt throughout the Muslim world and perhaps most of all in Central Asia, where the great majority of the people were of Turkic origin and regarded Turkey as their spiritual and cultural mentor.

The death near Bukhara in 1922 of Enver Pasha, once the strong man of Turkey, who had thrown in his lot with the Basmachi rebels against the Bolsheviks, sounded as it were the death knell of Turkish and Muslim temporal power and prestige. Moreover, with the rise of nationalism all over the Muslim world and the new wealth resulting from the exploitation of oil, the old Islamic traditions and way of life were everywhere being weakened. All these circumstances aided the Soviet regime in their task of undermining the social and cultural power of Islam within the Soviet Union. But although the outward observance of Islam is probably less there than in any other part of the Muslim world, its underlying influence is still very much alive. In spite of the closing of mosques, the secularization of education and the steady stream of atheist propaganda, the vast majority of Central Asians would readily admit to being Muslims, and many if not most would strongly resent any suggestion that they were not.

Language

Very little information is available about the languages spoken in Central Asia before the Muslim conquest, and still less about the written languages. It seems probable that since the sixth century, Turkic speech of one kind or another was in general use all over the Steppe Region, Semirech'ye, the Turkmen country, and in the rural areas of Transoxania. In the oases of Transoxania and in what is now Tadzhikistan, Iranian languages probably predominated, and today a form of Persian perfectly intelligible to Persians and Afghans is spoken in Tadzhikistan and to a considerable extent in the cities of Bukhara and Samarkand. After the Muslim conquest, classical Arabic became the religious and literary language which was taught in all the schools and was universally used by men of letters. Persian was also taught in the religious schools and was written and spoken by the urban intelligentsia. A third language of cultural intercourse was Chagatay. This was a literary language, named after one of Chingiz Khan's sons, which came into vogue at the beginning of the fourteenth century and had its apogee in the fifteenth century. It was a Turkic language but was written in the Arabic character and made use of a considerable Arabic and Persian vocabulary.

Up to the middle of the nineteenth century, when the cultural impact of the Russians first began to be seriously felt, these three traditional languages symbolized a kind of common Arabo-Irano-Turkic culture. As the more advanced material civilization of the Russians made itself felt, so the old nationless Muslim society, the Umma, began to disappear and languages based on popular dialects began to appear. On the eve of the Revolution, however, only three languages had achieved any kind of literary form in Central Asia. One of these was Kazakh, which was created in the middle of the nineteenth century and was used by such writers as Chokan Valikhan (1837-65) and Abay Kunanbay (1845-1904). It partially replaced Chagatay in the Steppe Region and was also used by the Kirgiz. The other languages were so-called literary Uzbek, which first appeared in the eighteenth century but by the end of the nineteenth century had only a limited vogue, and Turkmen of which examples can be found in the work of the poets Molla Azadi and Makhtum Kuli writing at the end of the eighteenth century.

While, however, the old Muslim Umma was breaking up, a new unifying tendency appeared in the Jadid movement which has been more fully described elsewhere. An important aim of this movement was the creation of a common Turkic language to be used by all the Turkic peoples of Russia. It was to be based on the southern dialect of Crimean Tatar, and Gasprinskiy, the founder of the Jadid movement, propagated it unceasingly in his magazine *Terjuman*. But the centrifugal tendencies of budding national consciousness militated against the unifying force of the pan-Turkic movement, and the language of *Terjuman* therefore made no progress.

Before the beginning of the Soviet regime the peoples of Central Asia had never been subjected to anything approaching a linguistic policy, that is to say, an attempt to change and regulate by legislation established languages or methods of writing them. Linguistic policies are generally of two kinds. There is the policy initiated by the government of a country in order to change or develop national language in accordance with national requirements. Such a policy often aims at the dropping of foreign accretions and the adoption of new and more practical scripts and orthographies. Examples of this are the policies adopted by Kemal Atatürk in Turkey and the orthographical reform of Russian introduced after, but devised before, the Revolution. There is also the policy which seeks to compel subject alien peoples either to abandon their own languages in favour of another or to change them in certain specified ways. The Soviet linguistic policy is in a special category in the sense that being inseparably associated with the nationalities policy it has concerned itself not only with the changing of languages but with their creation and, in some instances, with the abolition of the national status of newly created languages. With the vast prescriptive authority which the Soviet Government acquired after the end of the Civil War, it could probably have done what Gasprinskiy failed to do, namely, create a single Turkic literary language for the use of all the Turkic peoples of the USSR. There were, however, strong political objections to such a course, and the Soviet Government not only took note of the natural tendencies working against unification, but deliberately developed them still further. Thus, for example, although the differences between the languages of the Kazakh, Kirgiz and Karakalpak peoples are merely dialectal, the decision taken for political reasons to constitute them as separate nations resulted in their being artificially endowed with separate literary languages.

Soviet linguistic policy passed through several phases, and its trend was not always consistent. After the frontier delimitation of 1924, which was ostensibly carried out on the basis of language, the first sign of an officially controlled linguistic policy was the introduction from 1929 onwards of a so-called Unified Latin Alphabet which arbitrarily replaced the Perso-Arabic character in which Central Asian languages had hitherto been written. Some ten years later this in turn was replaced by modified Cyrillic alphabets which served the double purpose of encouraging the use of Russian and of emphasizing dialectal, phonetic and grammatical differences among the vernacular languages by allotting certain special letters to each language.

As the likelihood of the various Muslim nationalities of Central Asia ganging up against the Soviet regime lessened, so the emphasis on linguistic differences became less pronounced. Indeed, from 1959 onwards, there was a general tendency to play down national distinctions of all kinds including that of language. But three basic aims have been declared throughout: first, 'the "completion" and "enrichment" of existing languages, the widening of their scope and the transformation of tribal and community languages into developed national languages with a rich terminology and vocabulary'; secondly, the removal of the large Arabic and Persian loan vocabulary inherited from the Muslim conquests; and thirdly, the establishment of Russian as 'a second native language'. The first of these aims was to a large extent achieved by 1960: immense efforts and a great deal of genuine scholarship was directed towards the systematization of languages whose literary form was either under-developed or non-existent. Grammars and dictionaries were produced for all of them and they all acquired their own literatures and surprisingly large numbers of newspapers and periodicals. But it can hardly be said that any of them reached the stage when it could be used as the medium of instruction in higher, and particularly in scientific, education. The elimination of the Persian and Arabic loan vocabularies made less progress than was expected. The borrowing of Persian and Arabic words in order to express new ideas and new objects ceased with, if not before, the Revolution. New words were either formed from the languages themselves, or, much more often, taken from Russian. The replacement of existing words by Russian or Russianized international words was carefully controlled. Thus, most political expressions became Russian while cultural expressions remained Persian or Arabic. For example, *inqilab* the Arabic word for 'revolution' became *revolyutsiya*, while the Arabic *edebiyat* was still used for 'literature' in all the Central Asian languages. The Persian and Arabic element remaining in the written Turkic languages of Central Asia is probably as large today as it is in the Turkish language of Turkey.

The third aim, the promotion of Russian as the 'second native tongue', was the most important for it related to the ultimate aim of all Soviet and Communist planners of the Soviet multi-national state, that is to say, the making of Russian as the *first* language of the State and the medium of primary and secondary instruction in education. Judging from the constant complaints of the low standard of Russian reached in the middle and secondary schools, progress in this matter did not come up to official expectations or requirements. Much, nevertheless, was achieved. Owing to the far greater spread of education and the universal teaching of Russian in the primary and secondary schools, the Russian language penetrated much more deeply into all walks of life in Central Asia than English did in India, even during the British period. The use of Russian as a written lingua franca all over the Soviet Union and even among the peoples of Central Asia became general, but its use as a spoken lingua franca among the Muslims of the USSR, nine-tenths of whom speak closely inter-resembling Turkic languages, remained uncommon. Inside the nationalities, the language of the hearth, except in the rare instances of intermarriage, remained the mother tongue. It is likely to remain so for many generations just as it has done in parts of Wales long after Welsh ceased to be the medium of education.

The reactions of the Muslim peoples of Central Asia to the linguistic reforms were very mixed. When the Arabic alphabet was first replaced by the Unified Latin Alphabet, the standard of literacy was still very low and opposition was mainly confined to the clergy. Official propaganda did not have much difficulty in arousing the people's interest in national languages or in demonstrating that the Latin alphabet was far easier to learn and write than the Arabic. The later introduction of the Cyrillic alphabet did not excite any particular resentment among the people, few of whom realized that one of the objects of the reform was to cut them off from the people and culture of Turkey, where the Latin alphabet remained in vogue. The educational dislocation caused by the change was to some extent balanced by the advantage of having to teach one alphabet instead of two. Much greater opposition was caused by the introduction of Russian words, often as it seemed quite unnecessarily. For example, no one could understand why the word *ustad*, of Persian origin but used all over the Middle East and Central Asia and even in the Arabic-speaking countries, in the sense of 'artisan' or 'expert' should be replaced by the Russianized word *master*. The official insistence on the spelling of Russian loan-words exactly as in Russian rather than in such a way as to conform to the phonetics of each language also seems to have been resented, although not so much in Central Asia as in the Muslim republic of Azerbaydzhan.

The work of systematizing and developing the national languages of Central Asia was initiated by the Communist Party and largely carried out by Russian scholars. Although it was conducted with great skill and assiduity and was accompanied by much interesting literature, it has largely escaped the attention of Western scholars. But the interest of the Russians in Central Asian languages was, and always had been, mainly academic and only rarely showed itself in intercourse with the local population. Russian civil and military officials were never compelled by regulation to learn the local languages and very few of them ever did so. The local population were – and still are – expected to know Russian and if they did not do so, official business was carried out through the medium of interpreters. In India, by contrast, all British officials in British Government service had to pass examinations in at least one Indian language and, except in some of the northern provinces, always had to learn another language as well. In the Army, the speaking of English between British officers and Indian ranks, even Indian officers, was strongly discouraged. The reluctance of Russians to learn local languages and thus to associate themselves more closely with Central Asian culture, is something to which the people have probably become resigned; but adverse mention of it has sometimes found its way into the vernacular press. Thus, in 1957 some articles appeared in the Kazakh magazine *Kazakh Adebiyety*

(Kazakh Literature) which criticized the attitude of the Party to Kazakh culture in general and made special mention of the failure of Russians working in Kazakhstan to learn the Kazakh language, suggesting that this ought to be compulsory. These articles evoked a strong official reproof. While admitting that 'business correspondence is not conducted in Kazakh everywhere that it should be', it was stated clearly that 'no one has the right to make a knowledge of Kazakh an obligatory condition of work in Kazakhstan'.[60] Kazakhstan is, perhaps, an extreme case since, according to the 1959 census, the Kazakhs constitute only 29 per cent of the population of the Kazakh SSR.

Education

Before the Soviet regime there were no accurate statistics showing the percentage of literacy among the peoples of Central Asia. It is, however, probable that in 1880, by which time the whole of the Steppe Region and of Turkestan except for the two khanates of Bukhara and Khiva had passed under Russian rule, not more than 1 per cent of the Muslim population was literate. At the time of the Revolution, it was not more than 3 per cent. From this it might be assumed that nothing much had happened in the realm of education either before or during the Tsarist regime. In the formal Western sense this might be true, but it is important to remember that there was a tradition of Islamic learning and instruction which went back to the ninth century; there was also an old-established oral literature which fostered the development of memory and imagination. During the latter part of the Tsarist period, too, there was an increasing interest in education, on the part not only of the Russian authorities but also of Muslim reformist elements. There is good reason to believe that even without the Revolution there would have been a sharp increase in literacy as well as movement towards the introduction of higher educational establishments for the local population.

Like other imperial governments with large backward colonial territories to administer, the Russian Government was confronted with a serious dilemma. Would education make the people of Central Asia more or less difficult to handle? Again, if education were to be the order of the day, should it be on Russian or on Muslim lines? In the Russian empire an additional complication existed in the fact that since the middle of the sixteenth century, that is to say long before the Russian Asian empire came into existence, the Muslims of the former khanates of Kazan' and Astrakhan' had constituted a considerable part of the population of metropolitan Russia. The Russians had made use of the Tatars during their early penetration of the Kazakh Steppe and had even encouraged Tatar mullas to propagate Islam among the Kazakhs, whose practice of religion had hitherto been extremely casual. The result of this was that the first Kazakh schools established at the end of the eighteenth century in Orenburg and Omsk were virtually run by Tatars, on purely Muslim lines. By 1820 the Russians had realized that Tatar and Muslim culture was gaining a hold over the Kazakhs and they therefore started to establish schools run on Russian lines.

Apart from the school for interpreters founded at Orenburg in 1850, most of these schools were primarily intended for Russians; but a limited number of Kazakhs were also admitted. During the rise of Great Russian nationalism in the 1850s, interest in the assimilation of the Kazakhs for the better consolidation of the empire increased and the Government began to favour the system evolved by the well-known Russian orientalist N. A. Il'minskiy. According to this system the Kazakhs were to be gradually introduced to Russian culture through the medium of their own language transcribed into the Cyrillic alphabet. Kazakh intellectuals, of whom Ibrahim Altynsaryn was the principal, were quite ready to lend their support to a system in which Kazakh was to be the medium of instruction. Progress was, however, very slow and was hampered not only by the rigidity of the Russian educational system but by the lack of funds, which were not enough for the education of Russians, let alone of Muslims. In addition, there was a considerable body of opinion among the military authorities that education of any kind would merely 'put ideas into the heads' of the Kazakhs. It was perhaps because of this that the greatest progress in education was made in the Turgay *oblast*, which was administered directly by the Ministry of the Interior. In 1897, this *oblast* could boast 71 schools with 2,000 pupils, of whom 52 were girls.

Before the coming of the Russians education of any kind was virtually unknown in the Kazakh Steppe. In Turkestan, however, the situation was entirely different. Although, according to

Barthold, Turkestan in the nineteenth century was one of the most backward countries in the whole Islamic world, Bukhara retained its previous reputation as a centre of theological education and attracted students not only from all over Turkestan but also from the Volga region. During the first half of the century, as a result of the improved economic situation of the khanates, the building of *madrasahs* in Samarkand, Kokand and Andizhan, which had been discontinued in the eighteenth century, was resumed. In addition, *mektebs* and mosque schools were again in a fairly flourishing condition, and it can be said that in 1867 when the Governorate-General of Turkestan was established, education on traditional Muslim lines was on the upgrade. Kaufman's policy of cold-shouldering Islam was extended to the Muslim schools, and he did not in any way interfere with their curriculum or with the influence exercised by Bukhara on the *madrasahs* situated outside the jurisdiction of the khanate. The only difficulty the *madrasahs* experienced was in the collection of revenues from the properties they owned inside the khanate.

Kaufman believed that the best way to undermine the influence of Muslim education was to create Russian schools to which Central Asian children would be admitted. This would have the double advantage of drawing away Muslim children from the Muslim schools and of bringing Muslim and Russian children together. A commission to study the subject was formed in 1871 and a project for creating Russian schools of various grades with a limited number of vacancies for local children was gradually brought into effect from 1875 onwards. It was not a success, the average number of local entrants in the new schools being not more than 4 or 5 per cent of the total; moreover, this number tended to diminish rather than increase. The Russians were inclined to attribute this failure to the 'unpreparedness' of the local population for the European system of education, but the real cause lay elsewhere. According to Russian law, only orthodox religious instruction could form part of the school curriculum. Consequently, in the new schools Muslim children received no religious instruction whatever. But according to Islamic tradition, religion was not merely a part of education, but its essential basis. For Muslim parents, therefore, a school without religious instruction was no school at all. Even the later relaxation of the Russian law in this matter had little effect. Another reason for the failure was that the Russians had supposed that the urban population would take more kindly to education than the country folk and nomads. They therefore concentrated most of their efforts in the towns, only to find that the new schools were much more popular among the Kazakhs of the Syr-Dar'ya *oblast* and the Kirgiz of the Semirech'ye *oblast*. This of course was because the Kazakhs and Kirgiz were comparatively unaffected by Islamic educational tradition.

Two other kinds of school came into existence parallel with Kaufman's system. The first was the so-called Russo-native school (*Russko-tuzemnaya shkola*). These were schools for Muslim children only, their primary object being to acquaint the children with Russian culture through the medium of their own language and also with the elements of the Russian language. The originator of this idea was a wealthy Tashkent merchant, Sayyid 'Azim, who had traded with the Russians long before the capture of Tashkent and was an ardent admirer of Russian culture. He proposed to turn one of the Tashkent *madrasahs*, that of Ishan Quli, into a school where Muslim boys would be taught the Russian script, Russian law, arithmetic and various trades; but where the precepts of the shariat would be taught at the same time. Although this proposal cut right across Kaufman's policy of replacing rather than reforming the Muslim schools, Kaufman gave it favourable consideration and a committee was set up to examine its possibilities. It was, however, not put into effect in Kaufman's time owing, it was said, to the absence of suitable teachers.

The first Russo-native school, on somewhat different lines from those proposed by Sayyid 'Azim, was opened in 1884 under Governor-General Rosenbakh in the house of Sayyid Ghani, the son of Sayyid 'Azim. It was treated with suspicion at first but under the enlightened headmastership of V. P. Nalivkin, the great Russian orientalist and student of Central Asian affairs, it made gradual progress. More schools were opened and according to available statistics there were 89 of them in Turkestan by 1911. The principle was extended to the Kazakh Steppe, and by 1913 the Steppe Region had 157 schools. Pierce is hardly correct in saying that they were intended for both Russian and native children, and in any event only the latter attended them. Muslim children continued to attend the Russian schools in the same small numbers as before. Pierce sums up the Russian achievement in education in Central Asia as follows:

The education of a few hundred interpreters, minor officials, and traders was no revolution of the sort Il'minskiy had in mind for transforming the Kazakhs into devoted Russified subjects of the Tsar. Nor did it accomplish what Von Kaufman had envisaged for the Uzbeks, whose schools, through a policy of international neglect, he hoped would fall into disuse and either be supplanted by Russian schools or be transformed into institutions more in keeping with Russian aims of modernizing the native culture and outlook and 'drawing closer' natives and Russians.

Definite accomplishments, on the other hand, were the introduction of new thought in a small segment of native society, the creation of a native intelligentsia, and the appearance of native schools of a reformed type.

The other kind of school which made its appearance at the turn of the nineteenth century was the so-called New Method (*usul-i-jadid*) school which was part and parcel of the Jadid movement. Since this was essentially a modernist movement, the primary object of the Jadid schools was to bridge the gap between orthodox Muslim traditionalism and the requirements of modern life. The founders of the movement were Tatars, who, as Muslims having to a large extent adopted the Russian way of life, were in a good position to interpret it to the more backward Muslims of Central Asia. The appearance of the New Method schools coincided with that of the Russo-native schools with which they were soon in competition. Barthold, writing in 1927, complained that no reliable information was available about the number of Jadid schools which existed at the time of the Revolution. The Russian authorities themselves were slow to appreciate the spread of the Jadid movement, and in a statistical survey of the Fergana *oblast* published in 1908, it was admitted that information about the New Method schools had now been collected for the first time 'although they had appeared in the oblast some 10 or 12 years previously'. They were mainly established in the larger towns where they were much more successful than the Russo-native schools, partly because they attracted the considerable number of Tatar settlers there, and partly because they were recognized as Muslim schools even though they broke to some extent with tradition. In 1910 there were in Tashkent 8 Russian Russo-native schools and 16 New Method schools, and in

Kokand in 1911 there were 2 Russo-native schools with 162 pupils and 8 New Method schools with 530 pupils. No details are available of the number of non-Tatar Muslim children who attended the Tatar schools, but there were several instances of existing *mektebs* adopting the New Method. Thus out of 30 *mektebs* in the town of Turkestan in 1910 one was a New Method school with a Tatar teacher, while two others were gradually adopting the New Method. These latter must have been Uzbek schools, for the number of Tatars in the town at that time was very small. In Kazalinsk, too, in addition to a Tatar New Method school founded in 1903, there was a Kazakh New Method school with a Kazakh teacher. The New Method schools also found their way to the khanate of Bukhara, where the opposition of the orthodox clergy was even stronger than it was in Russian Turkestan. The first school was opened in 1908 but closed at the instigation of the clergy in 1910. There were, however, the beginnings of enlightenment in Bukhara, especially among the merchant classes, and many more schools were opened in 1912 and 1913. But they were all finally closed by order of the Emir in 1914.

During the last years of the Tsarist regime, when the authorities had begun to apprehend the growing influence of the Jadid movement and its New Method schools, there grew up what Barthold has described as 'an alliance between Russian conservatism and old-style Islam'. The government began to take an interest in the *madrasahs*, whose number had greatly increased during the period of Russian rule. They were placed under official administrative and financial control and a system of inspection was inaugurated. Even the policy of not interfering in the curriculum of the *mektebs* showed signs of being changed, and in 1907 a plan was put before the Duma for the introduction of compulsory primary education throughout the empire. This plan had the support of such pioneers in Muslim education as Ostroumov and Nalivkin, but for political and financial reasons it was never put into effect.

The position of the Russian Government *vis-à-vis* Islamic education at the outbreak of the Revolution has been summed up by Barthold as follows:

The alliance of Russian conservatism with old-style Islam completely changed the [Russian] attitude towards the old Muslim school. In 1876 it seemed that 'Russian influence in the East was confronted with an important and lofty task – that of breaking the intellectual shackles of Mohammedanism and of bringing the natives into the orbit of a humane existence'; in 1907 the Muslim school could be compared with the ancient Russian Christian school; the *madrasah* course was recognized as 'a very serious one' compatible with the real requirements of the people's life and as only susceptible of gradual and cautious extension in the sense of the introduction into it of 'elements of modern knowledge', and not of radical dismemberment. With the victory of the Revolution, conservative aims in the sphere of the school, as in all other spheres, were replaced by other aims, which have not yet produced definite results.[61]

The development of general and technical education was one of the first aims of the new Soviet regime, and the comparatively rapid success which it attained was probably the most outstanding of its achievements. Detractors of the regime have always insisted that the Soviet Government's aim in introducing education was purely political and economic, that it did not take into consideration the needs of the people and that it rode roughshod over all religious and traditional susceptibilities. Even if this were partly, if not wholly true, it cannot be denied that the development of public instruction in the widest sense of the term has contributed greatly to the people's general welfare. It is also one of the most striking examples of Soviet Russian determination, dynamism and imperviousness to sentimental considerations. Whether more lasting and in the long run more beneficial effects can be achieved by a more deliberate process and a more liberal curriculum and whether education may not promote rather than obscure the idea of opposition to colonialism are matters still in the realm of conjecture.

The considerable conservative opposition to its educational policy which the Soviet regime encountered was, except in the matter of female education, practically confined to the clergy. The idea of literacy is certainly no less and possibly even more attractive to Asian than to European peoples and the only reason why the standard of education in most Asian countries is so low is that governments, whether imperial or national, either cannot or will not provide the necessary funds and stimulus. After some early difficulties and hesitation the Soviet Government has always made ample financial provision for the education of the Muslim republics and has adhered much more closely than any other imperial power to the principle of equal educational opportunity without regard to race or social status. The results have been remarkable. Exact figures of Muslim literacy are not available owing to the Soviet practice of including in their statistics the European settlers, who in 1959 amounted to about seven and a half million, or over one-third of the total population of Central Asia and Kazakhstan, but there is little doubt that since 1955 the percentage of literacy has been three or four times higher than in any other Muslim country in Asia.

The decree of January 23, 1918, on 'freedom of conscience and religious societies' laid down that 'the teaching of religious doctrines is not permitted in any state, public or private educational institution where general educational subjects are taught'. The Soviet administration in Tashkent was not in a position to enforce this law immediately, and for a time the Muslim schools continued much as before. But just as the security brought by the Russians in the nineteenth century had given a fillip to education and culture, so the collapse of that security during the Civil War wrecked the system to such an extent that, even without Soviet determination to destroy it, it would have taken years to recover. The establishment of Soviet secular schools dates from the 8th All-Russian Party Congress of 1919, which demanded urgent steps for the abolition of religious influence from education and the creation of schools in which the local languages would be the medium of instruction. By November 1921 there were 1,117 Soviet schools with an enrolment of 84,970 Muslim pupils. But at the end of 1923 these figures had dropped to 678 and 31,054 owing to the fact that in 1922 the Central Government had cut off its educational subvention to Turkestan and forced the government there to rely on its own resources. To meet this situation the authorities in Turkestan decided to see if the Muslim schools could not in some way be adapted to Soviet requirements, and in 1922 most of the Waqf endowments, which had earlier been expropriated, were restored and a system of administering the Waqfs as well as of selecting and approving textbooks for use in Muslim schools was established under the Republican Commissariat of Education. This system was continued to some extent after the national delimitation of 1924, for although it soon became clear that no compromise between Islam and Communism was possible, the total elimination of the Muslim system of education could not be realized immediately. 250 Muslim schools were said to be still operating legally in 1927, and it is probable that the last of them did not disappear until after the introduction of compulsory primary education in 1930. This measure had been preceded in 1929 by the establishment of the Latin alphabet in place of the Arabic and it is from then that the secularization of education became a foregone conclusion. Even in the more backward republics such as Turkmenistan, compulsory primary education made remarkable progress. In 1937–8, according to official statistics, 94 per cent of all the children in Turkmenistan were attending primary schools. This figure included non-Muslim settlers, but in Turkmenistan the number of these did not at that time exceed 15 per cent. Later, four-year compulsory education was extended to seven-year, but as a result of World War II, the achievement of this target was delayed and the exact number of Muslim children who had completed seven-year education before the educational reforms of 1958 cannot be extracted from the statistics, which include all nationalities. A clearer picture of the proportion of Muslims attending higher education establishments was, however, available by 1961. This showed a somewhat higher proportion of non-Muslims than their percentage of the population in various republics would seem to warrant. Thus, in Uzbekistan where non-Muslims only constituted about 20 per cent of the population in 1959, they accounted for over 30 per cent of the students in higher educational establishments. When, however, this situation is compared with that prevailing thirty years ago, when there were no higher educational establishments which Muslims could attend, progress can be seen as remarkable. One of the many criticisms levelled against the prevailing system of education in Central Asia is that being uniform with the general Soviet system in every respect except that of language, it takes no account of differences in various national cultures and outlook. However true this may be there is no doubt that one of the main attractions of education for the Muslims lies in this very fact of uniformity: the same standards of preliminary, secondary and higher education obtain throughout the Union, and academic posts whether in the social sciences or in technology appear to be open to all alike. It is worth noticing that at the time of writing, the President of the Academy of Sciences of Uzbekistan is an Uzbek geologist of international standing who did not learn to read until he was nineteen.

One of the greatest problems which faced the Soviet educational authorities was the extent to which local languages should be the medium of instruction. After the Revolution of 1905, as a result of representations made by Gasprinskiy, the Russian Government ostensibly accepted the principle that primary education should be in local languages, that is, in the children's mother tongue, and a regulation to that effect was published in 1907. In spite of this, however, Four-Year programmes drawn up for the Russo-native schools in the same year contained no mention of the use of local languages, and it appears that Russian remained the official medium of instruction. There were, in consequence, no officially recognized textbooks in local languages. From the very beginning of the Soviet regime the use of local languages as the universal medium of instruction among the nationalities was a prominent feature of educational policy and, after the introduction of compulsory primary education in 1930, textbooks were printed in the Unified Latin Alphabet, which had been taken into use the year before. But *pari passu* with the Soviet policy of encouraging national languages went Soviet insistence on the importance of Russian as 'a second mother tongue'. Up to 1958 the study of Russian beyond the 4th class seems to have been compulsory, but in 1958 it was announced that it was now for parents to decide whether their children should attend schools where Russian or the national language was the medium of instruction, and if they chose the latter, whether they should take Russian as a subject. Up to 1960 it was not known what proportion of children opted not to take Russian as a subject at all, but it seemed unlikely that it was a high one, for although Russian may nominally have been voluntary, a knowledge of it was essential for almost any kind of professional advancement. In the same way, although university lecture courses for subjects such as medicine were offered in the local languages, a doctor who knew no Russian would not be expected to go very far. The authorities have always made it clear that Russian should be regarded as a superior language, and however much importance has been attached to the development of national languages there has never been any question of any of them being considered on a par with Russian as a medium of higher education. This would of course be arguable in respect of such Asian languages as Armenian and Georgian with a long and unbroken literary tradition, but it is difficult to see how Central Asian languages, which have no such tradition, could ever become fully adequate as educational media as long as Russian intellectual and philological mentorship persists.

Literature

The literature of the peoples of Central Asia falls into two distinct categories – oral literature which was characteristic of nomadic peoples such as the Kazakhs, Kirgiz and Turkmens up to the nineteenth century, and written literature characteristic of the sedentary and urban peoples, of which Central Asian language examples date back to the fourteenth century. Neither of these literatures has so far attracted much attention in the West, but in Russia they were made the subject of exhaustive study, particularly during the Soviet regime. The work of such Central Asian philosophers as Ali ibn Sina (Avicenna) and Al Biruni has, of course, a world-wide reputation; but before the fourteenth century all such work was written either in Arabic or Persian and is not generally regarded as part of Central Asian literature. Soviet writers claim the works of such Persian poets as Rudaki, Ferdausi, Sa'adi and Omar Khayyam as part of the Tadzhik literary heritage and therefore as Central Asian literature; but this has never been accepted in the West and still less in Persia.

The oral literature of the Turkic nomads displays three forms: first, there are the ritual songs associated with weddings, funerals, partings, wrestling matches and the like; secondly, tales and legends consisting mainly of love stories and fairy tales; finally, and most important of all, the epic poems. To much of the literature expressed in the first two forms it is difficult to assign a date. There are, however, certain general guides which are of some interest. The first is Mahmud al-Kashgari's *Diwan Lughat at-Turk*, or Treasury of the Turkic languages, which is in fact a dictionary compiled about 1077 in Arabic by a Turk from Kashgar. This extraordinary work, which was not discovered until the nineteenth century, contains a large number of quotations from songs, stories and epics which were current at the time it was written. Another guide to dates is the appearance in oral literature of Arabic words. This, however, is not a very precise indication since the use of such words is in general rare in oral

literatures and besides, very little is known of the progress of
Islamic influence among the nomads, particularly among the
Kazakhs. The epics are more easily dated since they mainly
consist of accounts of historical events and were almost certainly
composed during or immediately after these events.

Most of the ritual songs are peculiar to individual tribes and
communities and are of great interest as well as possessing high
poetical merit. An important collection of these songs was made
by the Russian scholar V. Radlov between 1856 and 1907 and
some good examples of them have been given in English by
Thomas G. Winner in his book *The Oral Art and Literature of the
Kazakhs of Russian Central Asia* (Cambridge University Press,
1958). Some of them take the form of singing competitions
between men and women and seem to indicate that the position
of Kazakh women was nothing like so abject as is often made out.
The tales and legends are much more universal and often have
their counterparts all over Asia. The epics, too, are by no means
confined to one nationality or area, although versions of the same
epic may vary somewhat according to language and people.
This goes for some of the better known epics such as Alpamysh,
Dede Korkut and Kör Oghlu which are widely known among
all Turkic peoples, particularly the last which is also known
among the Iranian population of Tadzhikistan under the name of
Gurguli. Kazakh literature is probably the richest in epics and
contains some which are not known elsewhere. The basis of the
epics is usually some historical event. Although such events
seldom relate to a period earlier than the fourteenth century, the
epics often contain other matter which is of much greater
antiquity. Traces of such matter can be found in Mahmud
al-Kashgari's dictionary, and even in the Orkhon inscriptions
which relate to the period AD 600–800. The exploits of real or
imaginary heroes form an important part of the epics, which also
contain a great deal of lively and dramatic description.

Although the composition of long epic narratives tended to
die down during the nineteenth century, particularly after the
final establishment of Russian rule and the beginning of stabilization of the nomads, oral literature as a whole remained vigorous,
although after the Revolution it took on a very different form.
The resistance of the Kazakhs to Russian encroachment during
the first half of the nineteenth century, and particularly the revolt

of Kenesary Kasim, was the subject of a great many poems and songs which were frowned upon by the Soviet authorities and will probably die out altogether. Some of the revolutionary oral literature composed at the time of the 1916 Revolt is, however, still extant. After the Revolution, the first tendency was not only to exploit the extraordinary facility of Kazakh and Kirgiz *akyns* or bards in oral composition for propaganda purposes, but also to transcribe as much as possible of the traditional epics and legends. The first tendency still persists, but after the Second World War there was a marked change in the official attitude towards the traditional epics and particularly towards those which tended to glorify the prowess of the people in their fight with the Russians. Many of the transcriptions which had been made were found to contain matter which did not accord with Soviet ideology, and such matter was described as spurious interpolation and eliminated. A vigorous official campaign against the epics was conducted in 1952 and particularly against the Kirgiz epic *Manas*. This attack met with considerable opposition and was marked by a controversy of a kind hitherto unknown between the two organs of the Central Committee of the Kirgiz Communist Party, *Sovetskaya Kirgiziya* and *Kyzyl Kirgzstan*, the one attacking the epic for its subject matter (the resistance of the Kirgiz to the Chinese invaders) and the other defending it as being a truly popular composition. A conference to discuss the matter was convened in Frunze in June 1952 and from this a new theory of the development of epic form was worked out to apply not only to *Manas*, but to all epics. This was expounded in a leading article in *Literaturnaya Gazeta* on July 1, 1952. It was explained that 'epics of a fundamentally popular character are not infrequently handed down to us spoiled by alien stratification . . . The Kazakh epic *Koblandy-Batyr*, of whose popular foundation we may judge by certain little-known versions, was published in Marabel's version which is strongly corrupted by Islamic ideas of fighting for the faith and destroying the "infidel". The Kirgiz epic *Manas* has also been subject to considerable corruption. One excerpt from *Manas*, which has been widely read in Kirgiz and in Russian, is saturated with pan-Islamist and military-adventurist ideas alien to the Kirgiz people.' The result of this reassessment was that while the original decision to abolish the epics altogether was rescinded, they were only to be allowed to exist in a carefully

expurgated form. The original epics as they came from the mouth
of the bard and were handed down from generation to generation
are, therefore, doomed to extinction, except in so far as transcriptions of them exist outside the Soviet Union.

Central Asian written literature has never provided the same
reflection of manners and morals as the oral literature. With one
or two notable exceptions such as Babur's Memoirs, the so-called
classical literature of the Central Asian peoples was written in
verse. If that part of Persian literature which Soviet writers claim
for Tadzhikistan is excluded, this classical literature was confined
to what are now Uzbekistan and Turkmenistan. By far its
greatest exponent was Mir Ali Shir, or Alishir Navai as he is
nowadays known to the Uzbeks, Navai ('the melodious') being
the *takhallus* or *nom de guerre* which he appended to his writings in
the Chatagay language. He also wrote a considerable amount in
Arabic and Persian but to this work he appended the name Fani,
or 'transitory'. Ali Shir was unquestionably a poet of great merit,
to whose work, however, very little attention has been paid by
Western orientalists. (His name was unaccountably excluded
from the first edition of the *Encyclopaedia of Islam*.) A number of
other minor poets are mentioned in modern histories of Uzbek
literature, those whose works dealt principally with religious and
mystical themes being generally stigmatized as 'reactionary'. Also
described as a classical writer is Muqimi, a lyrical and satirical
poet who wrote in the second half of the nineteenth century. The
principal figure of Turkmen literature is Makhtum Quli, who
flourished between 1730 and 1780, although the exact dates and
other details of his life are not known. His popularity, which is
still considerable, was due to his breaking away from the medieval
tradition of writing in a language incomprehensible to the
ordinary people. Other popular writers who followed Makhtum
Quli were Mamed (Muhammad) Veli Kemine and Mulla Nepes.
These are all names to conjure with in Turkmenistan and their
work is regarded as part of the literary heritage of the Turkish
peoples and as such figures largely in the Turkish Encyclopaedia
of Islam. They do not, however, appear in the first edition of the
Western *Encyclopaedia of Islam*.

No full and objective assessment of Central Asian classical
literature has yet been made and it is unlikely that it will be made
during the Soviet regime. The literary histories of the various

Central Asian peoples which have been written during the present regime are harshly critical of work which cannot somehow be made to fit in with present-day Marxist ideological and realistic standards. Literature which consists exclusively or mainly of poetic imagery or fantasy without carrying any practical message is thought to be hardly worth perpetuating.

At the beginning of the second half of the nineteenth century, before Russian cultural influence had begun to be felt, Islamic society in Central Asia was still at a medieval level. Literacy stood at not more than 2 per cent, and intellectual life and thought were associated more with classical Arabic and Persian learning than with indigenous artistic and literary production. As elsewhere in the Islamic East, men of letters were largely dependent for their livelihood on kingly or clerical patronage. Since the passing of the Timurid dynasty, patronage of the arts, where it existed at all, had been confined to the Uzbek khanates of Bukhara, Khiva and Kokand. With the annexation of Kokand by the Russians and the considerable circumscription of the territory, influence and wealth of Bukhara and Khiva, the further decline in the already mediocre state of literature and the infiltration of Russian cultural influence were inevitable. Poets like Firqat (1858–1909) and Ahmed Kalla (1827–97) knew Russian well and were familiar with Russian literature, and the former did the first translation of a Russian classic – Tolstoy's *What Men Live By* – into Chagatay, or old Uzbek as it is now called, in 1877. Writers like Hamza Hakim-zadeh (1889–1929) were much influenced by the Tatar Jadid movement, which itself derived its modernist ideas from Russian inspiration. Nevertheless, except in the introduction of prose writing as distinct from poetry, it was not until the twentieth century that literature published in Turkestan began to show any marked signs of Russian influence. Surveys made by Russian orientalists and officials between 1908 and 1912 on the reading matter available in Turkestan showed that publications in local languages issuing from lithographic presses consisted partly of translations from Arabic religious literature and partly of secular literature made up of translations from the Persian, and original works either in local languages or in other Turkic languages such as Tatar.

Although the nomad Kazakhs had no classical literary tradition other than their oral epics, and although there were no cities which could form centres of learning, it was in Kazakhstan that writing on modern lines first developed. This was partly because the Kazakhs were culturally and linguistically more homogeneous than the other peoples, and partly because they were the first to feel the effect of Russian influence. In addition to the Russian troops and peasant settlers, there were in Kazakhstan a number of political exiles such as Dostoyevskiy, Korolenko and Taras Shevchenko who interested themselves in Kazakh affairs and exercised a profound influence on the small number of Kazakh intellectuals. As a result of this and of the peace and security which developed under Russian rule during the second half of the nineteenth century, the practice of literature grew apace. The Kazakh intelligentsia was roughly divided into two groups: the national traditionalists who rejected Russian culture and concerned themselves exclusively with classical Arabic and Persian literature and with Kazakh traditional folk lore; and the modernists who were affected by Russian culture and who aimed at breaking down much of the old tribal tradition and at making Kazakhstan into a modern nation. Of the latter school the three main figures were Chokan Vali-khan, Ibrahim Altynsaryn and Abay Kunanbay. All three had an excellent knowledge of Russian and of Russian literature, and the last two had had a traditional education and were well versed in Arabic and Persian literature. Their intellectual roles varied considerably: Chokan Vali-khan concerned himself principally with interpreting Kazakh culture to the Russians and produced little original writing in the Kazakh language; Altynsaryn (1841–99) was primarily an educational reformer who worked hard at modernizing and systematizing the Kazakh language. He himself was virtually the first Kazakh to use prose as a medium. As a creator of original literature both in prose and verse Abay Kunanbay, generally known to the Kazakhs simply as Abay, was the greatest of the three. Abay's earlier work showed the influence of Islamic classical writing and thought in Arabic and Persian; but he became disillusioned with these, and his later writing is pre-occupied with his own Kazakh cultural heritage and with what he regarded as Russian and Western enlightenment. His often declared distaste for Islamic dogma has always been strongly approved of by the Soviet authorities; but in his own day he incurred the displeasure not only of the Russian authorities on account of his close contacts with Russian revolutionary exiles, but of the traditionalists among his own people.

The division of the Kazakh intelligentsia into Western and traditionalist groups persisted into the twentieth century. With the 1905 Revolution and the partial relaxation of official restrictions on political writing in the Kazakh language, the conflict of views between these two groups became more marked. The Westerners continued their demand for reforms based on Russian models and the adoption of Western skills and 'know-how', although in the minds of some of them this was with the object of enabling the Kazakhs to secure their independence more quickly. The traditionalists, on the other hand, while displaying less interest in Islam and in classical Islamic learning, had become more nationalist and anti-Russian in their outlook. The most important representative of the Westerner group was the poet and journalist Toruaygyr (1893–1920), while the outstanding Kazakh nationalist was Baytursun (1872–1928). The latter's early activities were mainly concerned with the development of the Kazakh language, and this remained an abiding interest with him for the whole of his life. Unlike Altynsaryn, who advocated the adoption of a modified Cyrillic alphabet, he invented a simplified form of the Arabic script. Gaoled for his revolutionary activities in 1910, he was one of the leaders of the anti-Russian Kazakh nationalist movement known as Alash Orda, which emerged after the 1917 Revolution. In 1919, he joined the Bolsheviks and became Commissar for Education in the Kirgiz (Kazakh) ASSR on its formation in 1920. Later, however, his nationalist attitude became offensive to the Soviet authorities and he faded into obscurity.

Before describing the development of written literature during the Soviet regime, a few words must be said about the birth of journalism in Central Asia. The first newspaper to appear in a Central Asian language was *Tuzemnaya Gazeta* or Native Newspaper, *tuzemnyy* being a word which is nowadays considered highly derogatory. This newspaper was under official Russian control, its first director being Ostroumov, a well-known Russian orientalist, who was assisted by the Uzbek poets Muqimi and Firqat. Although the language in which it was printed was in no sense popular, the paper had a considerable vogue among the intelligentsia, its circulation in 1906 being 3,600. It lasted until the Revolution, but by then was competing unsuccessfully with privately printed Tatar newspapers. As with modern writing in general it was the Kazakhs who led the way in journalism. After 1905, a number of newspapers and periodicals in the Kazakh language began to appear. The most popular of these was *Qazaq* edited by Baytursun, who even in 1913 was voicing those nationalist sentiments which were eventually to be his downfall during the Soviet regime. 'The modern Kazakh intelligentsia,' he wrote, 'having received their education in Russian schools and Tatar *madrasahs* already begin to feel contempt for the Kazakh language, and begin to speak Russian or Tatar among themselves. That is a bad sign. If it should continue further, then we shall have once and for all said goodbye to the Kazakh language and along with it, to the Kazakh people as an independent nation.' *Qazaq* was published in Orenburg and had at one time a circulation of 8,000, which far exceeded that of any other newspaper or periodical. Some of the others were published outside Kazakh territory – *Serke* in St Petersburg, *Ayqap* in Troitsk, and *Zaman Tili* and *Alash* in Tashkent. No other Central Asian journalistic activity approached that of the Kazakhs; small newspapers which appeared from time to time in Turkestan were more in the nature of pamphlets, such as those issued between 1901 and 1906 by Munavvar Qari, leader of the Young Bukharans, an offshoot of the Jadid movement.

It will be seen from the foregoing that on the eve of the Revolution the development of literature as a vehicle of artistic or popular expression or as a medium for official, nationalist or clerical propaganda was not great. Printing in Central Asian languages was strictly limited and was confined to direct lithography, that is, reproduction from material written by hand on stone surfaces. The only languages which were beginning to assume definite literary form were Kazakh and Turkmen.

Although writing on political subjects was subject to severe official control, such imaginative literature as appeared was quite spontaneous and the authorities seem to have made no attempt to mould it to suit their requirements. The Russian influence which began to show itself in the new prose writing was the result not of official inspiration or encouragement but of the natural interest in Russian literature which followed the learning of the Russian language by the intelligentsia. Although great literary figures like Muhammad Iqbal, Rabindranath Tagore and Prem Chand did not appear in the short-lived Tsarist regime in Central Asia as they did in India, there is every reason to suppose that they would have done so had the regime continued.

It is not easy to describe the development of literature during the first forty-five years of the Soviet regime. Directly the Soviet regime became firmly established, that is to say, after the creation of the republics in 1924, writing and publishing of every kind came under strict official control. The control of literary production, in respect both of its contents and its literary forms, by hierarchies of one kind or another was not of course a new phenomenon; it had occurred both in the Islamic world and in medieval Europe. There had also been more recent instances of the mass production of literature written to the dictates of official or religious bodies in order to meet a popular demand resulting from a sudden increase in literacy. The quality of such literature has usually been mediocre, and it has disappeared with the rise of private enterprise in writing and publishing. The circumstances in which literatures were created in Soviet Central Asia and Kazakhstan seem to be without any previous parallel. To begin with, the average of literacy over the whole region in 1917 was not more than 3 per cent. Secondly, apart from some embryonic writing in Kazakh and Turkmen, nothing in the way of a national written literature had ever existed. Finally, the idea of literature, where it had penetrated at all, was associated with religion, legend and, for a brief period, with national consciousness, all of which subjects were an anathema to the new Soviet regime. What the Soviet Government set out to do was first of all to abolish illiteracy and then to provide reading matter organized in 'national literatures' and written in national languages which had been officially apportioned and systematized. These literatures were to be 'national in form and socialist in content', which meant in effect that apart from the language in which they were written, they would conform to certain literary criteria laid down by the Communist Party for the whole of the Soviet Union and were to be a vehicle for official propaganda on carefully restricted subjects ranging over the positive merits of socialism and Communism and the iniquities of imperialism, capitalism, religion and nationalist survivals.

From the point of view of practical achievement the increase in the practice of writing and of publishing during the past 40 years is astonishing and can perhaps best be illustrated by the following figures for Kazakhstan: in 1913, 13 books were published with a total print order of 4,000. In 1957, 1,194 books were published with a total print order of 6,906,000. In the same year there were in circulation 483 newspapers and 11 periodicals.

Taken on the basis of population, publishing of all forms of literature in Central Asia was soon far to exceed that in any of the other Muslim countries in Asia, and with one or two exceptions the standard of printing and production was much higher. The technical literary quality of modern Central Asian literature in the 1960s was probably as good if not better than that of Middle Eastern literature and it was free from the pernicious rubbish circulating either in original writing or in translation in many non-Soviet Muslim countries. Some of the novels of such Kazakh writers as Auezov and Mukanov, of the Turkmen writer Kerbabayev, and the memoirs of the Tadzhik writer Sadreddin Aini, are works of undoubted literary merit, and many other examples could be cited. The extent to which Central Asian literature reflected the spirit of its peoples, however, is quite another matter. The standard of contemporary literature produced in Turkey, Persia and the Arab countries was certainly not to be compared with the great literature of the past, but it did serve as a mirror of modern living conditions in these countries and gave expression to a wide variety of ideas on political, sociological and artistic subjects. Moreover, a large part of the literature published in the Middle East consisted of translations of foreign works selected without any regard to their ideological content, thus providing some insight into the progress of ideas in the outside world. There was very little of all this to be found in modern Central Asian literature: there were some good descriptions of the countryside, and some information was to be gleaned about life in factories and collective farms; but there was no ventilation of controversial views, no translation from modern foreign literature except from Russian. Prolific though they were, Central Asian writers seemed to lack spontaneity and to be leaning over backwards in order to meet official requirements. Judging by the steady stream of official criticism, they were not very successful in this and looked at from the western angle their task seems to have been an impossible one; for the Party required national writers to produce works of a characteristic national flavour about nations which were supposed to be rapidly losing their distinguishing national characteristics. When, however, they not unnaturally looked for such characteristics in the past, they were liable to be accused of reactionary tendencies. On the whole, the claim that Central Asian literatures have already been 'created' seems to be premature, but the eventual emergence of an entirely new but vigorous and representative Central Asian literature cannot be excluded.

Fine Arts, Drama, Cinema, Radio and Television

The fine arts, as the term is understood in the West, barely existed in Central Asia before the Soviet period. Since Islam forbade the representation of the human form, painting was at a very low ebb and sculpture was non-existent. Musical skill was held in high esteem but its development was hampered by the total absence of notation. The creative arts found expression in architecture, ceramics, embroidery and carpet-weaving, but except in the first, achievements were not outstanding either in workmanship or in inspiration. During the period of relative security which followed the Russian conquest there were signs of development in all these creative arts in the practice of which the Russian Government showed no disposition to interfere.

The drama as it developed in China, India and the West had little vogue in Central Asia until the Soviet regime, although in Azerbaydhan the plays of Fathali Akhund were being performed to enthusiastic audiences some years before the Revolution. Probably the first and only theatrical performance given in a local language in Central Asia before the Revolution was that arranged by Mahmud Khoja Behbudi of his play *Padarkush* (The Parricide), performed in Tashkent in 1913. There was, however, no lack of native talent. Entertainment was provided by strolling players. The Kazakh *akyn* (bard) and the Turkmen *bakhshi* (folk minstrel) sang improvised songs and ballads to the accompaniment of traditional musical instruments. In Uzbekistan, the *maskharabaz* (jester) imitated animals and men, sometimes performing in market squares or on platforms by the roadside whole scenes portraying unjust judges, dishonest merchants, mullas and others. There were also puppet shows, the *chadir-i-khayal* or 'tent of apparitions' which used marionettes, and the *dast kurchak* or hand puppets, whose main character was a kind of Punch, Pahlivan-i-kachal, 'the bald hero'. It is noteworthy that all these names, with the exception of *akyn*, are of Persian origin.

From the very beginning of the Soviet regime the development of the fine arts and drama was actively and enthusiastically encouraged and even organized by the authorities. As elsewhere in the Soviet Union, the primary purpose was considered to be political and ideological propaganda, but they were also designed to educate the people in the canons of culture and taste, both of these being conditioned by the Marxist principle of socialist realism. The production of painting, sculpture and music in conformance with the dictates of a ruling hierarchy is by no means a new phenomenon in the history of art, and when artists are compelled to embody prevailing religious or other principles in their compositions their work need not necessarily be impaired provided they have behind them a great artistic tradition. The fact that Fra Lippo Lippi was something of a freethinker and a rebel against contemporary conventions did not prevent him from producing great religious paintings. In Central Asia, how-ever, the fine arts started, as it were, from scratch: artists were suddenly required to produce painting, sculpture and formal music which were not only entirely new to them as forms of expression, but were to act as vehicles for entirely new ideas. It is therefore not surprising that their productions, although con-siderable in quantity, seemed to lack spontaneity and genuine character. Tendencies to 'hark back to the past' were frowned upon by the authorities, who steadily maintained the Marxist-Leninist aesthetic principle that the main purpose of art was the propagation 'of the great ideals of communism and the immortal-ization of the memory of those who devoted their lives to the struggle for the people's happiness'. There has at the same time been much official concern at the decline in artistic craftsmanship which, not perhaps unnaturally, seems to have accompanied the inculcation of western styles in art. If condemnation of the cult of personality is maintained there is some hope that the arts of carpet-weaving and woodcarving may be rescued from the obsession with political portraiture from which they suffered up to the 1950s. But the figure of Lenin will probably remain a popular artistic theme for many years.

Up to the early 1960s the effect of the new art on modern life and decoration was unsatisfactory. In the absence of fine specimens of their own native arts with which to decorate their homes, people have had to fall back on *objets d'art* supplied by the shops, many of them in the worst possible taste. On July 28, 1960, *Pravda Vostoka* reported that an exhibition of amateur art held in Termez was full of objects 'embroidered in cross-stitch and showing monstrous cats of various colours, misshapen psyches and cupids, gleaming Marys and Dianas, maimed faces of the poets we hold dear, coarse crimson roses, garlands of forget-me-nots, little wreaths and sugary cherubs minus wings'. Similar tendencies to abandon traditional styles and motifs in favour of the crudest examples of Western bad taste can, of course, be observed in other Asian countries which have been subjected to Western influences. But traditional arts and crafts are disappearing far more quickly in Soviet Asia than elsewhere, and although the authorities constantly inveigh against bad taste there can be little doubt that it is the regimentation of art on unfamiliar lines and the confusion of art with propaganda which are largely responsible.

It is perhaps too early to say to what extent the artificial creation of fine arts in Central Asia has contributed to the cultural education of the people or how far it has actually promoted the practice of socialism. For people making their debut in the graphic and plastic arts socialist realism would be likely to have a stronger appeal than for people acquainted to some extent with more abstract forms of art; and it is possible that the people of Central Asia may eventually slough off the untypical forms and styles which they have been constrained to adopt, and develop something of their own. That they will be unable to do so in present circumstances can be deduced from the following example of official art criticism taken from the newspaper *Kommunist Tadzhikistana* of November 18, 1959. 'The attitude of the citizen-painter to life' should find artistic expression in demonstrating the transformation of banal scenic and accidental atmospheric effects by the beauty and power of man's purposeful producing activities. On the other hand, a painting representing a large hydro-electric power station somewhere in Tadzhikistan, makes it obvious that the artist's main interest is not to 'sublimate the grandiosity and might of the structure' but 'to show the commonplace of evening light' which transforms this 'great and significant subject' into a 'sugary daub'. The same admiration for nature disqualified another painting called 'The Building of Communism'. This represented high-voltage masts and a highroad with lorries carrying machinery. In this case it is the artist's admiration of the colour which mountains assume with the coming of night which destroys the ideological value of his work; for 'the great principle of party spirit completely excludes passive naturalistic objectivism and demands from the painter clarity and precision of his ideological conceptions'. All these, explains the newspaper, are embodied in another picture, 'The Way to Town'. There, the artists 'with great love and passion fill the spaces with bulldozers, excavators, cranes and masts' by means of which they 'convey with spirit the speed and rhythm of our time'.

The introduction of the drama and the opera has been much more popular – in every sense of the word – than have the fine arts. It has brought colourful entertainment into the lives of people whose only form of amusement was occasional displays by acrobats, performing animals, minstrels and highly unedifying dancing done by boys. Moreover, although the theatre has been officially used as a propaganda medium, it has also brought to the people stage productions of familiar legends such as *Leyla and Majnun* and *Farhad and Shirin* as well as selected scenes and episodes from the well-known and loved oral epics such as *Manas*, *Alpamysh* and *Korkut Ata*. There are now theatres in all the principal towns of Central Asia, and in the republican capitals there are at least two – one Russian and one national. All the theatres maintain their own repertory companies, which are able to give a wide range of performance including not only original work by local playwrights, but translations into local languages of many Russian plays and operas as well as of works by Shakespeare, Molière, Verdi, Puccini, and even Jack London. The popularity of all forms of stage production was quickly established and has never waned, although a marked preference has always been shown for older works and especially for those on traditional themes. Playwrights, producers and actors have always been subjected to a steady stream of official criticism, the actors in particular being taken to task not only for bad acting but for their disreputable private lives. The principle has been laid down that 'before one can attempt to bring culture to others one must be cultured oneself'.

The ballet and orchestral music have proved just as popular in Central Asia as the theatre; the old inhibitions about the appearance of women on the stage either as actors or dancers have long been thrown to the winds and ballet troupes of both sexes exist in all the Republics. Most of the classical Russian ballets are regularly performed, and native talent, particularly in Tadzhikistan, has been applied to the adaptation of traditional themes with traditional music. Great strides have been made in the notation and orchestration of music, and some Western influence on new musical composition is becoming apparent. Up to 1960, however, there was little sign of the garbling of Eastern with Western musical idioms which has occurred, for example, in modern Greek music.

Lenin considered that of all the arts the cinema was the most important and the most effective as a means of spreading Communist enlightenment among the masses; consequently, the Soviet regime has devoted proportionately more effort to the development of the film industry than to that of any other medium of propaganda. In 1915 there were said to be 52 cinemas throughout Turkestan and the Steppe Region; and today there are approximately 7000 stationary and mobile cinemas in operation. The first film studios in Central Asia were established in Tashkent and Stalinabad (now Dushanbe) before the Second World War. Documentary, instructional and feature films were already being produced here when the main Soviet studios Mosfilm and Leninfilm were evacuated to Alma Ata, Tashkent and Stalinabad from European Russia in 1941. During the war the bulk of Soviet film production was carried out in Central Asia; this included a considerable number of patriotic and war propaganda films and several documentaries. After the end of the war, all the existing film studios in Central Asia were completely reconstructed and extended and some new ones were built, particular attention being paid to those specializing in the production of documentary and instructional films. This and the dubbing into local languages of Russian and foreign films of all kinds has so far been the main function of the Central Asian studios, the production of full-length feature films having been considerably hampered by the lack of scenarios and the absence of capable scriptwriters. It does not look as if the popularity of the cinema was in any way affected by the introduction of television, although the popular preference for full-length feature films apparently continued to be unsatisfied.

'The main task of Soviet sound and television broadcasting is to mobilize the workers of our country in order to translate successfully into reality the Seven-Year Plan and the whole programme of the large-scale construction of communism in the USSR.' This statement, appearing in the newspaper *Turkmenskaya Iskra* on May 7, 1961, would not seem to suggest that radio and television programmes have a very high entertainment value. There have, indeed, always been complaints about the dullness of programmes; nevertheless the amount of listening and viewing seems to be very large and on the increase. The first radio broadcasting transmitters were established in Central Asia in the 1930s. By far the most powerful station was that at Tashkent, which can be heard throughout the region and whose broadcasts are boosted and rediffused from the republican transmitters. Rediffusion has been the preferred method of broadcasting in the rural areas, and the making and use of wireless sets without a licence has always carried severe penalties. Official reports on the number of rediffusion points and sets operating in the various republics are very inconsistent but the following details for Kazakhstan published in the newspaper *Kazakhstanskaya Pravda* on April 1, 1961, are of some interest: there were then 3,000 radio diffusion points with some 970,000 extensions as well as over 500,000 receiving sets. Kazakh radio was then broadcasting not only in Kazakh and Russian but also in Uzbek, Uygur, German, Korean and Chechen.

Television transmissions were being relayed to Central Asia from Moscow, Leningrad and Kiev in 1955, and by 1960 there were 2 television transmitters in Uzbekistan, 4 in Kazakhstan, 1 in Tadzhikistan and 1 in Kirgizia. There was no transmitter in Turkmenistan, but parts of the Republic were served by Baku. In addition to the transmitters, there were a number of relay stations in each of the republics. Statistics for the number of television sets in use vary in the same way as for radio sets. In 1960 there were said to be up to 25,000 sets in use in Alma-Ata alone, but only 5,000 throughout Tadzhikistan.

Soviet writers claim that whereas the Tsarist Government pursued an active policy of Russification in Central Asia, the

Soviet regime enabled the peoples to develop their own national cultures without let or hindrance; that they have only borrowed from the Russian and other peoples of the Soviet Union those features of their cultures which are superior or complementary to their own. This, however, is not at all the impression which is gained from a careful study of Soviet writing on the whole region during the past forty years and from visits to the region itself. Indeed, whatever the Soviet intention, there can be no doubt that the region has become more Russian since the end of the Tsarist regime in 1917. To begin with, there are more than three times as many Russians there as in Tsarist times; and Russian influence is clearly observable in every branch of culture except in those like religion which it is planned to eradicate altogether. Russianization is, of course, merely one form of the Westernization which in varying degrees has affected almost all the Muslim countries of Asia. The difference is that except in isolated instances such as the dress and language reforms in Turkey, no government of an Asian Muslim country whether national or imperial, has ever proposed to enforce the introduction of Western culture by means of legislation, or formally to declare its superiority to Muslim culture. Today, apart from the 40 million Muslims in India, who are not subjected to any kind of cultural regimentation, and some 30 million in China, the only considerable body of Muslims living under non-Muslim rule is the 25 million of the Soviet Union.

Even if the Soviet contention that no pressure of any kind has been brought to bear on the Muslims of Central Asia were true, it can hardly be denied that Westernization has penetrated more deeply into Soviet Central Asia than into any of the adjoining Muslim countries of South Asia and the Middle East. The main reason for this is the importance attached and the priority given by the Soviet Government to compulsory primary education and to education in general, the nature of the education imparted being essentially non-Asian in character. The educational systems of many of the non-Soviet Muslim countries have been effected by Westernization, although not to the extent of permanently excluding Islamic religious instruction, but no national government of a Muslim country has so far launched an educational campaign of such intensity and insistence as that launched by the Soviet Government in Central Asia in 1930. Other reasons are the collectivization and mechanization of agriculture, the extensive development of modern means of communication – railways, motor roads, civil aviation, radio and television, the substitution of modern irrigation technique for the ancient *qanat* system, and last but by no means least the conscription of Muslims into the predominantly Westernized Soviet armed forces.

Belief in the absolute superiority of Western 'know-how' and of Western methods of production, transport, hygiene and the like is by no means confined to the Soviet Union; it is widely held not only in Europe and America, but by the ruling groups in the majority of Asian and African countries. Only in the Soviet Union, however, is the conviction openly expressed that full realization of the material benefits of Western civilization necessitates a complete transformation of traditional cultures and the dropping of all practices which conflict with the Western or Soviet notion of progress. The Russian administrators of Muslim Central Asia, whether Tsarist or Soviet, have always maintained that Islam in particular acted as a brake on progress and material well-being and the present regime has sedulously propagated the view that the increase in productivity and material welfare is in direct proportion to the 'Sovietization' of culture and the decline of Islam. There is so far no means of proving or disproving the validity of this assertion. While it is probably true that no independent Muslim country where Islamic culture is still predominant has attained the same degree of productivity, literacy, public health and material well-being, it is equally true that no Muslim country outside the Soviet Union contains, or has ever contained, such a high proportion of non-Muslim settlers employed in every branch of human activity. It is noteworthy that the Soviet authorities are far from being satisfied either with the state of productivity in the Muslim lands or with the extent to which they have been able to substitute Soviet for traditional culture, and they evidently believe that further regimentation of culture and further colonization are necessary in order to achieve their aims.

EPILOGUE

The facts are really not at all like fish on the fishmonger's slab. They are like fish swimming about in a vast and sometimes inaccessible ocean; and what the historian catches will depend, partly on chance, but mainly on what part of the ocean he chooses to fish in and what tackle he chooses to use – these two factors being, of course, determined by the kind of fish he wants to catch. . . .

Much of what has been written in English-speaking countries in the last 10 years about the Soviet Union, and in the Soviet Union about the English-speaking countries, has been vitiated by this inability to achieve even the most elementary measure of imaginative understanding of what goes on in the mind of the other party, so that the words and actions of the other are always made to appear malign, senseless or hypocritical. History cannot be written unless the historian can achieve some kind of contact with the mind of those about whom he is writing.

E. H. Carr.
What is History? pp. 18 and 19

THESE TWO quotations from one of the relatively few writers who have striven to write objectively about the Soviet Union seem to me particularly relevant to the history of Soviet Central Asia. If, however, history is, as Carr contends, 'a continuous process of interaction between the historian and his facts', the task of the historian of Soviet Central Asia is rendered peculiarly difficult by the rigid official control not only of historiography, but of first-hand impartial observation both before and after the Revolution. In addition, collateral source material on Central Asia in the Soviet period is probably scantier than on any other part of the Soviet Union, being confined to the accounts of refugees whose experiences were limited to certain periods and regions, and none of whom had access to official archives. The would-be impartial historian of Soviet Central Asia, therefore, not only finds himself gravely short of reliable and relevant source-material but is hard put to it to establish any kind of 'contact with the mind of those about whom he is writing'; and this, in Carr's view, really disqualifies him from writing at all.

The poverty of the available source-material on the history of Central Asia under the Tsarist and Soviet regimes, and particularly under the latter, can best be apprehended by comparing it with that available to the historian of the British period in India. Even in Tsarist times, Central Asia was a closed country compared with India; for foreigners travel was difficult, and prolonged residence limited to the representatives of one or two remote mining concessions like the Spasskiy Copper Works near Karaganda; literature on the subject of government policy and the state of national feeling was subject to strict censorship; and the local press was confined to one or two officially controlled Russian newspapers and a few small and frequently suppressed vernacular papers appearing in the first decade of the twentieth century. Nevertheless, the facts of the Russian military conquest of the region, the nature and development of the Russian administrative system and details about the way of life of the various peoples of Central Asia were available from the works both of Russian travellers and scholars and also of expert observers and scholars like Schuyler and Curzon who were able to carry out tours lasting many months. There were also fairly close contacts between Central Asian cultural and commercial elements and those of adjoining Muslim countries. But since the consolidation of the Soviet regime in 1927, information available to the historian has been entirely confined to that contained in the Soviet press and literature which, from the beginning of the regime, have been subject to the most rigid censorship. This material, while providing a vast mass of accurate and detailed information about officially controlled material and cultural developments, affords no direct reflection of the working of men's minds or of the progress of ideas. This means that the historian is constrained to read between the lines and thus run the risk of exaggeration and misinterpretation. The historian of India, by contrast, is confronted by an *embarras de richesses*. From the earliest years of British power in India, freedom of travel and of prolonged and even permanent residence, except in the frontier districts, was open to people of all nations prepared to grant similar facilities in their own countries and even of many which were not. In addition to a wealth of State papers, reports of all-party commissions and the like, there were innumerable books of memoirs and travel by serving and retired British officials, businessmen, missionaries and politicians of all parties. These works contained not only detailed descriptions of Indian life, the British administration and various economic and agricultural problems, but also strong and frequent criticisms of the foreign and domestic policies of the British Government of India. During the second half of the nineteenth century a large English and even larger vernacular press came into being, a considerable section of which was nationalistic and anti-British. At the same time there were no restrictions on the travel or residence abroad of any Indians including those with extreme nationalist and anti-British views. It was even possible for such Indians to become members of the British parliament and to engage in violent criticism of British policy towards India. With access to material of this kind the historian not subject to official or ideological dictation can achieve 'some kind of contact with the mind of those about whom he is writing', whether they be Indian or British.

But although detail is lacking on a wide range of material and spiritual matters relating to Central Asia which would normally be necessary in order to sustain Carr's definition of history as 'an unending dialogue between the present and the past', it may still be possible to treat the available material in such a way as to arrive at some broad conclusions on the lines of Barthold's fifteen so-called theses in which he summed up his dissertation on Turkestan delivered in 1900. With the reservation that some of these conclusions are only tentative and could be modified or set aside by the opening up of new sources of information, they may aid in arriving at a more balanced judgement on the impact of the West on the peoples of Central Asia, that is to say, how they have fared both materially and spiritually under the Russian Tsarist and Soviet regimes.

Before attempting to adduce any conclusions from the foregoing and, as it may seem to many readers, sketchy narrative, it would be as well to mention one circumstance which, in spite of the difficulties just referred to, seems to make it worth while treating the Tsarist and Soviet regimes in Central Asia together. In 1917 imperial Russia not only suffered signal defeat at the hands of Germany, but underwent a change of regime, of system of government and of *weltanschauung* more fundamental than any previously experienced by a great world power. In spite of this, the frontiers of the Asian empire of the Tsars remained precisely the same and have been jealously defended by the Soviet regime without suffering the slightest secession or encroachment from outside. Whether or not the Soviet contention of the non-colonial and non-imperial character of the Soviet Union is accepted, this single territorial fact alone would justify the attention now being paid by the present writer and by many others to the past history and current affairs of that part of the former Russian Asian empire with the largest indigenous population. If, (to repeat Carr's quotation from Croce's *History as the Story of Liberty*) 'the practical requirements which underlie every historical judgment give to all history the character of "contemporary history" because, however remote in time events thus recounted may seem to be, the history in reality refers to present needs and present situations wherein those events vibrate', then this phenomenon of the colonies of the former Russian empire remaining firmly within the Soviet state frontiers, while the colonies of the Turkish, German, French, Dutch and British empires have nearly all achieved complete, if in some instances, precarious independence, is indeed deserving of constant and cumulative study.

The following are some of the conclusions which the impartial student of Central Asian history might be expected to form from the data available:

1. The impact of the West on Central Asia caused by the coming of the Russians has been the greatest formative influence to which the region has been subjected since the impact of Islam in the seventh and eighth centuries. Westernization as introduced by the Tsarist and Soviet regimes has not yet superseded the Islamic way of life in Central Asia but its effect has probably been more far-reaching than in other Muslim countries. This is due partly to the presence of a much greater proportion of non-Asian settlers and partly to the much more rapid growth of education on Western lines. In no Muslim country outside the USSR have the rulers, whether native or alien, deliberately aimed at the eradication of Muslim culture.

2. Considering its short duration, the Tsarist administration

of Central Asia achieved a great deal in respect of security, communications and urban development. In education and irrigation it achieved little. The vast scheme of white colonization put into operation at the beginning of the twentieth century was badly conceived and executed. It was, however, an important factor in the extension of the Revolution into Central Asia, since on the one hand it antagonized the local population against the Tsarist regime, and on the other introduced a large non-Asian element into the population which made the development of local nationalism and the freeing of the country from white domination virtual impossibilities. It was the completeness of the Russian conquest, the rapid consolidation of Russian rule, the creation of a military and civil communications system, the securing of the Persian and Afghan frontiers, and the development of Russian influence in western China which made possible the continuity of Moscow's control over an area vital to the Russian or Soviet state as a whole.

3. The process of nation-forming among the Central Asian peoples began before the Revolution in the relatively secure conditions introduced by the Tsarist regime and with the gradual break-up of the old Muslim Umma. It was actively discouraged by the Tsarist Government, which never formulated any plans for eventual self-government for any of the Central Asian peoples. The unco-ordinated and badly organized nationalist movements aiming at autonomy, although not necessarily at separation from Russia, which developed in the first year of the Revolution were given short shrift by the Bolshevik government set up in Tashkent by the non-Asian settler element in the Central Asian population. Whether or not the Basmachi revolt can fairly be described as a nationalist movement, it was this which decided the Soviet leaders to meet trouble half-way by a kind of homeopathic treatment taking the form of the Nationalities Policy and the eventual creation of five Union republics covering the territory formerly administered by the Governorates-General of Turkestan and the Steppe Region and the khanates of Bukhara and Khiva.

4. Although the self-government and full sovereignty claimed for the national republics by the Soviet Government were and are by Western standards purely fictitious, there can be no doubt that the general line of policy followed by the authorities since 1919 made for a great increase in the range of professional

opportunity open to the Muslims of Central Asia. The rigours of the anti-religious and anti-nationalist campaigns were to a considerable extent mitigated by the positive attractions of an improved standard of living and of general and technical education. Had the Great Purge of 1937–8 and the consequent mass defection of Muslim troops to the Germans in World War II been followed by a Soviet instead of a German defeat, the spell of Russian domination over Central Asia, which was barely disturbed by the Revolution, might have been broken. In the event, however, the end of the War found the Soviet Government in a mood of greatly increased confidence and the Muslim population of Central Asia further deprived of the ability and even of the will to resist. The transfer during the War of industrial plant and technical personnel was followed by further non-Asian colonization and by a powerful and largely successful drive to speed up technical training, industrialization and the mechanization of agriculture.

5. The death of Stalin and the subsequent repudiation of some of his methods and policies probably had less fundamental effect in Central Asia than elsewhere. There may have been some temporary decline in the Great Russian chauvinism fostered from the mid-1930s onward, but there was no reduction in the measure of central control exercised through the medium of the Communist Party.*

6. The Soviet campaign to do away with the traditional way of life induced in the first place, according to Soviet contention, by Islam and feudalism and prolonged by Tsarist imperialism, pan-Islam and pan-Turkism, has been largely, but not completely successful. Nomadism has virtually disappeared; tribal, clan and family loyalties no longer play a dominant part; education is entirely secular, the *shariat* (canon law) no longer operates and traces of *'adat* (customary law) are little more than vestigial;

---

* An important proof of this control is the fact that with one single and only temporary exception, the vital post of Chairman of the Committee of State Security in all the republics has always been held by a non-native, and usually by a Russian. The exception was the appointment of a Kazakh, Arstanbekov, as Chairman of the Kazakh State Security Committee in March 1960. This was thought to have been brought about by the serious riots by the *non-Asian* workers on the building of the Temir-Tau metallurgical plant in October 1959. Arstanbekov was replaced by a non-Asian, Yevdokimenko, in November 1963.

Western work and living habits have taken a more general hold than in most other Muslim countries; the Russianization of Central Asian languages and the use of Russian itself are rapidly increasing; finally, Western, that is, Russian styles and genres in art and literature (although not in music) are now almost universal.

7. For over forty years the peoples of Central Asia have been effectively segregated from any political and cultural influence which might have emanated from Turkey, Persia or Afghanistan. During the past ten years the Soviet Government seems to have been more concerned with establishing normal commercial and diplomatic relations with these countries than with pursuing what was at one time thought to be their aim of drawing them into the Soviet Union or at least making satellite countries of them. The case of China is different and the Sino-Soviet rift, if it continues, must have an effect on Soviet policy not only towards South-West and South Asia, but also towards the Muslim republics of Central Asia, abutting as they do on western China. The widening of this rift in the early 1960s and the possibility of its permanence may well have played a part in the decision taken at the time of the 22nd Party Congress to aim at the eventual abandonment of the present so-called federative system of the Soviet Union and to aim instead at the creation of a multi-national unitary state. The Soviet Government may have felt that the creation of the republics as national political units, although originally intended to remain notional and formal, was developing, or might develop into something real and that the right of secession included in the 1936 Soviet Constitution might come to be taken seriously with the emergence of China as a new and powerful pole of attraction. It seems likely that the right of secession, if it appears at all in the new Constitution now in the process of formulation, will be expressed somewhat differently.

The year 1965 will be the centenary of the Russian capture of Tashkent, which marks the beginning of effective Russian domination over the whole region now occupied by the four republics of Soviet Central Asia and Kazakhstan. It is unlikely that this anniversary will pass unnoticed in Central Asia and whatever the nature of the celebrations they will serve to under-line an undeniable fact, namely, that whatever the correct definition of the present political status of the Central Asian peoples – colonial, dominion, autonomous or sovereign – their destinies have lain in Russian hands for upwards of a hundred years and are likely to remain so. For them, therefore, the Western impact has meant primarily that their way of life and work and their culture have become progressively more and more Russian, and that the means of national expression have dwindled correspondingly and now seem destined to disappear altogether. It also means that whether organized as Governorates-General, union republics, autonomous republics or autonomous *oblasts*, the peoples of Central Asia have never been in a position to exercise any collective responsibility as nations.

For the historian the history of the Central Asian peoples under the Western impact postulates two comparisons: the first is with the Western colonial empires of the nineteenth and early twentieth centuries; the second with the formerly colonial territories which have acquired independence during the past twenty years. Some, and particularly American, historians have found that the Tsarist administration of Central Asia compared favourably with, for example, the British administration of India. But although as a latecomer in the field of Asian empire-building, Russia may have learned something from Britain's early mistakes in India and elsewhere, the Russian administration of Central Asia displayed much the same mixture as other colonial administrations of altruism and cupidity, of accident and design, of indulgence and oppression, of sincerity and hypocrisy, of satiety and expansionism, of the selfless devotion and tireless energy of individuals, and of the neglect and obtuseness of governments. When, too, account is taken of disparities in size and homogeneity of population, in distance from the homeland, and in the distractions caused by foreign wars and domestic disturbances, the Russian achievement in improving the material condition of the peoples of the Tsarist Asian empire was, on balance, not much different from the British and French achievement. One marked difference can, however, be noted: whether by neglect or design, the Tsarist Government did far less than Britain or France to prepare its subject peoples for responsible self-government.

The second comparison is far more striking. The standards of living, public health, education, technical 'know-how', communications and productivity in Central Asia are much higher than those in the great majority of African and Asian countries, whether colonial or independent, the only obvious exceptions being Japan and Israel. This is the result not of a natural process of national evolution, not of experience gained in the rough-and-tumble of international relations, nor of what has been described as 'self discovery demanding a reassessment of national interests', but simply of the application of a modernized and efficient form of administration to colonial territories acquired by force of arms during a previous regime. Membership of the United Nations, diplomatic representation abroad, participation as individual states in international conferences and, perhaps most important of all, the opportunity to follow a policy of neutralism, all these are run-of-the-mill experiences which have not so far fallen to the lot of the Muslim peoples of Central Asia. On the other hand, the Central Asian republics are relieved of all responsibility in the settlement of minority and border disputes, as well as in a whole range of matters which are a constant burden to national governments elsewhere. By contrast with the steady proliferation of independent although in many instances economically unviable states which is going on elsewhere this arrangement can be seen to have some practical advantages and might even be less un-ethical than the premature abdication of control over backward peoples unprepared for independence. But it could never succeed, either in the Soviet Union or elsewhere, without the presence of a strong paramount tutelary power. It is all the more contradictory that the Soviet Union should continue to press for the creation of more and more independent nation-states in Africa and Asia while manifestly aiming at the abolition of national distinctions inside the Soviet Union itself and at the fusion of all nationalities in a unitary state with one uniform culture.

APPENDIX

In the following translated extract from *Aziatskaya Rossiya* (Asiatic Russia)[62] the word 'Kazakh' has been substituted throughout for 'Kirgiz' in the original. At the time the book was published the Kazakhs were always officially referred to as Kirgiz and the Kirgiz as Kara Kirgiz.

One of Peter the Great's 'fledglings', I. K. Kirillov, a secretary of the Senate and a geographer and statistician, produced an interesting memorandum about the Kazakhs who had accepted Russian subjection. He proposed that in order to secure this region for Russia a town should be built on the River Or'. This he said would be necessary not only to keep the Kazakhs in subjection and to seal off Bashkiria, but also in order to open the way for trade to Bukhara and India. Kirillov also proposed the building of a town on the Aral Sea in order to control 'the far-flung territory of Bukhara'. The project was approved and the Orenburg expedition was fitted out. Kirillov and Tevkelev left Ufa with a considerable force in the spring of 1735.

At the mouth of the River Or' Kirillov founded Orenburg, the present Orsk (Orenburg was later transferred to another place, at first to Mt. Krasnaya, and in 1742 to its present site). Kirillov congratulated the Empress on the acquisition of a new Russia: in his dreams he already saw himself on the shores of the Aral Sea and insisted on the necessity of building forty-five towns between Orenburg and the Aral. Instead of this, however, he had to tackle the task of putting down a Bashkir revolt. But he was able to establish some iron and copper factories on the River Ik . . .

Kirillov's dreams about the establishment of trade with South Asia never materialized, but the Government paid serious attention to the Orenburg district. In the first place Kirillov's idea about the 'enclosure of Bashkiria' was put into operation. Up to that time the Asiatic nomads had had free and easy access to the Bashkirs, who regularly responded to all kinds of intrigue and occasionally revolted. Kirillov's successors, Tatishchev and Neplyuyev, finally subdued the Bashkirs and surrounded Bashkiria with a ring of Russian 'lines', of which the principal was the Orenburg or Yaik line. It began at Gur'yev at the mouth of the Yaik (Ural) River on the Caspian Sea and went upstream to the town of Verkhneyaitsk, now Verkhne-Ural'sk. Here the line left the Yaik and at Petropavlovsk Fort crossed to the River Uy, a tributary of the Tobol. Beyond this the frontier went eastward along the River Uy, through the town of Troitsk to Ust'Uysk, and then along the River Tobol. In all the line was 1,780 versts* long.

Adjoining the main line were several secondary lines which had been constructed earlier. From the point where the main line turned eastwards along the River Uy another line went northeastwards to the River Miass covering the Chelyabinsk positions. The line then went by way of the Miass to its junction with the River Iset' and along the Iset' to its junction with the River Tobol. The Iset' line protected the Shadrinsk and Yalutorovsk *uyezds*. From the mouth of the Miass there went the great Yekaterinburg line westwards through Shadrinsk to Yekaterinburg and on through the Ural mountains, Krasnoufimsk, Kungur and Osu, where it came to an end on the River Kama. Another branch of the main line went from Orenburg to Samara – the so-called Samara line.

There was thus constructed a large parallelogram of which the Rivers Kama (from the town of Osa) and Volga (to the town of Samara) constituted the western side, the Yekaterinburg line from Osa to Ust-Miass the northern side, the Rivers Miass and Yaik (to the mouth of the Or'), protected by the Iset', Uy and Yaik lines the eastern side, and finally the Orenburg line from Orsk to Orenburg (the River Yaik) and the Samara line the southern side. Inside this parallelogram was Bashkiria and access from the Steppe to the susceptible Bashkirs was thus cut off.

But the protection of this line required a large number of men – the local Yaik and Orenburg Cossacks were not enough, and it was for this reason that the Government energetically took up the question of increasing the Russian population in this area.

* A verst is approximately equal to two-thirds of a mile.

At first the authorities (in 1744 the Orenburg expedition had already become the Orenburg province) tried to increase as much as possible the number of the local Cossacks since they were the most reliable guardians of Russian soil in these parts. Against a cunning, fleet and bold enemy such as the Kazakhs only the Cossacks could operate with success; regular troops were far less effective in this region since they were not able to pursue a fast-moving enemy. The Cossack on the other hand with his two horses, his rifle and his lance was a source of terror for the Kazakhs. The Cossacks moved out from the line into the Steppe and established posts there surrounded by trenches. . . .

These lines did not constitute a *state* frontier but the limit of stable settlement. Beyond that began the Steppe the Kazakh inhabitants of which were regarded as subjects of Russia. They were, however, bad and restless subjects with whom a difficult guerrilla war had constantly to be waged. After carrying out a raid or plundering a merchant's caravan, the Kazakhs could disappear into the Steppe with impunity.

Gradually the Kazakhs became more and more bold. The Kalmyks, their greatest enemies in the Steppes of Central Asia, had disappeared, having been subdued by China in the middle of the eighteenth century. At the same time the Muslim world with every generation became more hostile to Russia. The khans of Khiva, Bukhara and Kokand, believing that Russia was not in a position to get at them, constantly spurred the Kazakhs on to hostile action. Fortunately, however, there was constant internal dissension among the Kazakhs, whose popular masses were hostile to the khans. But the local Russian authorities were not able to take advantage of this dissension; usually they supported the khans who with oriental cunning shifted the responsibility for keeping the people quiet on to the Russians and Russia. In addition, the Russian Government itself acted in such a way that the influence of Muslim organizations among the Kazakhs increased: from the time of Catherine II we tried to educate the Kazakhs in the belief that by this means they would be weaned away from their brigandish way of life. But for this purpose we sent into the Steppe Tatar mullas from Kazan who merely preached hatred towards the Russians.

At the end of the eighteenth century our actual frontier with Central Asia presented itself as a curved broken line: it began at the Caspian Sea and then went along the River Uy to Zverino-golovskaya, and thence in a straight line to Omsk; from Omsk the frontier followed the Irtysh River to its upper reaches, and ended at the Altay. The Lesser and Middle Kazakh hordes, who only nominally recognized Russian dominion, had shifted the direction of their roaming and now reached this line; at the beginning of the nineteenth century part of them (the Bukeyev horde) received permission to settle within the confines of Russia.

A practical means of pacifying this region would have been the establishment of a series of forts and the destruction of the power of the small khans, that is to say, the subjection of the Kazakhs to Russian State rule. It was, however, difficult to build towns in the sterile sandy spaces of Central Asia; and it was almost impossible to move a settled population there. Graphic proof of this can be found in the insignificant change which took place in the main Orenburg line: only in 1810 was the Novo-Iletskaya line established, which embraced the small Iletsk district; later, in 1835, a new line was extended from Orsk direct to Troitsk. Formerly the protective line had gone along the River Ural; now it went a little back from the river in a north-easterly direction. This was the sum total of the small progress made by the Russian settled population in the Orenburg district in a whole century.

Meanwhile, the main line formed three sides of a rectangle. If this rectangle could be closed, the district would become Russian the Kazakhs would become as cut off from external and anti-Russian influences as the Bashkirs had been earlier.

A glance at the map shows clearly that the basis of the fourth enclosing line would have to be the great rivers flowing into the Aral Sea. Along their course lay the khanates hostile to Russia – Khiva, Bukhara and Kokand. Only by subduing these could the Kazakh country become Russian not only in name but in fact. In consequence, Russia had to move on to the Steppe by the two routes indicated by Peter the Great: from one side it was absolutely necessary to traverse the Steppe from the Caspian Sea to the Aral Sea; and from the other side to approach by way of the Irtysh to the lakes of Zaysan, Balkhash and Issyk-Kul'; and from there to move westwards to the Aral Sea.

Difficult in itself, this task was complicated by the political relations of Russia with certain West European powers, especially after Russia had occupied a dominating position in Europe thanks to the glorious events of 1812 to 1815. Russia at that time took precedence among the European powers, who were afraid lest she should occupy the same position as that occupied by France in the time of Napoleon I. Consequently, they took up a disapproving attitude to every extension of Russian power. The advance of Russia in Asia, both in Central Asia and in the Far East, excited the liveliest apprehension, particularly in Britain, who feared that her invulnerability would be destroyed if the Russian frontiers approached those of India. Britain had expended great efforts in order to destroy Napoleon when he had threatened her Indian frontiers; but what had seemed a conqueror's dream very difficult of realization now became a real danger in view of the new and continuing advance of Russia in Central Asia. Many of the obstacles encountered in this advance by Russia were created by Britain.

From the beginning of the nineteenth century Russia was firmly established on the eastern shore of the Caspian Sea. Our wars with Persia forced us to pay attention to the Turkmens roaming between the Atrek and Gurgan rivers, who in 1819 had come under the protection of Russia. At the same time our Government had again, and this time more energetically, begun to take action against the Kazakhs. In 1822 the statute in respect of the Siberian Kazakhs worked out by Speranskiy, the Governor-General of Siberia, had been confirmed. With all its unavoidable shortcomings this statute did weaken the tribal basis and the power of the khans among the Kazakhs, gave the people an opportunity of choosing their own rulers, and established administrative centres in the heart of the Steppe. Simultaneously, even during the rule of the Emperor Nicholas I, settlers started to penetrate the Kazakh Steppe – peasants from the interior provinces and Cossacks from the fortified line. At the same time towns were established in the Steppe: Akmolinsk (1832), Kokpekty (1844), and Kopal.

Another fundamental aspect of our policy in Central Asia now became clear: the Kazakhs, like the Kalmyks before them, were under the strong influence exercised by the khanates of Kokand, Khiva and Bukhara. Pacification of the Steppe was only possible by terrorizing or subduing these khanates, who adopted a bold attitude towards Russia and not only considered themselves unassailable but encouraged others in the same belief. From this followed the conclusion that it was necessary to deliver a decisive blow against the khanates, and by the 1850s the Russian Government had adopted this course. In 1839 General Perovskiy had tried with a force of 4,000 men to penetrate from Orenburg to Khiva. This operation had not succeeded, mainly because it had been undertaken during the winter. In the ensuing years forts were built in the Steppe, which later became the towns of Turgay and Irgiz (both in 1845), and of Raimsk and Aral'sk at the mouth of the Syr-Dar'ya; this allowed us to put on to the Aral Sea naval schooners and even steamers, which greatly facilitated the movement of troops.

In 1853 Perovskiy repeated his operation, this time with far greater success; he was able to gain possession of a considerable part of the course of the Syr-Dar'ya, upwards of 400 versts; and the important Kokand fort of Ak-Mechet' was captured and re-named Perovsk. On the Siberian side also our territory had by the end of Emperor Nicholas I's reign extended to Lake Balkhash and along the valley of the River Ili to Lake Issyk-kul'.

It was the Kazakhs who had brought the Russians to this point. At the request of the sultans of different tribes of the Kazakhs of the Middle Horde the Government more than once sent forces of Cossacks to their aid; the area of indirect Russian influence on the Kazakhs kept on extending and gradually began to include the Greater Horde as well. This circumstance caused dissatisfaction to the Chinese Government since some tribes of the Kazakhs of the Greater Horde considered themselves subjects of the Celestial empire. It also displeased both the Kazakhs and the Kokand khanate which exercised considerable influence on them. China, however, protested very weakly. In the 1840s, one of the sultans of the Greater Horde, Kenesary, was able to collect around him many tribes of this Horde. He became a hero of the Kazakhs and hoped to unite all the Kazakhs into one independent people. The dreams of Kenesary met with a lively response from many Kazakhs and his activities left a deep impression on the history of western Siberia and the Orenburg district. Nevertheless he was not able to bring all the Greater Horde over to his side; in addition, the sultans who were hostile to him in order to maintain their own position were obliged to approach the Russian Government with a request that they should be accepted as Russian subjects. The Emperor Nicholas I gave his agreement to this and in the summer of 1846 five tribes of the Greater Horde took the oath of subjection to Russia. At the same time troops were sent to Lakes Balkhash and Ili against Kenesary. He fled to Chinese territory and was there killed. The remaining Kazakhs of the Greater Horde then declared their wish to accept Russian subjection and some hundreds of Cossacks were despatched into the Steppe with the object of traversing the whole of Kazakh territory up to the Chinese border. The Kazakhs met the Cossacks and presented them with bread and salt on a gold plate as a sign of their willingness to submit. The Cossacks ordered them to take them as far as the Chinese frontier and at a point 30 versts from it they chose a suitable place for a town which was given the name of Kopal (1851). Shortly after the fortified town of Vernoye* was founded on the site of the ancient city of Almata. In this way were formed the Russian domains to the south of Lake Balkhash, which from the main River Ili flowing into Balkhash made up the *oblast* of Semirech'ye.

Higher up the Ili in the district of Kuldja dwelt a mixed population of Dungans, Taranchis and Chinese. A serious disturbance began in this area which extended to the Russian frontier districts. The Chinese Government was not able to bring peace to Kuldja and in 1871 it was occupied by Russian troops. Ten years later, with the object of maintaining good neighbourly relations with China, Russia returned Kuldja to her and only then was the frontier between our and Chinese territory delimited. As we gradually moved into the Steppe we acquired a firm frontier – the Pamirs.

Thus, by the end of Emperor Nicholas I's rule, the *fourth* side of the rectangle began to close and inside it were Kazakhs who were now subjects of Russia. In the West this line went from the Caspian Sea to the Aral Sea and farther along the River Syr-Dar'ya where it came to an end at the fort of Perovsk; in the east from the Chinese frontier it began with Semirech'ye; and it only remained to join the fortified town of Vernoye with a cordon to Fort Perovsk for the Kazakh territory to be cut off from external influences hostile to Russia as was Bashkiria in the eighteenth century. The Emperor Alexander II set himself this urgent task in the first years of his reign.

* So called, while it remained a fortress (ukrepleniye). On its achieving the status of city (gorod) it became Vernyy.

In St Petersburg it had already been decided to begin an attack on the khanates from two sides – from Perovsk and Vernoye. But before military operations could be begun from our side our position in Semirech'ye underwent a grave danger. This distant province was of course occupied by a small Russian force based on the 'fortress' of Vernoye, which itself had in fact hardly been fortified at all. The Kokandis, foreseeing the Russian attack, themselves invaded Semirech'ye in 1860 and started to work up the Kazakhs. A large force of 20,000 Kokandis laid siege to the Russian piquet at Uzun-Agach, not far from Vernoye. Lieut.-Col. Kolpakovskiy (later Military Governor of Semirech'ye) went from Vernoye to the relief of the Russian troops with a force of 800 men and 6 guns. In spite of the great courage of their cavalry, the Kokandis were defeated and fled from Uzun-Agach. This victory strengthened our position in Semirech'ye and showed the natives the need for respecting Russian power. By 1864 our troops under the command of Chernyayev, Verevkin and Kolpakovskiy, memorable figures in the chronicles of Turkestan, captured the towns of Turkestan, Chimkent and others. The line was now closed up and extended from the Aral Sea to the Alatau mountains. The Steppe had been crossed and the Russians were now firmly established in a very rich and fruitful region. The time was now past when expeditions had to be provisioned down to the last crust from Orenburg.

But our occupation of the new line did not bring peace to the Central Asian Steppes. The khanates of Khiva, Kokand and Bukhara, in their half-brigandish existence, did not appreciate the significance of the events which had taken place nor had they a proper understanding of the power of Russia. Remembering our many failures in the past, the Asiatic nomads attributed these to their own cleverness and strength; they had no desire to reconcile themselves to the new situation and to see around them Russian garrison towns. Incited from outside, they plundered our merchants, attacked small detachments, and detained not only our traders but our ambassadors, and incited the native population of the towns captured by us to start a *ghazavat*, or holy war, against the infidels. They were not brought to their senses either by the brilliant feat of Russian troops under the command of M. G. Chernyayev, when with a force of 2,000 men and 12 guns he took by storm one of the most important cities of the region – Tashkent, surrounded as it was by a 20-verst wall defended by a force of 30,000 with 50 guns, by the brilliant victory of Generals Romanovskiy and Kryzhanovskiy at Irdzhar or by the capture of the forts of Khodzhent, Ura-Tyube and Andizhan. And they were not deterred by the formation of a new Governorate-General of Turkestan (1867), the first head of which was K. P. Kaufman.

The hostile action of the Asiatics brought the Russian troops to the walls of what was a holy city for all Muslims, Samarkand. On May 1, 1868 on the Zeravshan River before this city, a force of 3,500 Russians under the command of Kaufman, defeated a great army of the Emir of Bukhara. On the following day Samarkand, 'the focus of the world' and the capital of Tamerlane who had once been so terrible to Russia, surrendered. Almost five hundred years after Tamerlane's fearful attack on Russia (1395) our troops captured the town where lay his tomb. After this new victory of ours the Emir of Bukhara was obliged to conclude a peace according to which he recognized the former conquests of Russia, surrendered the Zeravshan district (Samarkand and Katta-Kurgan) and paid Russia an indemnity.

The lesson given to Bukhara had no effect on Khiva and Kokand. In 1873 General Kaufman undertook his famous campaign to Khiva in which Russian troops had to undergo the terrible hardship of crossing the desert. Khiva was captured and under a peace treaty the Khan acknowledged himself the vassal of the Russian empire, paid an indemnity and ceded all his territory on the right bank of the Amu-Dar'ya, out of which there was formed the Amu-Dar'ya sector. The Russians were granted the exclusive right of navigation on the Amu-Dar'ya and of carrying on duty-free trade.

Russia's victory was accompanied by the abolition of slavery and of the shameful trafficking in people in Khiva and Bukhara. In the summer of 1875 a revolt broke out in Kokand. In spite of the victory of a small force of 16 companies of infantry and 9 squadrons of Cossacks at Makhram, where a force of 50,000 Kokandis were defeated by General Kaufman, the revolt continued, and the main forces of Kokand to the number of 70,000 men were concentrated near Andizhan. The suppression of this revolt was entrusted to M. D. Skobelev, who with a handful of men went through the whole Kokand khanate breaking up the rebel gangs. In 1876 the Fergana *oblast* was formed out of the Kokand territories. After this the only people in the Transcaspian Steppe who remained unsubdued were the Turkmens and the Tekes living on the frontier with Afghanistan, which had come under the domination of Britain. The Russian Government now decided to put a curb on the Tekes. The first expedition of 1879 had not been crowned with success, but in 1880 a force of 11,000 was put under the command of Skobelev with Kuropatkin as his Chief of Staff. The force had to traverse a sandy desert and preparations for this campaign began in May 1880. In December the Russians laid siege to the Teke stronghold, and on January 12, 1881, they captured it by storm, in spite of the desperate and heroic defence of 25,000 Tekes. Later a force under Kuropatkin occupied Ashkhabad, but only on March 27, after the Emperor Alexander had come to the throne, did the leader of the Tekes surrender his sword to Skobelev.

The Afghans now laid claim to the southern part of the Merv district and adopted a threatening attitude towards Russia; but a brilliant victory won by a small force under General Komarov at Kushk in 1885 brought the Afghans to heel and made it possible for Russia to establish the precise frontier of the Transcaspian *oblast* with Afghanistan; the delimitation of this frontier (1887) gave us the territories along the Rivers Murgab and Kushk. Shortly after this the Afghans and Chinese, the first from the west, and the second from the east, began to occupy the high uninhabited plateau of the Pamirs, the southern frontier of which was formed by the Hindukush range, with India lying beyond. The Pamirs had formerly formed part of the territory of Kokand, but this desert plateau, which was useless for human habitation, had not been occupied by us. The British also hoped to profit by the circumstance in order to keep our frontier at a distance from India. However, by the will of the Emperor Nicholas II, now fortunately ruling over us, the Russian forces occupied the Pamirs (1895), cleared it of Afghans and Chinese and built a fortress there. Under a Russo-British Agreement only a narrow strip of Afghan territory separates our territories from the Hindukush, the frontier of British India. Thus, our acquisition of Turkestan was completed with the annexation of the Transcaspian *oblast* and the Pamirs only a quarter of a century ago and within the recollection of the present generation.

BIBLIOGRAPHICAL NOTE

WHAT FOLLOWS IS merely a list of those works (mainly in English) which the author found most useful in compiling the present book and which in his opinion provide the best background for further study of the subject. Many of them, and particularly those by Park, Pierce and Zenkovsky contain excellent bibliographies which there seems no point in repeating here.

Classical works on pre-Revolutionary Central Asia are Schuyler's *Turkistan* and the numerous writings of Barthold, of which only a few have been translated out of Russian.

The most abundant source of information on the recent and current cultural affairs of Central Asia is *Central Asian Review* (quarterly since July 1953). This periodical provides a cumulative analysis of Soviet writing (books, periodicals and newspapers) published since 1953.

In addition to the background books listed below, the following works of reference should be noted:

Great Soviet Encyclopaedia, 2nd Edition.
Everyman's Concise Encyclopaedia of Russia by S. V. Utechin.
Smaller Soviet Encyclopaedia.
Peoples of Central Asia by Laurence Krader. 1962. Bloomington and The Hague.

CHAPTER I

Tokarev. Ed. *Etnografiya Narodov SSSR* (Ethnography of the Peoples of the USSR). 1958. Moscow.
Barthold. *K Istorii Orosheniya Turkestana* (History of Irrigation in Turkestan). 1913. St Petersburg.

CHAPTER II

Gibb. *The Arab Conquests in Central Asia.* 1923. London.
Barthold. *Turkestan down to the Mongol Conquest* (English Translation). 1958. London.
— *Four Studies on the History of Central Asia.* 3 vols. 1956. Leiden.
Caroe. *Soviet Empire.* 1953. London.

CHAPTER III

Barthold. *Istoriya Kul'turnoy Zhizni Turkestana* (History of the Civilization of Turkestan). 1927. Leningrad.
Holdsworth. *Turkestan in the 19th Century.* 1959. London.
Schuyler. *Turkistan.* 1876. London.

CHAPTER IV

Pierce. *Russian Central Asia, 1867–1917.* 1960. Berkeley and Los Angeles.
Aziatskaya Rossiya. 1914. St Petersburg.
Khalfin. *Politika Rossii v Sredney Azii (1857–68).* 1960. Moscow.

CHAPTER V

Pierce. *Russian Central Asia, 1867–1917.*
Bennigsen and Quelquejay. *The Evolution of the Muslim Nationalities of the USSR and their Linguistic Problems* (English Translation). 1961. London.
Barthold. *History of the Cultural Life of Turkestan.*

CHAPTER VI

Pipes. *The Formation of the Soviet Union.* 1954. Cambridge, Mass.
Zenkovsky. *Pan-Turkism and Islam in Russia.* 1960. Cambridge, Mass.
Bailey. *Mission to Tashkent.* 1946. London.
Ellis. *Transcaspian Episode.* 1963. London.

CHAPTER VII

Park. *Bolshevism in Turkestan, 1917–27.* 1957. New York.
Bennigsen and Quelquejay (*op. cit*).

CHAPTER VIII

Park (*op. cit*).
Baymirza Hayit. *Turkesta im Zwanzigsten Jahrhundert.* 1956. Darmstadt.
Economic Bulletin for Europe. *Regional Economic Policy in the Soviet Union: The Case of Central Asia.* 1957. Geneva.

CHAPTER IX

Barthold. *History of the Cultural Life of Central Asia.*

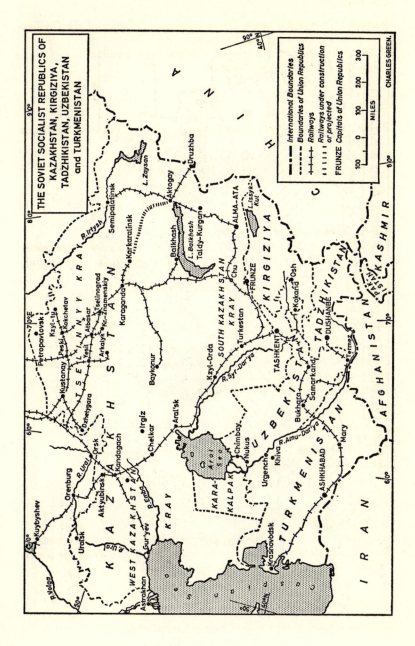

THE SOVIET SOCIALIST REPUBLICS OF KAZAKHSTAN, KIRGIZIYA, TADZHIKISTAN, UZBEKISTAN and TURKMENISTAN

International Boundaries
Boundaries of Union Republics
Railways
Railways under construction or projected
FRUNZE Capitals of Union Republics

MILES
100   0   100   200   300

CHARLES GREEN.

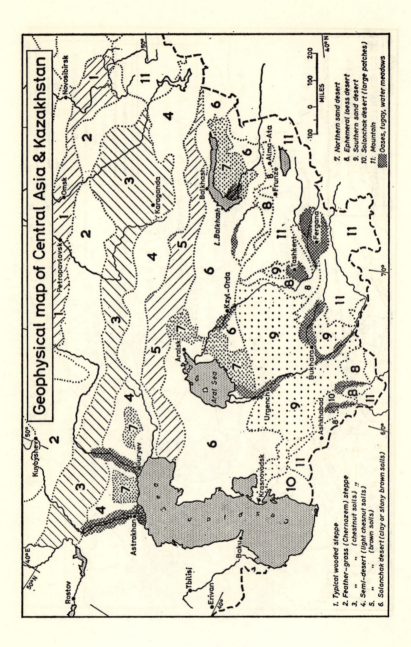

Geophysical map of Central Asia & Kazakhstan

1. Typical wooded steppe
2. Feather-grass (Chernozem) steppe
3.   "   "   (chestnut soils) "
4. Semi-desert (light chesnut soils) "
5.   "   "   (brown soils)
6. Solonchak desert (clay or stony brown soils)

7. Northern sand desert
8. Ephemeral loess desert
9. Southern sand desert
10. Solonchak desert (large patches)
11. Mountain
▨ Oases, tugay, water meadows

MILES
0   100   200

40°N

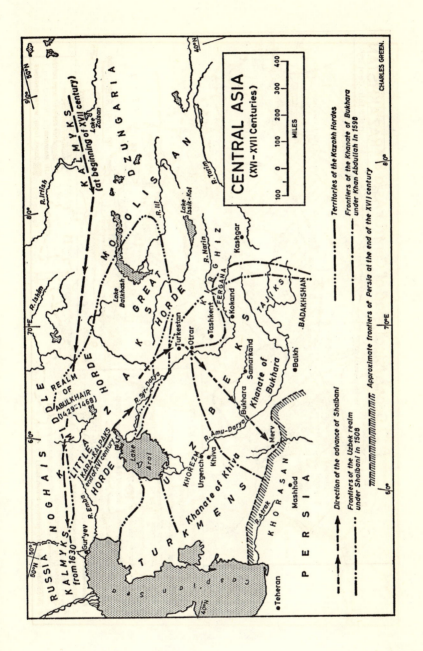

CENTRAL ASIA
(XVI - XVII Centuries)

MILES

100	0	100	200	300	400

Territories of the Kazakh Hordes

Frontiers of the Khanate of Bukhara
under Khan Abdullah in 1598

Approximate frontiers of Persia at the end of the XVII century

Direction of the advance of Shaibani

Frontiers of the Uzbek realm
under Shaibani in 1508

CHARLES GREEN.

RUSSIA

K A L M Y K S
(at beginning of XVII century)

KALMYKS
from 1630

Lake Zaisan

D Z U N G A R I A

M O G O L I S T A N

R.Irtish

R.Ishim

R.Ili

Lake Issik-Kol

R.Tarim

Lake Balkhash

G R E A T   K A Z A K   H O R D E

Kashgar

K I R G H I Z

R.Narin

FERGANA

Kokand

Tashkent

Turkestan

Otrar

TAJIKS

BADAKHSHAN

NOGHAIS

M I D D L E

H O R D E

REALM
OF
ABULKHAIR
(1429-1468)

K A Z A K

LITTLE
HORDE

KARA-KALPAKS
end of XVI century

R.Emba

R.Syr-Darja

Gur'yev

U Z B E K S

Khanate of
Bukhara

Bukhara

Samarkand

Balkh

Lake Aral

KHOREZM

Urgench

Khiva

R.Amu-Darya

Khanate of Khiva

Merv

T U R K M E N S

KHORASAN

Mashhad

R.Atrak

P E R S I A

Teheran

C a s p i a n   S e a

249

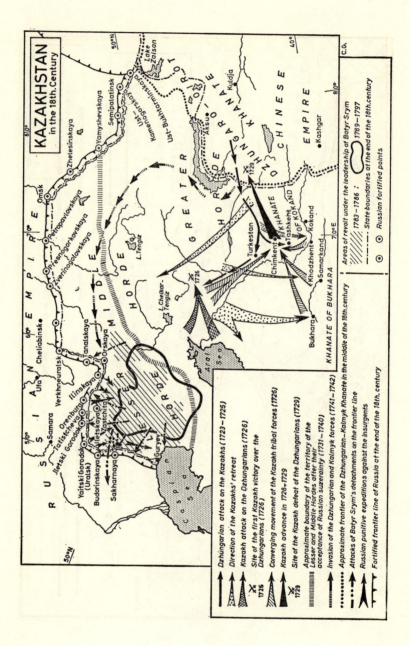

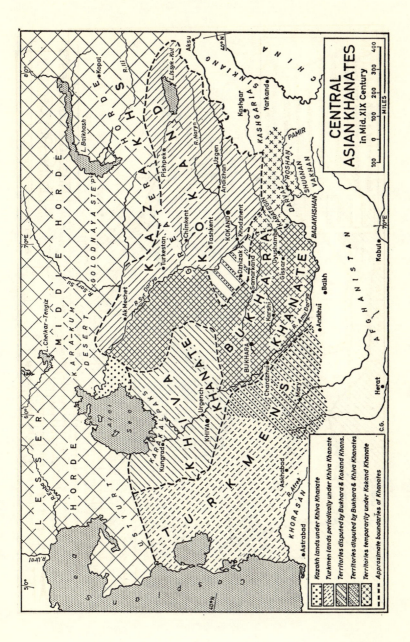

CENTRAL
ASIAN KHANATES
in Mid. XIX Century

MILES
100   0   100   200   300   400

Kazakh lands under Khiva Khanate
Turkmen lands periodically under Khiva Khanate
Territories disputed by Bukhara & Kokand Khans.
Territories disputed by Bukhara & Khiva Khanates
Territories temporarily under Kokand Khanate
Approximate boundaries of Khanates

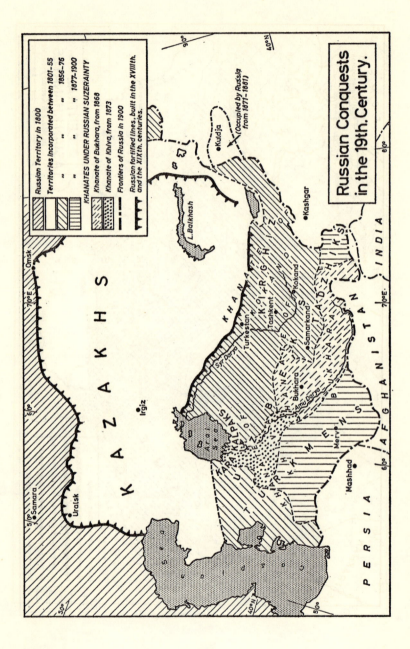

Russian Conquests in the 19th. Century.

Russian Territory in 1800

Territories Incorporated between 1801–55

"   "   "   1856–76

"   "   "   1877–1900

KHANATES UNDER RUSSIAN SUZERAINTY

Khanate of Bukhara, from 1868

Khanate of Khiva, from 1873

Frontiers of Russia in 1900

Russian fortified lines, built in the XVIIIth. and the XIXth. centuries.

(Occupied by Russia from 1871–1881)

Kuldja

Kashgar

L. Balkhash

Omsk

K A Z A K H S

Irgiz

Samara

Uralsk

KHANATE OF K. O. KIRGHIZ

Tashkent

Turkestan

Syr Darya

Kokand

Samarkand

T A D Z H I K S

K H A N A T E   O F   B U K H A R A

Bukhara

Amu Darya

KARA-KALPAKS

UZBEKS

KHANATE OF KHIVA

T U R K M E N S

Merv

Mashhad

A r a l   S e a

C a s p i a n   S e a

P E R S I A

A F G H A N I S T A N

I N D I A

40°N

90°

70°E.

60°

60°

70°E.

50°

40°N

50°

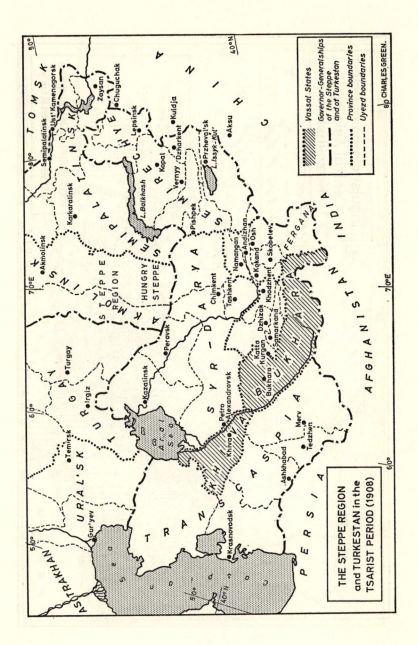

THE STEPPE REGION
and TURKESTAN in the
TSARIST PERIOD (1908)

Vassal States
Governor-Generalships
of the Steppe
and of Turkestan
Province boundaries
Uyezd boundaries

© CHARLES GREEN.

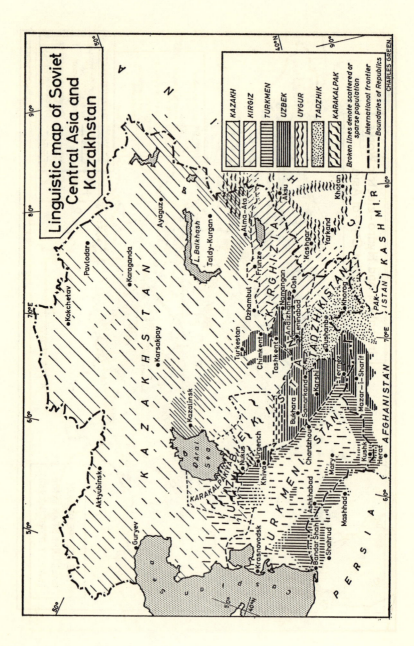

Linguistic map of Soviet Central Asia and Kazakhstan

KAZAKH
KIRGIZ
TURKMEN
UZBEK
UYGUR
TADZHIK
KARAKALPAK

Broken lines denote scattered or sparse population
International frontier
Boundaries of Republics

CHARLES GREEN.

Kokchetav
Pavlodar
Karaganda
Ayaguz
L. Balkhash
Taldy-Kurgan
Alma-Ata
Frunze
Aksu
Kashgar
Khotan
Yarkand
KASHMIR
Karsakpay
Turkestan
Dzhambul
Namangan
Andizhan
Osh
Leninabad
Khorog
[PAK.] ['STAN]
Chimkent
Tashkent
Dushanbe
Termez
Kzalinsk
Karshi
Samarkand
Mazar-i-Sharif
AFGHANISTAN
Aktyubinsk
Bukhara
Nukus
Urgench
Chardzhou
Kushk
Guryev
Khiva
Mary
Herat
Ashkhabad
Mashhad
Krasnovodsk
Bandar Shah
Shahrud
PERSIA

KAZAKHSTAN
KIRGHIZIA
TADZHIKISTAN
UZBEKISTAN
TURKMENISTAN
KARAKALPAKIA
Aral Sea

254

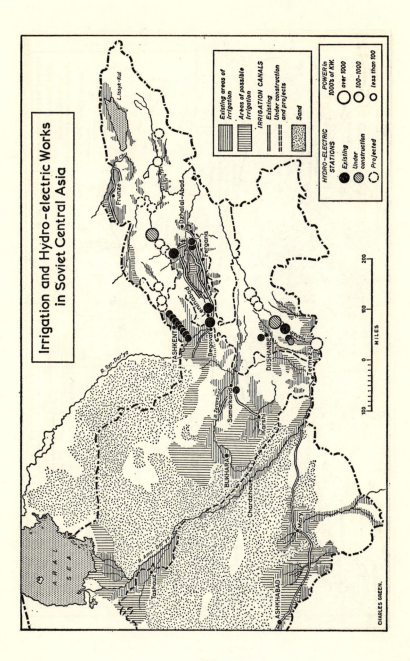

Irrigation and Hydro-electric Works
in Soviet Central Asia

Legend

Existing areas of irrigation
Areas of possible irrigation

IRRIGATION CANALS
Existing
Under construction and projects
Sand

POWER in 1000's of KW.
over 1000
100-1000
less than 100

HYDRO-ELECTRIC STATIONS
Existing
Under construction
Projected

R. Syr-Dar'ya
L.Issyk-Kul
Frunze
Dzhalal-Abad.
Fergana
TASHKENT
Begovat
Leninabad
DUSHANBE
Nayak
Termez
R.Zerovshan
Samarkand
Karshi
BUKHARA
Chardzhou
Mary
Tashauz
ASHKHABAD
R. Amu Dar'ya
ARAL SEA

MILES
200 100 0 100

CHARLES GREEN.

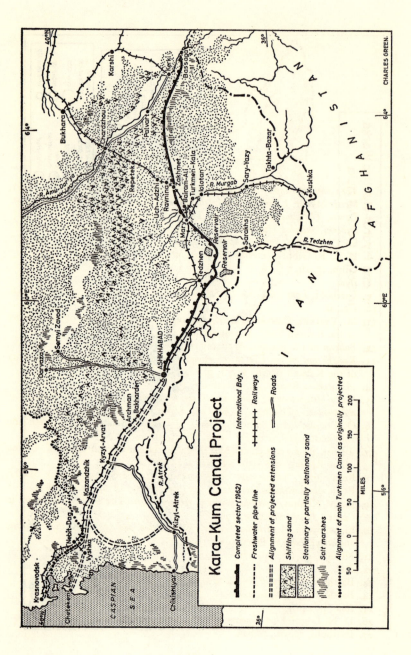

Kara-Kum Canal Project

Completed sector (1962)
Freshwater pipe-line
Alignment of projected extensions
Shifting sand
Stationary or partially stationary sand
Salt marshes
Alignment of main Turkmen Canal as originally projected
International Bdy.
Railways
Roads

MILES

50   0   50   100   150   200

CHARLES GREEN.

U.S.S.R.

A F G H A N I S T A N

I R A N

C A S P I A N   S E A

Krasnovodsk
Cheleken
Nebit-Dag
Vyshka
Kazandzhik
Kizyl-Arvat
Bakharden
Archman
ASHKHABAD
R. Atrek
Kizyl-Atrek
Chikishlyar
Darvaza
Sernyi Zavod
R. Amu-Dar'ya
Bukhara
Karshi
Chardzhou
Pitnyak
Repetek
Uch-Adzhi
Ravnina
Zakhmet
Mary
Bairam-Ali
Turkmen-Kala
Iolotan
R. Murgab
Tedzhen
Reservoir
Reservoir
Sarakhs
R. Tedzhen
Sary-Yazy
Takhta-Bazar
Kushka
Kerki

NOTES

1. *The Changing Map of Asia*, ed. East and Spate, 4th edition, London, 1961.
2. Henri Moser, *L'Irrigation en Asie Centrale*, Paris, 1894.
3. Lewis, *The Emergence of Modern Turkey*, London, 1961, p. 1.
4. *Ocherki Obshchey Etnografii*, Aziatskaya Chast' SSSR, Moscow, 1960.
5. Sir Olaf Caroe, *Soviet Empire*, London, 1953, p. 31.
6. H. A. R. Gibb, *The Arab Conquests in Central Asia*, London, 1923.
7. Gibb, *op. cit.*
8. *Ibid.*
9. Barthold, *Four Studies on the History of Central Asia*, vol. I, Leiden, 1956.
10. *Op. cit.*
11. M. Vyatkin, *Ocherki po istorii Kazakhskoy SSR* (Outline of the history of the Kazakh SSR), Leningrad, 1941.
12. *Bulletin* of the Kazakh Academy of Sciences, June, 1955.
13. *Kazakhstan on the Eve of its Annexation to Russia*, 1957 official history of the Kazakh ASSR, vol. I, p. 224.
14. *Aziatskaya Rossiya*, St Petersburg, 1914.
15. Mary Holdsworth, *Turkestan in the Nineteenth Century: a brief history of the khanates of Bukhara, Kokand and Khiva*, London, 1959.
16. O. Chekhovich, 'Some Problems of Central Asian History (18th and 19th centuries)', *Voprosy Istorii*, No. 3, 1956.
17. 'British Policy in Central Asia in the Early Nineteenth Century', *Central Asian Review*, 1958, vol. VI, No. 4, p. 386.
18. Reza Qoli, 'Ambassade de Khorezm', translated by Charles Shefer, Ecole des Langues Orientales Vivantes, Paris, 1876, ser. 1, vol. IV.
19. N. A. Khalfin, *Politika Rossii v Sredney Azii* (The Policy of Russia in Central Asia), Moscow, 1960.
20. Maksheyev, *A historical survey of Turkestan and of the Russian offensive operations there*, St Petersburg, 1890.
21. Khalfin, *op. cit.*, pp. 178–9.
22. *Ibid.*, p. 206.
23. Barthold, *History of the Cultural Life of Turkestan*, p. 223.
24. Barthold, *op. cit.*, p. 223.
25. *Ibid.*, p. 246.
26. D. N. Logofet, *A Country without Justice*, St Petersburg, 1909, p. 153.
27. Barthold, *op. cit.*, p. 246.

28. *Ibid., op. cit.*, p. 250.
29. R. Pierce, *Russian Central Asia, 1867–1917*, p. 221.
30. *Ibid.*, chapter 18.
31. *Ibid.*, p. 281.
32. Lorimer, *The Population of the Soviet Union: History and Prospects*, Geneva, 1946.
33. Sharova, 'Pereselencheskaya politika tsarizma v Sredney Azii', *Istoricheskiye Zapiski*, VIII, 1940.
34. R. Pierce, *Russian Central Asia, 1867–1917*, p. 196.
35. Zenkovsky, *Pan-turkism and Islam in Russia*, Cambridge, USA, 1960, p. 216.
36. Safarov, *Kolonial'naya Revolyutsiya: opyt Turkestana*, Moscow, 1921, p. 64.
37. Vadim Chaykin, *K. Istorii Rossiyskoy Revolyutsii*, Moscow, 1922, vol. I, p. 133.
38. Chokayev, 'Turkestan and the Soviet Regime', *Journal* of the Royal Central Asian Society, vol. XVIII, July 1931, pt. 3.
39. Smaller Soviet Encyclopaedia. *Kokandskaya Avtonomiya.*
40. F. M. Bailey, *Mission to Tashkent*, London, 1946. Another valuable first-hand account is *The Transcaspian Episode* by C. H. Ellis: London, 1963.
41. Alexander Park, *Bolshevism in Turkestan, 1917–27*, New York, 1957, p. 59.
42. Ye. Kozlovskiy, *Krasnaya Armiya v Sredney Azii* (The Red Army in Central Asia), Tashkent, 1928.
43. Bennigsen and Quelquejay, *The Evolution of the Muslim Nationalities of the USSR and their Linguistic Problems.* English translation, Central Asian Research Centre, London, 1961.
44. Baymirza Hayit, *Turkestan in the Twentieth Century*, (*Turkestan im Zwanzigsten Jahrhundert*), Darmstadt, 1956.
45. Quoted by H. H. Munro in *When William Came*, 1929. Collected edition, p. 95.
46. Elie Kedourie, *Nationalism*, 2nd edition, London, 1961.
47. 'Regional Economic Policy in the Soviet Union: The Case of Central Asia', Economic Bulletin for Europe, United Nations, Geneva, November 1957, p. 49.
48. Alexander Park, *op. cit.*, chapter VI, 'The Drive for Economic Equalization'.
49. *Op. cit.*, p. 261.
50. *Op. cit.*, p. 61.
51. *Sovetskaya Etnografiya*, 1959, No. 1. An analysis of this article appeared in *Central Asian Review*, 1959, No. 4.
52. Henri Moser, *L'Irrigation en Asie Centrale*, Paris, 1894.
53. Owen Lattimore, *Studies in Frontier History*, London, 1962, p. 196.
54. E. Ginsberg, *Sociology*, London, 1955, p. 44.
55. MacIver, *The Modern State*, London, 1926, p. 325.
56. M. Vyatkin, *Ocherki po Istorii Kazakhskoy SSR* (Outline of the History of the Kazakh SSR), Leningrad, 1941, p. 321.
57. A. Bennigsen, Cahiers sur le Monde Russe et Sovietique, No. 1, 1959. La Famille Musulmane en Union Sovietique.
58. Baymirza Hayit, *Turkestan im XX Jahrhundert*, Darmstadt, 1956.

59. 'La Littérature anti-Religieuse dans les Republiques Sovietiques Musulmanes', 1957, published in *Revue des Etudes Islamiques*, Paris, 1958.
60. Kommunist Kazakhstana, No. 7, 1957.
61. Barthold, *History of the Cultural Life of Turkestan*, pp. 143–4.
62. *Aziatskaya Rossiya*, St Petersburg, 1914, vol. I, p. 29 *et seq.*

INDEX

Abbasid Caliphate, 22, 43
Abramzon, S. M., on social grouping, 182
Abd ul'Mu'min, death of, 27
Abulkhair Khan, 39, 51–2
Abdurrahman, Emir of Afghanistan, 83
'*Adat*, see Islam
Aden, 148
Afghanistan, 4, 5, 11, 14, 23, 29, 40; frontier delimitation of, 42, 51, 63; trade, 46; and Russian expansion, 61, 75, 244; and Great Britain, 61, 80–1, 83; and Bukhara, 82, 112; in 1917, 98; and Basmachi movement, 108–10; Tadzhiks in, 15, 153; agriculture, 161; foreign elements in, 174, 175; minorities in, 176; and Muslims, 177; communications with Soviets, 178; influence of, 232
Afghans, 16
Agabekov, G. S., *Memoirs* of, 175
Agrarian reforms, 135–6
Agricultural Bureau of the Central Committee, 146
Agricultural and Forestry Workers Union, 133
Agriculture, 2; collectivization of, 130–6, 168, 172; cotton, 157, 158, 160–1; livestock, 161; in Kazakhstan, 162
Ahmad Qavam as-Saltane, 30
Aini, Sadreddin, 217
Akhund, Fathali, 218
Ak-Mechet, 80, 240
Akmolinsk, 36, 68, 77, 239
Aktogay, 174
Alash Orda, 101–3, 129, 214
Ala-Tau Kirgiz, 55
Alatau Mountains, 242
Alexander II, Emperor, 241, 244
All-Kirgiz (Kazakh) Congress (3rd), 101

All-Russia-Muslim Congress, 91, 100, 104
All-Union Central Committee Presidium of Communist Party, 145–6
Alma-Ata, 15, 76, 102, 177, 222, 223, 241
Altay River, 238
Altynsaryn, Ibrahim, 199, 213, 214
Amanullah of Afghanistan, King, 176
Amu-Dar'ya River, 2, 4; settlement near, 10, 14, 46; records of, 19; course of, 45; and Russian expansion, 58, 86, 243; and railways, 71, 174; creation of flotilla, 84; Military Division, 119; Canal, 172
Anatolia, 23
Andizhan, 2, 15, 71, 109, 243; religious fanaticism in, 89–90, 187; education in, 200
Anglo-Russian Convention, 63
Angren River, 11
Arab Conquests, 16, 19–21
Arab population, 16
Arabic script, 34
Aral Sea, 2, 5, 10, 41, 171, 235, 238, 241, 242
Aralsk, 240
Armenia, Soviet policy in, 140; language of, 207–8
Arstanbekov, 169, 231
Arts, 218–25; fine arts, 218, 219
Ashkhabad, 4, 113, 146, 172, 244
Astrakhan khanate, 26, 48, 199
Atrek River, 11
Austrian imperialism, 147; Austrians in Turkestan, 98
Auezov, 217
Auliye-ata, *see* Dzhambul
Avicenna, 208
Azadi, Molla, 193
Azerbaydzhan, 197, 218; -is, 13, 150
Aziatskaya Rossiya, 52, 56–7, 67